The

of

Good Looks

THE PROSE AND POETRY OF

Cheryl Clarke,

1980 TO 2005

CARROLL & GRAF PUBLISHERS
NEW YORK

THE DAYS OF GOOD LOOKS
The Prose and Poetry of Cheryl Clarke, 1980 to 2005

Carroll & Graf Publishers
An Imprint of Avalon Publishing Group Inc.
245 West 17th Street
11th Floor
New York, NY 10011

AVALON
publishing group incorporated

Library of Congress Cataloging-in-Publication Data is available.

ISBN-10: 0-7867-1675-4
ISBN-13: 978-0-78671-675-3

9 8 7 6 5 4 3 2 1

Designed by Maria Elias
Printed in the United States of America
Distributed by Publishers Group West

To the memory of my mother,
Edna Payne Clarke (1917–2003),
whose days and good looks are with me always.

Contents

Essays

Part Three: Humid Pitch: 1991–1995

Poems

Part Five: The Days of Good Looks: 2000–2005

Poems

Essays

Introduction

The poems and essays in *The Days of Good Looks* represent twenty-five years of contribution to and controversy within the continuum of black writing. The Black Power and Black Arts Movements gave me the skills; gay and lesbian politics gave me the voice. I'll go back to *This Bridge Called My Back: Writings by Radical Women of Color* and what I said in my 1980 article, "Lesbianism: An Act of Resistance." I fully understood the intersection of race and sex for the first time when I met a group of black lesbians at a gay liberation conference in 1973. I quipped: "With these women out here, why am I in the closet?" From that day forward, for better and for worse, I haven't turned back. Soon after that first striking essay, came my famous critique of homophobia in the black community with "The Failure to Transform" in 1984, anthologized in *Home Girls: A Black Feminist Anthology*. You'll find both of these "classic" essays included here.

My 1982 poem, "Of Althea and Flaxie," from my first book of poems, *Narratives: Poems in the Tradition of Black Women,* published by Kitchen Table: Women of Color Press and now out of print, established a mythology/genealogy of black lesbian love and solidified my reputation as a black lesbian poet. I still want to thank Cherríe Moraga, the late Gloria Anzaldua, Barbara Smith, and Elly Bulkin for publishing my early writing and involving me in the lesbian-feminist movement. Twenty-five years later I continue to affirm my deep commitment to lesbianism and feminism through my writing.

Living as a Lesbian, my 1986 collection of poetry, and still my bestseller, established me as a sexual outlaw, when really it was (is) the poetry that is the "outlaw." *Humid Pitch* (1989) and *Experimental Love* (1993) reaffirmed my continuing commitments to both the narrative and the lyric forms of poetry. I chose poems from these three collections that have not often appeared in print and which I have not often read in public. All three collections were published by Firebrand Press, then under the able editorship of Nancy Bereano.

Included also in this collection are poems and essays which appeared previously in early lesbian and gay journals and newspapers like *Thirteenth Moon, Sinister Wisdom, Conditions, Gay Community News,* which are no longer publishing, as well as hard to obtain anthologies, like *Theorizing Black Feminisms.* For me, writing has always been a way, a practice of changing my mind and others' minds and positions on sexuality, sexual politics, and sexual expression: as they are contextualized by race and gender; and as they contextualize race and gender.

The essay, "Transferences and Confluences," first published in *Dangerous Liaisons: Blacks and Gays Fighting for Equality,* reflects my ceaseless desire to think about Afro-American literature in a queer context; and the more recent essays, "Lesbianism 2000" (2001), "The Prong of Permanency, a Rant" (2004), and "Ecstatic Fallacies: The Politics of the Black Storefront" (2005) reflect my concerns about issues currently affecting queer communities: viz., changing lesbian politics, same-sex marriage, and the changing face of homophobia in the black community. "Pomo Afro Homo Vexing of Black Macho in the Age of AIDS," a previously unpublished essay, is struggling to become a longer work on reckoning with the impact of AIDS on black communities, especially black gay men.

Thanks again to all of you who have supported my work for all the years I've been writing. Welcome to all of you who are reading me for the first time. And thanks to my lovely editor, Don Weise for all his support for *The Days of Good Looks.* Good looking.

Cheryl Clarke
Jersey City, New Jersey
2005

Part One
Narratives: 1980–1985

Of Althea and Flaxie

In 1943 Althea was a welder
very dark
very butch
and very proud
loved to cook, sew, and drive a car
and did not care who knew she kept company with a woman
who met her every day after work
in a tight dress and high heels
light-skinned and high-cheekboned
who loved to shoot, fish, play poker
and did not give a damn who knew her 'man' was a woman.

Althea was gay and strong in 1945
and could sing a good song
from underneath her welder's mask
and did not care who heard her sing her song to a woman.

Flaxie was careful and faithful
mindful of her Southern upbringing
watchful of her tutored grace
long as they treated her like a lady
she did not give a damn who called her a 'bulldagger.'

In 1950 Althea wore suits and ties
Flaxie's favorite colors were pink and blue
People openly challenged their flamboyance
but neither cared a fig who thought them 'queer' or 'funny.'

When the girls bragged over break of their sundry loves
Flaxie blithely told them her old lady Althea took her dancing
every weekend
and did not give a damn who knew she clung to a woman.

When the boys on her shift complained of their wives,
Althea boasted of how smart her 'stuff' Flaxie was
and did not care who knew she loved the mind of a woman.

In 1955 when Flaxie got pregnant
and Althea lost her job
Flaxie got herself on relief
and did not care how many caseworkers
threatened midnite raids.

Althea was set up and went to jail
for writing numbers in 1958.
Flaxie visited her every week with gifts
and hungered openly for her thru the bars
and did not give a damn who knew she waited for a woman.

When her mother died in 1965 in New Orleans
Flaxie demanded that Althea walk beside her in the funeral
    procession
and did not care how many aunts and uncles knew she
    slept with a woman.

When she died in 1970
Flaxie fought Althea's proper family not to have her laid out
    in lace
and dressed the body herself
and did not care who knew she'd made her way with a woman.

Ruby the runaway

Women excite me and move me
in the way those old midnite conferences
with my rebel sister Ruby
made my childhood memorable.

Ruby left me for the girl next door
for what she said 'won't even be a minute'
and turned into 14 years
and I mourned my sentence to the cell of my parents
wishing Ruby would come back and bust me out.

My father gave me cigarettes
from his commissary chest of drawers
for the violence of his sex
and my mother allowed me to smoke them
for colluding her silence.

With a cigarette between my fingers
I practiced adulthood in front of my mirror daily.
I was grown.
Not like Ruby who never satisfied herself with symbols.

For the sake of appearances my mother made cold predictions:
'First cigarettes, then alcohol, then sex, then vee dee
or pregnant
or a bulldagger
like that black Ruby!'

I had had it all
except been pregnant or a bulldagger
and still longed for Ruby's soft buzz against my ear
cried to be black and grown like Ruby
to have my sentence commuted
to be protected from my father's intrusions
and my mother's indifference.

Escape was imminent.
Amidst my father's threats to keep my hem below my knees,
to sit with my legs together,
and my mother's admonition never to let the roots of my
    hair revert
and to ignore the male need to call me out of my name in
    the streets
I became engaged to Claude when I was sixteen.
Something Ruby was too wild to do.

Claude was arrogant, intrusive, and clumsy.
He was dumb and impudent
and never understood my body's resistance.
I went to work and lied about my salary.

Upon being told to hand over my check for
the joint account
I rebelled.
Claude snatched my pocketbook
fished out the check
saw my net was ten dollars more than his
and beat me with my pocketbook from the living-
room floor to the bathroom tile.

That ass-whipping amazed me to the point of
calling the police
and calling for the courage of Ruby's big fists.
Claude nearly broke my nose with the telephone receiver
locked me in the bathroom
answered the door.

I heard him assure the police we were having an argument
not a fight.
The door shut.
The closet opened and shut.

His footsteps faded from where I sat in terror
and indifference.
I heard the front door open and shut.
Ten minutes: I retched his name out.
No answer.
Euphoria.
Hysteria.

Twelve hours in the bathroom recalling Ruby's escape
I made decisions.
I heard the front door open.
I did not start.
Straight to the bathroom
he came
to relieve his bladder.

He pushed my rigid body off the toilet seat
where I had begun to live
in that twelve-hour isolation.
Chivas Regal dulls dexterity.
And clumsy Claude could never do two things at once
like grab me and pee.

I was out.
He was in.

I locked him in.
He was noisy to be out.
And so was I. Out. Out. Out.
Running to Ruby.

Women excite me and move me
in the way those old, midnite conferences
with my rebel sister Ruby made my childhood memorable.

Gail

Gail
Chicago nightingale
bred on blues and Bigger Thomas
and extreme weather.
Lover of cocaine and marijuana
on tropical and early mornings in summer
and one hundred years of solitude in winter.

Gail
toucan and nightingale.
Sitting reading Jung in a Newark food stamp office
and speaking in dreams of atavistic masks.

Gail
girl mother.
Brushing, braiding other women's daughters' hair between
    your thighs
before that marauding time of womb-swelling, scraping,
    and pillage.

Gail
plumed amazon.
Tearing up diary pages filed in boxes and drawers crowded with
scents and sachets

singing r&b in Spanish
beating out a latin two-step
with your fist.

Gail

midwest nightingale in an eastbound flight.

The johnny cake
(for Charley)

Death frees people for new experiences.
At the funeral of my friend's mother I was to learn this.
As no one in my family I cared about had died then
I knew nothing of grief.

It was hurricane season.
The mother's death had been sudden.
My friend and I drove 95 South like thieves.
Relentless as hunters.
Through torrents.
Through vaults of foliage.
Every now and then a palmetto.
The car and inexperience between us.
Miles and miles of curves and turns to his ancestral home
where would be the body.

We arrived at the bungalow.
The evening tropical.
The gnats persistent.
Her scent enveloping as the ocean
a woman, the aunt, welcomed us
with her body.

Eyes hazel like his
in that cocoa skin of theirs.
He cried onto her breast all night.
In rhythmic sorrow she rocked him.
I watched from my pallet on the floor.
Their noises kept me vigilant.

I rose early purposefully.
Already she was moving through the rooms.
Eyes topaz signals.
Nipples protuberant against the sheer and floral duster
The covers fell from me.
Following her I passed, looking askance,
at the black naked beauty of my sleeping friend,
and the lace shrouded corpse
of the mother.

In the kitchen
the aunt fed me peaches
and showed me city pictures
of her in bow ties and suspenders
leaning over the mother seated
and wearing eye glasses and dark suits
smoking cigarettes.
Behind them tables and tables

full of women and women.
Intense people.
Unceremoniously the aunt left
to comfort my friend again.

By noon the kitchen was stacked with food.
The rooms filled with the talk of bold
independent women comforting the aunt
and commending her on how well the body looked.
They were distant with my friend.
From their plates
they offered me forkfuls and spoonfuls
of the rich fare they'd brought.
They were solicitous of me.

My friend enters the yard
leaning heavily on the aunt
a mauve veil covering her face.
I walk behind them
cleaving wild roses
azaleas
and purple geraniums.
Through the surprising gauze
the aunt stares at me.
She strokes inside the thigh of my weeping friend.

The body lowered.
The geraniums planted.
The exequies complete.
My friend regains his sense of place.
Grows conscious of the aunt.
The family makes room for him.
He welcomes the bold
independent women back into the house.
Instead of cornbread
He asks the aunt to make johnny cake.

She laughs and grabs me like a playmate.
Pulls me into the kitchen.
We hold each other there
for long moments.
Tongues in throats.

In the other room
my friend and the bold
independent women talk
of cars
the weather
and the road I would travel back.

In the kitchen
the aunt slides her hand between my thighs.
The same hand she makes her dough with.
I pull my tunic above my breasts for her.

I hear them in the other room
talk of the mother
the aunt
their lives in the bungalow.

I welcome her hand inside my drawers.
And come for the first time
for the rest of the day.
With the same hand she kneads the dough
short
and asks nothing back.

I give her my tongue in places she does not remember.
And touch her there.

It bakes.
In the other room
voices recede to a far corner.

Butter oozes from the hot and ready bread.

Death frees people for new experiences.
I learned this at my friend's mother's funeral.
As no one I cared for had died then
I knew nothing of grief.

I left soon and by myself.
For the trip back
the aunt and my friend filled the car
with wild flowers
stolen melons
fallen cake.
The sky was stark.
There were gauntlets of foliage.
Every now and then a palmetto.

Cantaloupe

Wednesdays Mama'd skip from her station at the sink
to look out the window.
Jealous of her attention I'd follow behind.
She'd reach her hand back to my shoulder
without turnin round
pull me by her side
and yell down:

   'dozen egg
   five pound green
   fo ham hock.'

then smile to herself, pat and gently
shove me out the door
as would get me to do anything she ask.

Wednesdays make me think of horses and watermelon.
I'd take Mama's staples from the wild boy man
who hawked wild foodstuff from his horse drawn
wagon I longed to climb into.

Summers he'd be bare chest.
Cold weather he'd wear a plaid and fringe

scarf over head and ears.
Red beard.
Never spoke nor smiled
cept on hot days to sing out:

> 'watermelon
> red to the rine.
> three fo a quarter
> one fo a dime.'

There was always somethin else he'd draw from
the shadow corners of the wagon and give me—
orange, peach, cantaloupe
dependin on season.
I loved to pet the neck of his horse
russet as his beard.

Smilin from the window where she'd watch us
Mama'd call me.
He'd set his jaw, swell in his breeches
and just as gently as Mama sent me to him
send me back to her.

Never bein told
I discover that wild child man

my brother, my father.
Cantaloupe make me remember the
pink inner part of his lip
as he weigh Mama turnip and water cress
and the inside of Mama hand as she clean them.

    'watermelon
    red to the rine.
    three fo a quarter
    one fo a dime.'

would haunt the air long moments after
and haunt me still with memory of Wednesdays
and that brief intimacy.

if you black get back

Vashti
with her one brown
and one hazel eye
was an ugly and dirty little black girl
whose nappy hair could not hold a curl
whose name nobody even wanted to say
much less to play
with her
so in awe of browns and tans we were

Vashti
with her hard hazel eye
was dull in school
but broke no rule.
Teachers laughed openly at her stutter.
Frequently calling upon her to read aloud.
Cowed, her face swelling like an udder,
she would rise to the effort
and the humiliation.

Vashti's hair was never straightened.
To be black was bad enough.
To be black and have nappy hair

was just plain rough.
Boys terrorized her.
Girls scorned her.
Adults walked the other way
to avoid the play
of Vashti's eyes
marking their cruelty.

So black she could stand out in a coal bin.
So black she was most nearly blue.
So black it was a sin.
So black she could stop the dew.
Vashti learned to live
and love with pain.
Wore it like a coat of armor
rather resembling an armadillo.

Lesbianism:
An Act of Resistance

FOR A WOMAN to be a lesbian in a male-supremacist, capitalist, misogynist, racist, homophobic, imperialist culture, such as that of North America, is an act of resistance. (A resistance that should be championed throughout the world by all the forces struggling for liberation from the same slave master.) No matter how a woman lives out her lesbianism—in the closet, in the state legislature, in the bedroom—she has rebelled against becoming the slave master's concubine, viz., the male-dependent female, the female hetero-sexual. This rebellion is dangerous business in patriarchy. Men at all levels of privilege, of all classes and colors have the potential to act out legalistically, moralistically, and violently when they cannot col-onize women, when they cannot circumscribe our sexual, produc-tive, reproductive, creative prerogatives and energies. And the lesbian—that woman who, as Judy Grahn says, "has taken a woman lover"[1]—has succeeded in resisting the slave master's impe-rialism in that one sphere of her life. The lesbian has decolonized her body. She has rejected a life of servitude implicit in Western, heterosexual relationships and has accepted the potential of mutu-ality in a lesbian relationship—*roles* notwithstanding.

Historically, this culture has come to identify lesbians as women who, over time, engage in a range and variety of sexual emotional relationships with women. I, for one, identify a woman as a lesbian who says she is. Lesbianism is a recognition, an awakening, a reawakening of our passion for each (woman) other (woman) and for same (woman). This passion will ultimately reverse the heterosexual imperialism of male culture. Women, through the ages, have fought and died rather than deny that passion. In her essay "The Meaning of Our Love for Women Is What We Have Constantly to Expand," Adrienne Rich states:

> Before any kind of feminist movement existed, or could exist, lesbians existed: women who loved women, who refused to comply with behavior demanded of women, who refused to define themselves in relation to men. Those women, our fore-sisters, millions whose names we do not know, were tortured and burned as witches, slandered in religious and later in "scientific" tracts, portrayed in art and literature as bizarre, amoral, destructive, decadent women. For a long time, the lesbian has been a personification of feminine evil.
>
> . . . Lesbians have been forced to live between two cultures, both male-dominated, each of which has denied and endangered our existence . . . Heterosexual, patriarchal culture has driven lesbians into secrecy and guilt, often to self-hatred and suicide.[2]

The evolving synthesis of lesbianism and feminism—two women-centered and powered ideologies—is breaking that silence and secrecy. The following analysis is offered as one small cut against that stone of silence and secrecy. It is not intended to be original or all-inclusive. I dedicate this work to all the women hidden from history whose suffering and triumph have made it possible for me to call my name out loud.*

The woman who embraces lesbianism as an ideological, political, and philosophical means of liberation of all women from heterosexual tyranny must also identify with the world-wide struggle of all women to end male-supremacist tyranny at all levels. As far as I am concerned, any woman who calls herself a feminist must commit herself to the liberation of *all* women from *coerced* heterosexuality as it manifests itself in the family, the state, and on Madison Avenue. The lesbian-feminist struggles for the liberation of all people from patriarchal domination through heterosexism and for the transformation of all socio-political structures, systems, and relationships that have been degraded and corrupted under centuries of male domination.

However, there is no one kind of lesbian, no one kind of lesbian behavior, and no one kind of lesbian relationship. Also there is no

---

* I would like to give particular acknowledgment to the Combahee River Collective's "A Black Feminist Statement." Because this document espouses "struggling against racial, sexual, heterosexual, and class oppression," it has become a manifesto of radical feminist thought, action, and practice.

one kind of response to the pressures that lesbians labor under to survive as lesbians. Not all women who are involved in sexual-emotional relationships with women call themselves lesbians or identify with any particular lesbian community. Many women are only lesbians to a particular community and *pass* as heterosexuals as they traffic among enemies. (This is analogous to being black and passing for white with only one's immediate family knowing one's true origins.) Yet, those who hide in the closet of heterosexual presumption are sooner or later discovered. The "nigger-in-the-woodpile" story retells itself. Many women are politically active as lesbians, but may fear holding hands with their lovers as they traverse heterosexual turf. (This response to heterosexual predominance can be likened to the reaction of the black student who integrates a predominately white dormitory and who fears leaving the door of her room open when she plays gospel music.) There is the woman who engages in sexual-emotional relationships with women and labels herself *bisexual*. (This is comparable to the Afro-American whose skin color indicates her mixed ancestry yet who calls herself "mulatto" rather than black.) Bisexual is a safer label than lesbian, for it posits the possibility of a relationship with a man, regardless of how infrequent or non-existent the female bisexual's relationships with men might be. And then there is the lesbian who is a lesbian anywhere and everywhere and who is in direct and constant confrontation with heterosexual presumption, privilege, and oppression. (Her struggle can be compared to that of the Civil Rights activist of the 1960's who was out there on the streets for freedom, while so many of us viewed the action on the television.)

Wherever we, as lesbians, fall along this very generalized political continuum, we must know that the institution of heterosexuality is a die-hard custom through which male-supremacist institutions ensure their own perpetuity and control over us. Women are kept, maintained, and contained through terror, violence, and spray of semen. It is profitable for our colonizers to confine our bodies and alienate us from our own life processes as it was profitable for the European to enslave the African and destroy all memory of a prior freedom and self-determination—Alex Haley notwithstanding. And just as the foundation of Western capitalism depended upon the North Atlantic slave trade, the system of patriarchal domination is buttressed by the subjugation of women through heterosexuality. So, patriarchs must extoll the boy-girl dyad as "natural" to keep us straight and compliant in the same way the European had to extoll Caucasian superiority to justify the African slave trade. Against that historic backdrop, *the woman who chooses to be a lesbian lives dangerously.*

As a member of the largest and second most oppressed group of people of color, as a woman whose slave and ex-slave foresisters suffered some of the most brutal racist, male-supremacist imperialism in Western history, the black lesbian has had to survive also the psychic mutilation of heterosexual superiority. The black lesbian is coerced into the experience of institutional racism—like every other nigger in America—and must suffer as well the homophobic sexism of the black political community, some of whom seem to have forgotten so soon the pain of rejection, denial, and repression sanctioned by racist America. While most political black lesbians do not give a damn if white America is negrophobic, it becomes deeply problematic when the contemporary black political community (another male-dominated and male-identified institution) rejects us because of our commitment to women and women's liberation. Many black male members of that community seem still not to understand the historic connection between the oppression of African peoples in North America and the universal oppression of women. As the women's rights activist and abolitionist Elizabeth Cady Stanton pointed out during the 1850's, racism and sexism have been produced by the same animal, viz., "the white Saxon man."

Gender oppression (i.e., the male exploitation and control of women's productive and reproductive energies on the specious basis of a biological difference) originated from the first division of labor, viz., that between women and men, and resulted in the accumulation of private property, patriarchal usurpation of "mother right" or matrilineage, and the duplicitous male-supremacist institution of heterosexual monogamy (for women only). Sexual politics, therefore, mirror the exploitative, class-bound relationship between the white slave master and the African slave—and the impact of both relationships (between black and white and woman and man) has been residual beyond emancipation and suffrage. The ruling-class white man had a centuries-old model for his day-to-day treatment of the African slave. Before he learned to justify the African's continued enslavement and the ex-slave's continued disenfranchisement with arguments of the African's divinely ordained mental and moral inferiority to himself (a smoke screen for his capitalist greed), the white man learned, within the structure of heterosexual monogamy and under the system of patriarchy, to relate to black people—slave or free—as a man *relates* to a woman, viz., as property, as a sexual commodity, as a servant, as a source of free or cheap labor, and as an innately inferior being.

Although counter-revolutionary, Western heterosexuality, which advances male supremacy, continues to be upheld by many black people, especially black men, as the most desired state of affairs between men and women. This observation is borne out on the pages of our most scholarly black publications to our most commercial black publications, which view the issue of black male and female relationships through the lens of heterosexual bias. But this is to be expected, as historically heterosexuality was one of our only means of power over our condition as slaves and one of two means we had at our disposal to appease the white man.

Now, as ex-slaves, black men have more latitude to oppress black women, because the brothers no longer have to compete directly with the white man for control of black women's bodies.

Now, the black man can assume the "master" role, and he can attempt to tyrannize black women. The black man may view the lesbian—who cannot be manipulated or seduced sexually by him—in much the same way the white slave master once viewed the black male slave, viz., as some perverse caricature of manhood threatening his position of dominance over the female body. This view, of course, is a "neurotic illusion" imposed on black men by the dictates of male supremacy, which the black man can never fulfill because he lacks the capital means and racial privilege.

> Historically, the myth in the Black world is that there are only two free people in the United States, the white man and the black woman. The myth was established by the Black man in the long period of his frustration when he longed to be free to have the material and social advantages of his oppressor, the white man. On examination of the myth this so-called freedom was based on the sexual prerogatives taken by the white man on the Black female. It was fantasied by the Black man that she enjoyed it.[3]

While lesbian-feminism does threaten the black man's predatory control of black women, its goal as a political ideology and philosophy is not to take the black man's or any man's position on top.

Black lesbians who do work within "by-for-about-black-people" groups or organizations either pass as "straight" or relegate our lesbianism to the so-called "private" sphere. The more male-dominated or black nationalist bourgeois the organization or group, the more resistant to change, and thus, the more homophobic and anti-feminist. In these sectors, we learn to keep a low profile.

In 1979, at the annual conference of a regional chapter of the National Black Social Workers, the national director of that body was given a standing ovation for the following remarks:

> Homosexuals are even accorded minority status now . . . And white women, too. And some of you black women who call yourselves feminists will be sitting up in meetings with the same white women who will be stealing your men on the sly.

This type of indictment of women's revolution and implicitly of lesbian liberation is voiced throughout the bourgeois black (male) movement. But this is the insidious nature of male supremacy. While the black man may consider racism his primary oppression, he is hard-put to recognize that sexism is inextricably bound up with the racism the black woman must suffer, nor can he see that no women (or men for that matter) will be liberated from the original "master-slave" relationship, viz., that between men and women, until we are all liberated from the false premise of heterosexual superiority. This corrupted, predatory relationship between men and women is the foundation of the master-slave relationship between white and black people in the United States.

The tactic many black men use to intimidate black women from embracing feminism is to reduce the conflicts between white women and black women to a "tug-o'-war" for the black penis. And since the black lesbian, as stated previously, is not interested in his penis, she undermines the black man's only source of power over her, viz., his heterosexuality. Black lesbians and all black women involved in the struggle for liberation must resist this manipulation and seduction.

The black dyke, like every dyke in America, is everywhere—in the home; in the street; on the welfare, unemployment, and social security rolls; raising children; working in factories; in the armed forces; on television; in the public school system; in all the professions; going to college or graduate school; in middle management, et al. The black dyke, like every other non-white and working-class and poor woman in America, has not suffered the luxury, privilege, or oppression of being dependent on men, even though our male counterparts have been present; have shared our lives, work, and struggle; and, in addition, have undermined our "human dignity" along the way like most men in patriarchy, the imperialist family of man. But we could never depend on them "to take care of us" on their resources alone—and, of course, it is another "neurotic illusion" imposed on our fathers, brothers, lovers, husbands that they are supposed to "take care of us" because we are women. Translate: "to take care of us" equals "to control us." Our brothers', fathers', lovers', husbands' only power is their manhood. And unless manhood is somehow embellished by white skin and generations of private wealth, it has little currency in racist, capitalist patriarchy. The black man, for example, is accorded native elite or colonial guard or vigilante status over black women in imperialist patriarchy. He is an overseer for the slave master. Because of his maleness he is given access to certain privileges, eg., employment, education, a car, life insurance, a house, some nice vines. He is usually a rabid heterosexual. He is, since emancipation, allowed to raise a "legitimate" family, allowed to have his piece of turf, viz., his wife and children. That is as far as his dictatorship extends, for if his wife decides that she wants to leave that home for whatever reason, he does not have the power or resources to seduce her otherwise if she is determined to throw off the benign or malicious yoke of dependency. The ruling-class white man, on the other hand, has always had the power to count women among his pool of low-wage labor, his means of production. Most recently, he has "allowed" women the right to sue for divorce, to apply for AFDC, and to be neocolonized.

Traditionally, poor black men and women who banded together and stayed together and raised children together did not have the luxury to cultivate dependence among the members of their families. So, the black dyke, like most black women, has been conditioned to be self-sufficient, i.e., not dependent on men. For me personally, the conditioning to be self-sufficient and the predominance of female role models in my life are the roots of my lesbianism. Before I became a lesbian, I often wondered why I was expected to give up, avoid, and trivialize the recognition and encouragement I felt from women in order to pursue the tenuous business of heterosexuality. And I am not unique. As political lesbians, i.e., lesbians who are resisting the prevailing culture's attempts to keep us invisible and powerless, we must become more visible (particularly black and other lesbians of color) to our sisters hidden in their various closets, locked in prisons of self-hate and ambiguity, afraid to take the ancient act of woman-bonding beyond the sexual, the private, the personal. I am not trying to reify lesbianism or feminism. I am trying to point out that lesbian-feminism has the potential of reversing and transforming a major component in the system of women's oppression, viz., predatory heterosexuality. If radical lesbian-feminism purports an anti-racist, anti-classist, anti-woman-hating vision of bonding as mutual, reciprocal, as infinitely negotiable, as freedom from antiquated gender prescriptions and proscriptions, *then all people struggling to transform the character of relationships in this culture have something to learn from lesbians.*

The woman who takes a woman lover lives dangerously in patriarchy. And woe betide her even more if she chooses as her lover a woman who is not of her race. The silence among lesbian-feminists regarding the issue of lesbian relationships between black and white women in America is caused by none other than the centuries-old taboo and laws in the United States against relationships between people of color and those of the Caucasian race. Speaking heterosexually, the laws and taboos were a reflection of the patriarchal slave master's attempts to control his property via controlling his lineage through the institution of monogamy (for women only) and justified the taboos and laws with the argument that purity of the Caucasian race must by preserved (as well as its supremacy). However, we know that his racist and racialist laws and taboos did not apply to him in terms of the black slave woman just as his classist laws and taboos regarding the relationship between the ruling-class and the indentured servants did not apply to him in terms of the white woman servant he chose to rape. The offspring of any unions between the white ruling-class slave master and the black slave woman or white woman indentured servant could not legally inherit their white or ruling-class sires' property or name, just their mothers' condition of servitude.

The taboo against black and white people relating at any other level than master-slave, superior-inferior has been propounded in America to keep black women and men and white women and men, who share a common oppression at the hands of the ruling-class white man, from organizing against that common oppression. We, as black lesbians, must vehemently resist being bound by the white man's racist, sexist laws, which have endangered potential intimacy of any kind between whites and blacks.

It cannot be presumed that black lesbians involved in love, work, and social relationships with white lesbians do so out of self-hate and denial of our racial-cultural heritage, identities, and oppression. Why should a woman's commitment to the struggle be questioned or accepted on the basis of her lover's or comrade's skin color? White lesbians engaged likewise with black lesbians or any lesbians of color cannot be assumed to be acting out of some perverse, guilt-ridden racialist desire.

I personally am tired of going to events, conferences, workshops, planning sessions that involve a coming together of black and other lesbians of color for political or even social reasons and listening to black lesbians relegate feminism to white women, castigate black women who propose forming coalitions with predominantly white feminist groups, minimize the white woman's oppression and exaggerate her power, and then finally judge that a black lesbian's commitment to the liberation of black women is dubious because she does not sleep with a black woman. All of us have to accept or reject allies on the basis of politics, not on the specious basis of skin color. *Have not black people suffered betrayal from our own people?*

Yes, black women's experiences of misogyny are different from white women's. However, they all add up to how the patriarchal slave master decided to oppress us. We both fought each other for his favor, approval, and protection. Such is the effect of imperialist, heterosexist patriarchy. Shulamith Firestone, in the essay "Racism: The Sexism of the Family of Man," purports this analysis of the relationship between white and black women:

How do the women of this racial Triangle feel about each other? Divide and conquer: Both women have grown hostile to each other, white women feeling contempt for the "sluts" with no morals, black women feeling envy for the pampered "powder puffs." The black woman is jealous of the white woman's legitimacy, privilege, and comfort, but she also feels deep contempt . . . Similarly the white woman's contempt for the black woman is mixed with envy: for the black woman's greater sexual license, for her gutsiness, for her freedom from the marriage bind. For after all, the black woman is not under the thumb of a man, but is pretty much her own boss to come and go, to leave the house, to work (much as it is degrading work) or to be "shiftless." What the white woman doesn't know is that the black woman, not under the thumb of *one* man, can now be squashed by all. There is no alternative for either of them than the choice between being public or private property, but because each still believes that the other is getting away with something both can be fooled into mischanneling their frustration onto each other rather than onto the real enemy, "The Man."[4]

Though her statement of the choices black and white women have under patriarchy in America has merit, Firestone analyzes only a specific relationship, i.e., between the ruling-class white woman and slave or ex-slave black woman.

Because of her whiteness, the white woman of all classes has been accorded, as the black man has because of his maleness, certain privileges in racist patriarchy, e.g., indentured servitude as opposed to enslavement, exclusive right to public assistance until the 1960's, "legitimate" offspring, and (if married into the middle/upper class) the luxury to live on her husband's income, etc.

The black woman, having neither maleness nor whiteness, has always had her heterosexuality, which white men and black men have manipulated by force and at will. Further, she, like all poor people, has had her labor, which the white capitalist man has also, taken and exploited at will. These capabilities have allowed black women minimal access to the crumbs thrown at black men and white women. So, when the black woman and the white woman become lovers, we bring that history and all those questions to the relationship as well as other people's problems with the relationships. The taboo against intimacy between white and black people has been internalized by us and simultaneously defied by us. If we, as lesbian-feminists, defy the taboo, then we begin to transform the history of relationships between black women and white women.

In her essay "Disloyal to Civilization: Feminism, Racism, Gynephobia," Rich calls for feminists to attend to the complexities of the relationship between black and white women in the United States. Rich queries:

What caricatures of bloodless fragility and broiling sensuality still imprint our psyches, and where did we receive these imprintings? What happened between the several thousand northern white women and southern black women who together taught in the schools founded under Reconstruction by the Freedmen's Bureau, side by side braving the Ku Klux Klan harassment, terrorism, and the hostility of white communities?*[5]

So, all of us would do well to stop fighting each other for our space at the bottom, because there ain't no more room. We have spent so much time hating ourselves. Time to love ourselves. And that, for all lesbians, as lovers, as comrades, as freedom fighters, is the final resistance.

Endnotes

1. Grahn, Judy, "The Common Woman," *The Work of a Common Woman*. Diana Press, Oakland, 1978, p. 67.

*One such example is the Port Royal Experiment (1862), the precursor of the Freedmen's Bureau. Port Royal was a program of relief for "freed men and women" in the South Carolina Sea Islands, organized under the auspices of the Boston Education Commission and the Freedmen's Relief Association in New York and the Port Royal Relief Association in Philadelphia, and sanctioned by the Union Army and the Federal Government. See *The Journal of Charlotte Forten* on the "Port Royal Experiment" (Beacon Press, Boston, 1969). Through her northern bourgeois myopia, Forten recounts her experiences as a black teacher among the black freed men and women and her northern white women peers.

2. Rich, Adrienne, *On Lies, Secrets, and Silence: Selected Prose, 1966–1978,* W.W. Norton, New York, 1979, p. 225.

3. Robinson, Pat and Group, "Poor Black Women's Study Papers by Poor Black Women of Mount Vernon, New York," in T. Cade (ed). *The Black Woman: An Anthology.,* New American Library, New York, 1970. p. 194.

4. Firestone, Shulamith, *The Dialectic of Sex: The Case for Feminist Revolution,* Bantam Books, New York, 1972, p. 113.

5. Rich, op. cit., p. 298.

Black, Brave, and Woman, Too

This is a situation in which those of us who research minority and/or women writers are familiar with—having to rescue these figures from some comfortable, circumscribed shadow and place them in their own light. (Hull, G., "Researching Alice Dunbar-Nelson: A Personal and Literary Perspective," *Some of Us Are Brave*, p. 192.)

BLACK AMERICAN WOMEN have been objectified in the flesh, in the language, in the literature, and in the body politic for several centuries. Black women know we have shared and shaped the struggle, development, and triumph of the coerced immigrant, the Afro-American. Black women have been on the front line of the war for survival in the racist United States. We and our black brothers have worked together as partners, comrades, allies, and adversaries for that oft-thwarted goal—black liberation.

The Black Woman. Her loyalty to black people cannot be questioned. In fact, the presumption historically has been made that the black woman's primary commitment is black liberation. In order not to seem individualistic, the black woman did not—in action—necessarily distinguish her struggle from her people's, though she might muse publicly and privately, in letters, diaries, poems, on her double slave lot. The race and the struggle against racism occupied and preoccupied her. These preoccupations created a myopia. Race and all it means in the United States is overwhelming and consuming. One can understand how the black woman might low-profile her concerns over, for example, capitalism, labor, suffrage for women, "free love," abortion, international affairs, et al. The black woman would say to herself: "Time for all that later. Gotta triumph over this race thing. After all isn't racism the reason we're poor, unemployed, can't vote, can't love who we want to love, can't control our bodies, and are kept out of the international domain?" And like Sarah Douglass in 1837, the black woman affirm(s)ed, "I believe they despise us for our color" (Lerner, G., ed., *Black Women in White America: A Documentary History,* 1973, p. 362).

Black women cast our lot with black people. What else was really out there? The Women's Movement. Feminism. The women's movement and feminism have figured significantly in the lives and development of black women from the time of the great social movements of the early nineteenth century. Black women have a feminist tradition. But black women could not ally with white women solely on the basis of gender oppression. Far too much other contradiction was unresolved, namely, white skin and class privilege. At least we share the race and ex-slave status with all other black people. Of course, it has been argued that white women too have been slaves.

We cast our lot with black people. And did our duty. And while we were busy and productive—"behind the scenes," "in the background," and "being the backbone"—our achievements in politics, art, education, service, et al., were being credited to men or not credited at all—just taken and used. It is curious how black women built schools and churches, organized rebellions, hoed fields, ran old-age homes, plus kept households, raised children, worked like beavers all the days of our lives—all in the same day, all in the same lifetime. Yet, any time when attention has been focused on the contributions of Afro-Americans, it is black men who are dredged up from obscurity. The traditions black women have passed on to our daughters and sisters remained anonymous, with few exceptions.

The impetus of feminism, i.e., women interpreting our lives for, by, and about women, has been a rescuing force for the tradition of black women. However, we have had our invisibility to and betrayal at the hands of the predominantly white women's movement. When the contributions women have made to American culture are catalogued, those of black women are strangely omitted. In spite of the sometimes willful, sometimes unconscious exclusion of black women from the ritual of acknowledgment, black women are on the brink of synthesizing the politics of women's liberation and the politics of black liberation for our own personal-is-political development, as opposed to making all the sacrifices. *All the Women Are White, All the Blacks Are Men, But*

Some of Us Are Brave, edited by Gloria T. Hull, Patricia Bell Scott, and Barbara Smith, is part of that synthesis.

But Some of Us Are Brave, subtitled "Black Women's Studies," is an impressive work: nineteen theoretical, sociological, literary, pedagogical essays; six extensive bibliographic essays; a listing of approximately eighty-nine references in addition to the extensive references, bibliographies, and notes that document and accompany the essays; twenty black women's studies course syllabi; a catalogue of non-print materials on black women; and eleven black-and-white photographs of black women of all ages, backgrounds, classes, from as long ago as 1902. The credentials and experiences of the contributors—all black American women except one white woman contributor and two white women co-authors—certainly debunk any myths of "idiocy," "illiteracy," or "vacuousness" (p. xviii). *Brave* is a political, pedagogical tool for use by us. A survival manual for all of us stuck down here in this swamp of Western male letters. *Brave* attempts to free us from the quicksand—Helga Crane rescued from the quagmire, revisited, revised, and resuscitated!*

The guiding politics of *Brave* are black feminist. Its orientation is heavily literary, which is a critical flaw. Though not all the contributors identify themselves or their processes as feminist, without exception the writers are black-woman-centered. *Brave* is not an apologia. It is an assertion of black women's existence as

*Helga Crane is the protagonist in Nella Larsen's novel *Quicksand* (reprinted in 1971 by Collier Books, NY).

intellectual, sentient beings. Hull and Smith, both longtime advocates of the liberation of black women writers from the fetters of anonymity, eloquently and forthrightly introduce us in "The Politics of Black Women's Studies" to the challenge of black women's studies in their assertion:

> Black feminism has made a space for Black women's studies to exist and, through its commitment to all Black women will provide the basis for its survival . . .

> Only a feminist, pro-woman perspective that acknowledges the reality of sexual oppression in the lives of black women, as well as the oppression of race and class, will make Black women's studies the transformer of consciousness it needs to be. (pp. xx–xxi)

In the last fourteen years of acute political repression, only those academics most loyal to white male patriarchal education, i.e., the Ph.D., the tenured, the prolifically published and profusely adored dilettantes, have been retained in our once radical academic programs, e.g., black studies, women's studies. And black women's studies, if it is ever institutionalized, will suffer the same fate, even though the editors caution that this trend toward "respectability," individualism, "acceptance" is a "trap that Black women's studies cannot afford to fall into" (p. xxi).

Like the editors, I believe that pedagogy need not only exist in a college classroom. For black women's studies to be a "transformer of consciousness," it *must* somehow be consumed by the "supposedly 'ordinary' Black women whose 'unexceptional' actions enabled us and the race to survive" (p. xxi). I believe that the perpetuity of a radical black women's studies is dependent upon its distance from traditional white and male institutions of high learning and otherwise. In its philosophy and vision, *Brave* is adaptable to the struggle of naming ourselves to black women who exist and survive outside the academic colony and who are in need of a "pro-feminist" and "anti-racist" perspective in their lives.

I would suggest that "Visions and Recommendations" (p. xxxiii), co-authored by Hull, Scott, and Smith, be amended to read: "That Black women's studies be accountable to black women of all ages." Were it not for the three photographs of older black women reproduced in the text, one might presume that black women do not live beyond the age of forty.

The first section of *Brave* is devoted to "establishing the framework in which black women's studies can most successfully be taught" (p. xxx). Michele Wallace's herstoric article "A Black Feminist's Search for Sisterhood" (1975) is reprinted here and formally opens the volume. In her candid style, Wallace broke the silence of isolated black feminists by proclaiming our existence and our invisibility to one another. She was also the first to address the sexual politics in the black community from a feminist perspective, especially those politics which proliferated during the late sixties and early seventies, wherein "the 'new Blackness' was fast becoming the new slavery for sisters."

Strategically following Wallace's piece is the pivotal contribution to radical black feminist thought, "A Black Feminist Statement," prepared by the Combahee River Collective. Never before has there been a model of black feminist practice which iridesces all the factors of oppression and attempts to integrate our struggles against racism, sexism, class oppression, homophobia, violence against women, imperialism, et al. The intent of this statement is to give us a vision of revolution and the implements to effect and sustain a revolution. The piece attempts to synthesize all of black women's oppressions, chiefly race, sex, and class, into a dialectic of resistance and liberation.

The bibliographic listing by Patricia Bell Scott, "Selected Bibliography on Black Feminism," is comprehensive and educational, and certainly provides a resource for those who would teach or want to know about black women's herstorical considerations of ourselves as women. Scott's use of the term "feminist" is problematic. Many of the works listed are feminist, i.e., written by women who call themselves feminists. Many are not. I believe we must differentiate between black women in history who comment on women's struggle for "equality" or who can articulate a feminist line, and black women who postulate that women's liberation will be effected through the practice of woman-centered politics and the destruction of male supremacy. The latter are feminists. This bibliographic listing does not differentiate between those women who call themselves feminists and those who talk about women. Angela Davis, for example, is not a feminist, though she can articulate a feminist line. Inez Smith Reid, for another example, is decidedly anti-feminist. The glaring shortcoming of Joyce Ladner's work, as a third example, is that she did not adopt a feminist approach to her study of adolescent black women, *Tomorrow's Tomorrow* (1971). Yet, Davis's autobiography is listed as a "black feminist" work. Reid's and Ladner's works are listed under the category "The Contemporary Black Feminist Movement." While all our contributions are valuable, let us not create the illusion that any black woman who writes about black women is a feminist.

Novelist Alice Walker opens Section II, "Roadblocks and Bridges: Confronting Racism," with the satirical narrative "One Child of One's Own: A Meaningful Digression Within the Work(s)—An Excerpt." I must admit to my personal difficulty with "Our Mother"—Ama Ata Aidoo notwithstanding—the virtuous persona who goes about in her various bourgeois women's settings tersely calling white feminists to account for their racism and "educated and successful" black women to account for their anti-feminism. The piece is zany, nonetheless. At the very end Walker's form shifts from the narrative to a more expository form. Seeming truly to have become "Our Mother," the author formally concludes the piece with a warning to black women:

To the extent that Black women dissociate themselves from the women's movement, they abandon their responsibilities to women throughout the world. This is a serious abdication from and misuse of radical Black herstorical tradition: Harriet Tubman, Sojourner Truth, Ida B. Wells, and Fannie Lou Hamer would not have liked it. Nor do I. (p. 42)

Patricia Meyer Spacks, Judy Chicago, and Ellen Moers are then singled out and attacked by Walker, in a series of footnotes, as emblems of racist ignorance of the contributions of black women to art and letters. This digression would have been more meaningful within the text, especially the criticism of the Sojourner Truth Plate in Chicago's exhibit, "The Dinner Party":

The Sojourner Truth Plate is the only one in the collection that shows—instead of a vagina—a face. . . .

It occurred to me that perhaps white women feminists, no less than white women generally, cannot imagine Black women have vaginas. (pp. 42–43)

The historical, sociological Section III, "Dispelling the Myths: Black Women and the Social Sciences," offers three informative essays on the status of black women in the social sciences. However, Erlene Stetson's essay, "Studying Slavery: Some Literary and Pedagogical Considerations on the Black Female Slave," is the best of this section and one of the best in the collection.

Stetson's elucidatory and lengthy essay on the black slave woman is a thoughtful, well-written piece. She sets forth the problems of research and pedagogy in this neglected area of study. In her attempt to teach the herstory of the black woman as slave, Stetson allows her class to become a research body, reconstructing herstory from scattered sources, raising questions which provoke further inquiry, and tracing the sources of prevalent myths regarding the black woman's non-womanness (vaginalessness).

Stetson reports nineteen questions raised by her students for further inquiry, the most provocative for me being, "Were monogamous relationships possible between women, between white and Black women, or only between women and men?" For the sake of pedagogy, I would like to suggest an additional question for future black women's studies classes to ponder: What has been the impact on the psychology of black women of the political sanction of centuries of violence against black women? Within the previously discussed pedagogical framework, Stetson offers an interesting historical perspective on ante-bellum women, black and white. She raises thoughtful questions about the pedagogical uses of black women's slave narratives and provides a bibliographic listing of black women's slave narratives, which will be invaluable to any student of black women. However, Stetson does not seriously examine the differential brutality leveled against the black slave woman. She chooses not to be critical of how white women exploited the analogy between their oppression in marriage and the enslavement of blacks.

Beginning Section IV, "Creative Survival: Preserving Body, Mind, and Spirit," is Beverly Smith's bibliographic essay, "Black Women's Health: Notes for a Course," which is urgently relevant to Hull's and Smith's assertion that black women's studies must be connected to black women's lives. I can think of no one issue more critical to our survival than health, which black women have the least of, like everything else. The bibliographic materials are a mixture of clinical, but mostly literary references. I regret that the issue of aging is not raised here, as black women's health problems increase as we age and there are certain health concerns concomitant with aging. However, the neglect of the issue of black women's aging throughout this collection is regrettable.

Jacquelyn Grant's essay, "Black Women and the Church," is excellent herstoriography. It is a call to revolutionize the patriarchal god of Western culture, which black people have adopted, into a "holistic Black theology." And black women in the church must be catalysts for the transformation of the black church:

If, as I contend, the liberation of Black men and women is inseparable then a radical, split cannot be made between racism and sexism. Black women are oppressed by racism and sexism. It is therefore necessary that Black men and women be actively involved in combatting both evils. (p. 148)

At the end, Grant's essay rings with evangelism—and this always disturbs me. Perhaps it is my atheism. I have as little patience with a "black theology" as I do with a "feminist theology." Grant even capitalizes the word "god"! She says, in those opiate tones:

> Such a theology will "allow" God through the Holy Spirit *to work through persons* without regard to race, sex, or class. This theology will exercise its prophetic function and serve as a "self-test" in a church characterized by the sins of racism, sexism, and other forms of oppression. (p. 149; italics mine)

Well, now, all I can say is, like the lady in red: "i found god in myself & i loved her / i loved her fiercely."*

Michele Russell's essay, "Slave Codes and Liner Notes," is insightful, skillfully written, and attempts to use the medium of the blues as a repository of the traditions of poor black women. Of the blues, Russell says:

> They are the expression of a particular social process by which poor Black women have commented on all the major theoretical, practical, and political questions facing us and have created a mass audience who listens to what we say in that form [the blues]. (p. 130)

---

*Ntozake Shange, *for colored girls who have considered suicide when the rainbow is enuf* (Macmillan Publishing Co., Inc., New York, 1976), p. 64.

As exponents of the blues form, and thus exponents of poor black women, Russell chooses five black women singers whose music reflects the Afro-American's song of freedom: Bessie Smith, Bessie Jackson, Billie Holiday, Nina Simone, Esther Phillips. Of the five she discusses, Bessie Smith and Bessie Jackson were "city" blues singers, i.e., they sang songs written in the classical, though stylized, blues mode. Though she was influenced by Bessie Smith and sang blues songs, Billie Holiday was a jazz singer and must be viewed as one of the heaviest influences in modern jazz. Bessie Smith and Billie Holiday had broad appeal to the masses of black women, but Nina Simone and Esther Phillips did not. Nina Simone experimented with a broad range of material, blues being one, but appealed to or was limited to an elite set. Esther Phillips is a singer of the moment, not of the stature of Smith, Holiday, or Simone. Were it not for Dinah Washington, Little Esther would not know which note to bend. Also, no analysis of black women singers can depend solely on the songs they sang, for most had little control over their material. Lastly, no *serious* black feminist consideration of mainstream black women singers "of the past fifty years" would omit consideration of Aretha Franklin!

Lesbianism:

Women must not collude in the oppression of women who have chosen each other, that is, lesbians. (Barbara Smith, p. 51)

In the contributions of Barbara Smith, Beverly Smith, Gloria
Hull, and Lorraine Bethel, the issues of lesbianism, homophobia,
and the lesbian aesthetic are addressed. Why is it that, with the
exception of comments in Beverly Smith's essay on health, the
Combahee River Collective's statement, and Barbara Smith's speech
on racism and women's studies, the issue of lesbianism is relegated
to Section V, "Necessary Bread: Black Women's Literature"?

The fascinating and herstorical literary essays of Barbara Smith
("Toward a Black Feminist Criticism"), Lorraine Bethel ("'This
Infinity of Conscious Pain': Zora Neale Hurston and the Black
Female Literary Tradition"), and Gloria Hull ("Researching Alice
Dunbar-Nelson") rank as the best essays in the book, primarily
because they have integrated the lesbian aesthetic into their study
of black women's literature—unlike Mary Helen Washington[*] and
Michele Russell, the other two contributors to Section V, who do
not even include one "politically correct" statement on lesbianism.
Hull, Smith, and Bethel proclaim the woman-identification
explicit and implicit in the works of black women writers and set
forth the criteria for black feminist criticism.

Smith is the first critic to examine the works of black women
writers from a lesbian-feminist perspective. In order to accomplish

[*]Washington has edited two volumes of fiction by black women writers, not one
lesbian story or one out lesbian writer among or in them. This is homophobia by
omission.

this, she must necessarily expand the definition of lesbianism beyond sex. Smith comes to define the lesbian sensibility in black women's literature as that in which "the central characters are female, are positively portrayed and have pivotal relationships with one another" (p. 164). As she says of Toni Morrison's novel *Sula:*

> it works as a lesbian novel not only because of the passionate friendship between Sula and Nel, but because of Morrison's consistently critical stance toward the heterosexual institutions of male-female relationships, marriage, and the family. (p. 165)

Yet I do so wish that some of the present-day non-lesbian black women writers whom we so admire and write about would take the risk of incorporating a conscious lesbian aesthetic in their fiction, deal directly with sexual love between women, and take it out of the subliminal realm of imagination. I, frankly, am tired of teasing it out of their imagery.

Bethel develops a similar argument as Smith in her analysis of the life and work of Zora Neale Hurston. Bethel views lesbianism, as it is defined in the previously cited passage from Smith's essay, as the basis of black feminist criticism:

> Black woman identification, the basis of Black feminism and Black feminist literary criticism, is most simply the idea of

Black women seeking their own identity and defining themselves through bonding on various levels. (p. 184)

While Bethel and Smith address the lesbian aesthetic in the works of non-lesbian writers, Hull writes of her discovery that writer, activist, and publisher Alice Dunbar-Nelson's "woman-identification extended to romantic liaisons with at least two of her friends" (p. 191). The process of researching Dunbar-Nelson was not only a process of rescuing her from the shadow of Paul Laurence Dunbar, her first husband, but of rescuing her from the presumption of "genteel bourgeoise" heterosexuality. Were it not for a "Black feminist critical approach" to researching Dunbar-Nelson, the issue of her lesbianism might have been suppressed or considered a private matter. Hull establishes criteria for black feminist criticism which closely parallel the Combahee River Collective's criteria for black feminist practice and analysis, but the closest Hull comes to calling for a conscious appreciation and acknowledgment of lesbianism is "everything about the subject is important for a total understanding and analysis of her life and work." In spite of its gentility, this essay demonstrates movingly that one's deepest intellectual commitment is emotional. Just as Hull has rescued Dunbar-Nelson from obscurity, she has resuscitated our black lesbian herstory.

The connection between black women's studies and poor and working-class women is reflected in Michele Russell's pedagogical article, "Black-Eyed Blues Connections: Teaching Black Women." The author delineates a holistic teaching strategy for black women based upon her teaching experience in a community college in Detroit. This article, in spite of its omission of the issue of lesbianism, comes closest to addressing the role of black women's studies in the lives of common black women.

But I ask the question again: Why is lesbianism relegated to the realm of literary criticism? The issue of black lesbianism should have been integrated into every single essay prepared for this collection if we are truly serious about black feminist scholarship and practice. Lesbianism is not solely an aesthetic nor solely a sexual issue, nor an issue to be treated solely by lesbians. Black lesbianism is also an issue in the social sciences. There are stereotypes and myths about black lesbians that need "dispelling." In terms of pedagogy, black women need to be taught about our lesbianism just as we are taught about our slave history or our composers, writers, poets, welders. The black church will be a regressive, oppressive institution until it corrects not only its sexism but also its homophobia. Why is there no essay in this collection which bears the word "lesbian" in its title? The bibliographic essays on influential black women, nineteenth-century black women poets, black women novelists, black women playwrights, and black women composers are fabulous resources—with no references to black lesbians. I ask all the contributors who accept that a "feminist, pro-woman perspective is necessary to understand fully the experiences of black women" and who did not address lesbianism: How do you expect to fully understand the experiences of black women?

The issue of black women's sexuality, except as lifestyle and aesthetic, is not treated. If one were to slip over Beverly Smith's "Health" piece and one sentence of Erlene Stetson's piece on slavery, one might assume that black women feminists do not believe black women have vaginas either.

How can we bring black women's studies to women who are no longer young? Who are in prison? Who are workers? Who are not of the educated elite? It is impossible for one book to be all things to all people. Our needs as black women are immense, unexplored, barely articulated. *Brave* is a serious piece of work affirming the survival and triumph of black women in America. *Brave* is truly an act of courage and tenacity—consistent with the tradition of black women. I welcome *Brave* as part of the tradition of black women's contribution to the life, culture, autonomy, and herstory of black women.

The Failure to Transform: Homophobia in the Black Community

THAT THERE IS homophobia among black people in America is largely reflective of the homophobic culture in which we live. The following passage from the proposed "Family Protection Act" (1981, S. 1378, H.R. 3955), a venomous bill before the U.S. Congress, vividly demonstrates the depth of the ruling class' fear and hatred of homosexuals, homosexuality, and the homosexual potential in everyone (themselves included).

> No federal funds may be made available under any provision of federal law to any public or private individual, group, foundation, commission, corporation, association, or other entity for the purpose of advocating, promoting, or suggesting homosexuality, male or female, as a lifestyle. (p. 9, line 13, section 108)

Yet, we cannot rationalize the disease of homophobia among black people as the white man's fault, for to do so is to absolve ourselves of our responsibility to transform ourselves. When I took my black lesbian feminist self to the First National Plenary Conference on Self-Determination (December 4, 5, 6, 1981) in New York City, thinking surely that this proclaimed "historic meeting of the Black Liberation Movement" must include black lesbian feminists, I was struck by a passage from the printed flyer left on every seat:

> Revolutionary nationalists and genuine communists cannot uphold homosexuality in the leadership of the Black Liberation Movement nor uphold it as a correct practice. Homosexuality is a genocidal practice. . . . Homosexuality does not produce children. . . . Homosexuality does not birth new warriors for liberation . . . homosexuality cannot be upheld as correct or revolutionary practice. . . . The practice of homosexuality is an accelerating threat to our survival as a people and as a nation.

Compare these two statements—the first from the ultra(white)-right and the second from self-proclaimed black "revolutionaries and genuine communists." Both reflect a decidedly similar pathology: homophobia. If I were a "revolutionary nationalist" or even a "genuine communist," I would be concerned if my political vision in any way supported the designs of my oppressors, the custodians of white male privilege. But it is these black macho intellectuals and politicos, these heirs of Malcolm X, who have never expanded Malcolm's revolutionary ideals beyond the day of his death, who consciously or unwittingly have absorbed the homophobia of their patriarchal slavemasters. It is they who attempt to propagate homophobia throughout the entire black community. And it is they whom I will address in this writing.

Since 1965, the era which marked a resurgence of radical black consciousness in the United States, many black people of the post–World War II generation began an all-consuming process of rejecting the values of WASP America and embracing our African and Afro-American traditions and culture. In complete contrast to the conservative black bourgeoisie and to bourgeois reformist civil rights proponents, the advocates of Black Power demanded progressive remedies to the accumulated ills of black folk in America, viewed racism as international in scope, rescued Afro-American culture from anonymity, and elevated the black man to the pedestal of authority in the black liberation movement. In order to participate in this movement one-had to be black (of course), be male-oriented, and embrace a spectrum of black nationalist, separatist, Pan Africanist sentiments, beliefs, and goals. Rejection of white people was essential as well as rejection of so-called white values, which included anything from reading Kenneth Clark's *Civilization* to eating a t.v. dinner.

While the cult of Black Power spurned the assimilationist goals of the politically conservative black bourgeoisie, its devotees, nevertheless, held firmly to the value of heterosexual and male superiority. As Michele Wallace states in her controversial essay, "Black Macho" (1979):

> the contemporary black man no longer exists for his people or even for himself. . . . He has become a martyr. And he has arrived in this place, not because of the dependency inflicted upon him in slavery, but because his black perspective, like the white perspective, supported the notion that manhood is more valuable than anything else. (p. 79)

It is ironic that the Black Power movement could transform the consciousness of an entire generation of black people regarding black self-determination and, at the same time, fail so miserably in understanding the sexual politics of the movement and of black people across the board.

Speaking of the "sexual-racial antagonisms" dividing the Student Non-violent Coordinating Committee during the 1960s, Manning Marable assesses the dilemma of the black movement of that era:

> The prevailing popular culture of racism, the sexist stereotypes held by black men and women, and the psychological patterns of dependency which exploitation creates over several generations could not be uprooted easily. In the end the

Movement may have failed to create a new interracial society in the South because its advocates had first failed to transform themselves. (1980, p. 125)

Like all Americans, black Americans live in a sexually repressive culture. And we have made all manner of compromise regarding our sexuality in order to live here. We have expended much energy trying to debunk the racist mythology which says our sexuality is depraved. Unfortunately, many of us have over-compensated and assimilated the Puritan value that sex is for procreation, occurs only between men and women, and is only valid within the confines of heterosexual marriage. And, of course, like everyone else in America who is ambivalent in these respects, black folk have to live with the contradictions of this limited sexual system by repressing or closeting any other sexual/erotic urges, feelings, or desires.

Dennis Altman, in his pivotal work, *Homosexuality: Oppression and Liberation* (1971), says the following of Western culture:

The repression of polymorphous perversity in Western societies has two major components: the removal of the erotic from all areas of life other than the explicitly sexual and the denial of our inherent bisexuality. (p. 79)

That Western culture is limiting, few can deny. A tremendous amount of pressure is brought to bear on men, women, and children to be heterosexual to the exclusion of every other erotic impulse. I do not begrudge heterosexuals their right to express themselves, but rabid sexual preference is a stone drag on anybody's part. That the black community is homophobic and rabidly heterosexual is a reflection of the black movement's failure to "transform" its proponents with regard to the boundless potential of human sexuality. And this failure has prevented critical collaboration with politically motivated black lesbians and gay men. Time and again homophobia sabotages coalitions, divides would-be comrades, and retards the mental restructuring, essential to revolution, which black people need so desperately.

The concept of the black family has been exploited since the publication of the infamous Moynihan report, *The Negro Family: A Case for National Action* (1965). Because the insular, privatized nuclear family is upheld as the model of Western family stability, all other forms—for example, the extended family, the female-headed family, the lesbian family—are devalued. Many black people, especially middle-class black people, have accepted the male-dominated nuclear family model, though we have had to modify it because black women usually must work outside the home. Though "revolutionary nationalists and genuine communists" have not accepted the nuclear family model per se, they have accepted African and Eastern patriarchal forms of the family, including polygamy (offering the specious rationalization that there are more black women than black men). Homosexuality is viewed as a threat to the continued existence of the heterosexual family, because homosexual unions do not, in and of themselves, produce offspring—as if one's only function within a family, within a relationship, or in sex were to produce offspring. Black family lifestyles and homosexual lifestyles are not antithetical. Most black lesbians and gay men grew up in families and are still critically involved with their families. Many black lesbians and gay men are raising children. Why must the black family be so strictly viewed as the result of a heterosexual dyad?

And finally, why is the black male so-called left so vehement in its propagation of these destructive beliefs, and why have its proponents given such relentless expression to the homophobic potential in the mass of black people? Because the participation of open black lesbians and gay men in the black so-called liberation movement is a threat to the continued hegemony of dogmatic, doctrinaire black men who have failed to reject the Western institution of heterosexuality and the Christian fundamentalist notion of sex as "sin," no matter what doctrine or guru they subscribe to. Homophobic black intellectuals and politicos are so charged with messianic fervor that they seem like a perversion of the W.E.B. DuBois concept of the "Talented Tenth," the hypothesis that "the Negro race . . . is going to be saved by its exceptional men." Indeed, this homophobic cult of black men seems to view itself as the "exceptional men" who will save the black liberation movement from homosexual "contamination." Furthermore, the black intellectual/political man, by dint of his knowledge, training, and male privilege—and in spite of racism—has access to numerous bourgeois resources (such as television, radio, the stage, the podium, publications, and schools) whereby he can advance his reactionary ideologies and make his opinions known to the public at large.

Let us examine the rhetoric and ravings of a few notable black heterosexuals.

Chairman Baraka, Imamu Baraka, LeRoi Jones—whatever patriarchal designation he assumes—is a rabid homophobe. Wherever he makes his homophobic statements, his sexist invective is not far behind. From his early works on, this chameleon, the patriarch of the "new black poetry" of the 1960s, has viewed homosexuality as a symbol of a decadent establishment, as defectiveness, as weakness, as a strictly white male flaw.

In his first book of poems, *Preface to a Twenty Volume Suicide Note* (1961), in which he reveals himself as a versatile though imitative poet, Jones is homophobic and woman-hating. In a wildly imagistic poem, "To a Publisher . . . cut out," he free-associates:

Charlie Brown spent most of his time whacking his doodle, or having weird relations with that dopey hound of his (though that's a definite improvement over . . . that filthy little lesbian he's hung up with). (p. 19)

In the same poem, Jones debunks the myth of the black woman's superior sexual prowess: "I have slept with almost every mediocre colored woman / On 23rd St . . ." (p. 19).

In his notorious essay "American Sexual Reference: Black Male" (*Home,* 1965), Jones lays the ultimate disparagement on the American white man and white woman:

> Most American white men are trained to be fags. . . . That red flush, those silk blue faggot eyes. So white women become men-things, a weird combination sucking male juices to build a navel orange, which is themselves. (p. 216)

But Jones is at his heterosexist best in the essay "Black Woman" (*Raise Race Rays Raze,* 1971), which should have been titled "One Black Macho Man's Narcissistic Fantasy." He commands the black woman, with arrogant condescension, to "complement" her man, to "inspire" her man. He is laughable in his smugness, his hetero-sexist presumptions—to say nothing of his obvious contempt for women. It seems that his homophobic and misogynist attitudes have not abated since he embraced Marxism. Leroi-Imamu-Chairman-Jones-Baraka is an irreversible homophobe. Methinks he doth protest too much.

In another classic example of sixties-style black woman-hatred, playwright Ed Bullins attempts a portrayal of a lesbian rela-tionship in *Clara's Ole Man* (1965). The action is set in the North Philadelphia flat of Clara and Big Girl, Clara's "ole man," who is stereotypically "butch." Clara and Big Girl are not disparaged by their "ghetto" community, symbolized by two older, alcoholic black women who stay upstairs and by three juvenile delinquents, Stoogie, Bama, and Hoss, who take refuge from a police chase in the couple's apartment, a familiar haunt. It is only Jack, an outsider and an ex-Marine in pursuit of upward mobility through "college prep courses," who is too narcissistic to understand the obvious bond between the two women. Jack, whose intention is to date Clara, "retches" when he realizes Clara and Big Girl are lovers. *Clara's Ole Man* is a substanceless rendering of the poor black community, a caricature of lesbianism, and a perpetuation of the stereotype of the pathological black community. But Ed Bullins gained a great deal of currency among black and white "avant-garde" intellectuals for his ability to replicate and create caricatures of black life.

In that same year (1965), a pivotal year in the political development of black people, Calvin Hernton discusses the interrelationship of sex and racism in his popular book *Sex and Racism in America*. Hernton does not address the issue of homosexuality in any of his four essays, "The White Woman," "The Negro Male," "The White Male," and "The Negro Woman." In several homophobic asides Hernton is alternately dismayed by, presumptuous about, and intrigued by his observations of homosexual behavior:

The extent to which some white women are attracted to Negro lesbians is immensely revealing—even the Negro lesbian is a "man." It is not an uncommon sight (in Greenwich Village, for instance) to see these "men" exploiting this image of themselves to the zenith. (p. 113)

One man who seemed *effeminate* put coins into the jukebox, *swished* along side of me (p. 114). He had the appearance of a businessman or a politician—except for his eyes, which seemed to hold some dark secret, something in them that made me wonder . . . maybe this man was a homosexual. (p. 89) [ital. mine]

We can see from the few passages cited above that homophobia in the black community has not only a decidedly bourgeois character but also a markedly male imprint. Which is not to say, however, that homophobia is limited to the psyche of the black intellectual male, but only that it is he who institutionalizes the illness within our political/intellectual community. And rest assured, we can find his homophobic counterpart in black women, who are, for the most part, afraid of risking the displeasure of their homophobic brothers were they to address, seriously and in a principled way, homosexuality. Black bourgeois female intellectuals practice homophobia by omission more often than rabid homophobia.

Michele Wallace's *Black Macho and the Myth of the Superwoman* is a most obvious example. This brave and scathing analysis of the sexual politics of the black political community after 1965 fails to treat the issues of gay liberation, black lesbianism, or homophobia vis-à-vis the black liberation or the women's liberation movement. In "Black Macho," the opening essay, Wallace addresses the homophobia of Eldridge Cleaver and Amiri Baraka, but she neither calls it "homophobia" nor criticizes these attitudes as a failing of the black liberation movement. For the sake of her own argument regarding the black macho neurosis, Wallace exploits the popular conception of male homosexuality as passivity, the willingness to be fucked (preferably by a white man, according to Cleaver). It is then seen as antithetical to the concept of black macho, the object of which is to do the fucking. Wallace does not debunk this stereotype of male homosexuality. In her less effective essay, "The Myth of the Superwoman," Wallace omits any mention of black lesbians. In 1979, when asked at a public lecture at Rutgers University in New Jersey why the book had not addressed the issues of homosexuality and homophobia, the author responded that she was not an "expert" on either issue. But Wallace, by her own admission, was also not an "expert" on the issues she *did* address in her book.

The black lesbian is not only absent from the pages of black political analysis, her image as a character in literature and her role as a writer are blotted out from or trivialized in literary criticism written by black women. Mary Helen Washington's otherwise useful anthologies are a prime example of this omission of black lesbianism and black lesbian writers. In both *Black Eyed Susans* (1975) and *Midnight Birds* (1980), the editor examines the varied roles black women have played in the black community and how these roles are more authentically depicted in the fiction of black women than in the fiction of black men.

In her introduction to *Midnight Birds,* Washington speaks of the major themes of the material presented in this anthology: "women's reconciliation with one another," antagonisms with men, "areas of commonality among black and white women." Now, one would think with all the mention of these women-identified themes that there would be a lesbian story or two in the anthology. But again we are disappointed. There is no mention of lesbianism in the introduction, there are no open lesbian contributors to the anthology, and there is no lesbian story in the collection. And yet, we know there is certainly plenty of available work by black lesbian writers. For example, Audre Lorde's lesbian fiction piece, "Tar Beach," which appeared in *Conditions: Five, The Black Women's Issue* in 1979—prior to the publication of *Midnight Birds*—would have powerfully enhanced the collection. Washington knows that black lesbian writers exist. In a footnote to the previously mentioned introduction (p. xxv), Washington credits Barbara Smith's essay "Toward a Black Feminist Criticism" (*Conditions: Two,* 1977) as one of two pieces of writing which has challenged and shaped her thinking. Smith is a lesbian and she writes about lesbianism. The other piece Washington refers to, Adrienne

Rich's "Disloyal to Civilization: Feminism, Racism, Gynephobia" (*On Lies, Secrets, and Silence,* 1979) is written by a lesbian as well.

One of the most recent books to appear in the name of feminism is bell hooks' *Ain't I A Woman: Black Women and Feminism.* Hooks seems to purposely ignore the existence and central contributions of black lesbians to the feminist movement. Aside from a gross lack of depth in her analysis of the current women's movement in America, the most resounding shortcoming of this work of modern feminism is its omission of any discussion of lesbian feminism, the radicalizing impact of which distinguishes this era of feminism from the previous eras. Hooks does not even mention the word *lesbian* in her book. This is unbearable. Ain't lesbians women, too? Homophobia in the black movement and in the women's movement is not treated, yet lesbians historically have been silenced and repressed in both. In her statement, "Attacking heterosexuality does little to strengthen the self-concept of the masses of women who desire to be with men" (p. 191), Hooks delivers a backhanded slap at lesbian feminists, a considerable number of whom are black. Hooks would have done well to attack the institution of heterosexuality, as it is a prime tool of black women's oppression in America. Like the previously discussed writers, Hooks fears alienating the black community cum the black bourgeois intellectual/political establishment. And there is the fear of transformation, the fear that the word will generate the deed. Like her black male counterpart, the black woman intellectual is afraid to relinquish heterosexual privilege. So little else is guaranteed black people.

I must confess that, in spite of the undeniably homophobic pronouncements of black intellectuals, I sometimes become impatient with the accusations of homophobia hurled at the black community by many gay men and lesbians, as if the whole black community were more homophobic than the heterosexist culture we live in. The entire black community gets blamed for the reactionary postures of a few petit-bourgeois intellectuals and politicos. Since no one has bothered to study the black community's attitudes on homosexuals, homosexuality, or homosexual lifestyles, it is not accurate to attribute homophobia to the mass of black people.

Prior to the growth of the contemporary black middle class, which has some access to the white world, the black community—due to segregation North and South—was even more diverse, encompassing a world of black folk of every persuasion, profession, status, and lifestyle. There have always been upwardly mobile blacks, but until the late 1950s and early sixties there had never been so many opportunities to reap the tenuous fruits of affluence outside the traditional black community. The cordoning off of all types of black people into a single community because of race may be one influence on black attitudes toward difference.

The poor and working-class black community, historically more radical and realistic than the reformist and conservative black middle class and the atavistic, "blacker-than-thou" (bourgeois) nationalists, has often tolerated an individual's lifestyle prerogatives, even when that lifestyle was disparaged by the prevailing culture. Though lesbians and gay men were exotic subjects of curiosity, they were accepted as part of the community (neighborhood)—or at least, there were no manifestos calling for their exclusion from the community.

I can recall being about twelve years old when I first saw a black lesbian couple. I was walking down the street with my best friend, Kathy. I saw two young women walking together in the opposite direction. One wore a doo-rag, a Banlon button-down, and high-top sneakers. The other woman wore pink brush rollers, spit curls plastered with geech, an Oxford-tailored shirt, a mohair sweater, fitted skirt with a kick pleat, black stockings, and the famous I. Miller flat, sling-back shoe, the most prestigious pair of kicks any Dee Cee black girl could own. I asked Kathy, "Who are they?" "Bulldaggers," she answered. "What's that?" I asked again. "You know, they go with each other," Kathy responded. "Why?" I continued. "Protection," Kathy said casually. "Protection?" I repeated. "Yeah, at least they won't get pregnant," Kathy explained.

It is my belief that poor black communities have often accepted those who would be outcast by the ruling culture—many times to spite the white man, but mainly because the conditions of our lives have made us empathic. And, as it stands now, the black political community seems bereft of that humanity which has always been a tradition among Afro-American freedom fighters, the most illustrious of whom have come from the grassroots.

As a group and as individuals, black lesbians and gay men—sometimes obvious and sometimes not—have been as diverse as the communities we've lived in. Like most other people, we have been workers, church-goers, parents, hustlers, and upwardly mobile. Since black gay men and lesbians have always been viable contributors to our communities, it is exceedingly painful for us to face public denunciation from black folk—the very group who should be championing our liberation. Because of the level of homophobia in the culture in general, many black gay men and lesbians remain in the closet, passing as heterosexuals. Thus, when public denunciations of our lifestyles are made by other black people, we remain silent in the face of their hostility and ignorance. The toll taken on us because we repress our rage and hurt makes us distrustful of all people whom we cannot identify as lesbian or gay. Also, for those of us who are isolated from the gay or lesbian community, the toll is greater self-hate, self-blame, and belief in the illness theory of homosexuality.

In the face of this, open and proud black gay men and lesbians must take an assertive stand against the blatant homophobia expressed by members of the black intellectual and political community, who consider themselves custodians of the revolution. For if we will not tolerate the homophobia of the culture in general, we cannot tolerate it from black people, no matter what their positions in the black liberation movement. Homophobia is a measure of how far removed we are from the psychological transformation we so desperately need to engender. The expression of homophobic sentiments, the threatening political postures assumed by black radicals and progressives of the nationalist/communist ilk, and the seeming lack of any willingness to understand the politics of gay and lesbian liberation collude with the dominant white male culture to repress not only gay men and lesbians, but also to repress a natural part of all human beings, namely the bisexual potential in us all. Homophobia divides black people as political allies, it cuts off political growth, stifles revolution, and perpetuates patriarchal domination.

The arguments I have presented are not definitive. I hope that others may take some of the issues raised in this essay into consideration for further study. The sexual politics of the black liberation movement have yet to be addressed by its advocates. We will continue to fail to transform ourselves until we reconcile the unequal distribution of power in our political community accorded on the basis of gender and sexual choice. Visions of black liberation which exclude lesbians and gay men bore and repel me, for as a black lesbian I am obligated and dedicated to destroying heterosexual supremacy by "suggesting, promoting, and advocating" the rights of gay men and lesbians wherever we are. And we are everywhere. As political black people, we bear the twin responsibilities of transforming the social, political, and economic systems of oppression as they affect all our people—not just the heterosexuals—and of transforming the corresponding psychological structure that feeds into these oppressive systems. The more homophobic we are as a people, the further removed we are from any kind of revolution. Not only must black lesbians and gay men be committed to destroying homophobia, but *all* black people must be committed to working out and rooting out homophobia in the black community. We begin to eliminate homophobia by engaging in dialogue with the advocates of gay and lesbian liberation, educating ourselves about gay and lesbian politics, confronting and correcting homophobic attitudes, and understanding how these attitudes prevent the liberation of the total community.

Works Cited

Baldwin, James. *Another Country.* New York: Dial Press, 1968.

Baraka, Imamu Amiri. *Raise Race Rays Raze: Essays Since 1965.* New York: Random House, 1971.

Bullins, Ed. *Five Plays by Ed Bullins.* New York: Bobbs-Merrill Co., Inc., 1968.

Hernton, Calvin. *Sex and Racism in America.* New York: Grove Press, 1965.

Jones, LeRoi. *Preface to a Twenty Volume Suicide Note.* New York: Totem/Corinth, 1961.

———. *The Dead Lecturer.* New York: Grove Press, 1964.

———. "American Sexual Reference: Black Male." *Home.* New York: William Morrow and Co., Inc., 1966.

Staples, Robert. "Mystique of Black Sexuality," in Staples (ed.) *The Black Family: Essays and Studies.* Belmont, California: Wadsworth Publishing Co., Inc., 1977.

Wallace, Michele. *Black Macho and the Myth of the Superwoman.* New York: Dial Press, 1979.

Washington, Mary Helen. "In Pursuit of Our Own History," in M. H. Washington (ed.),

    Midnight Birds. New York: Anchor Books, 1980.

New Notes on Lesbianism

"BLACK LESBIANS" SOUNDS formidable and intimidating. Did not bell hooks in *Ain't I a Woman* (1981) avoid the issue of Black lesbianism in the context of her feminist arguments for reasons she has never been able to explain that we (lesbians) know? "Black lesbians"—it is stark and startling. Did not Alice Walker (Fall 1981), an avowed nonlesbian, state that she would prefer, among others, the term "womanist" to the name "lesbian"? "Black lesbians"—sounds like a Thelonious Monk tune. Lately, even I have been plying myself with such questions regarding my lesbianism: Why do I call myself a lesbian? Why do I elevate who I sleep with to politics? Why do I not pursue a more revolutionary politic—a polymorphous perverse vision of the world and of living? "Come out of the shoe box of lesbianism." "Do not be so cushioned in the narrow politics of sexual preference." "Are *labels* really necessary?" have been reverberating inside me regularly lately.

Black women like pretty names. Remember the names of Black girls in our lives growing up? Blossom. Queen Esther. Countess Peace. Floresta. "Black lesbians" is certainly different sounding.

What Black person or Black lesbian in Harlem, on Chicago's South Side, Atlanta, Newark, Brooklyn, L.A. can relate to Sappho or the Isle of Lesbos, where white women were said to have migrated to cavort and become amazons? I wonder if they held Black lesbians slaves? Lesbos, as Alice Walker suggests in her *Black Scholar* review of *Gifts of Power: The Writings of Rebecca Jackson (1795–1871)* (1981), was not the origin of lesbians. Lesbians like Black folk came into existence in what is now known as the Kongo, where language began (thus, Black lesbians' facility for talk, storytelling, and advice-giving). So, perhaps, for Black women to call ourselves lesbians is anachronistic as Black women have obviously been lesbians longer than all women, according to Walker. Is "womanist" any more viable though? It is not the name that the prevailing culture despises but rather the act . . . of lesbianism, womanism; the interdependence of women and women, the fucking, the eating, the smells, the juices, the vaginas that our enemies despise. If Black women called ourselves something more neutral like "Black azaleas," would other Black women be more willing to identify with the politics of woman-bonding? If we were to call ourselves "Black azaleas," instead of "Black lesbians," would Black women be more willing to identify their woman-bonding as political? Would the Black community be any more willing to accept our definition, our naming? "Black azaleas"—sounds like a less foreboding Monk tune. "Black Azaleas."

In *Black American Literature Forum* (Vol. 14, No. 4, Winter 1980), Black feminist critic Deborah McDowell takes issue with "Towards a Black Feminism Criticism," written by Black lesbian feminist Barbara Smith and published in *Conditions Two* (1977), for its lack of "precision and detail." McDowell demands that Smith and others like Smith who write from a—Gasp!!!—lesbian perspective, pin our aesthetic to the page or folk will get confused. Not only may Toni Morrison's *Sula* (1973) as Smith suggests, be interpreted as a—Gasp!!!—lesbian novel, we might also be able, based upon Smith's criteria, to interpret Jean Toomer's *Cane* (Liveright, 1975) from a lesbian perspective: i.e., some writers who are not lesbians might be interpreted as advancing a lesbian aesthetic or ideology inadvertently.

The term "lesbian" has been denigrated, degraded, and made synonymous with disease. And feminists (lesbians) have rescued and reclaimed it as Black folk have rescued and reclaimed "black." And "lesbian" *can* mean "nigga" as June Jordan tells us in *Civil Wars,* especially if it's Black lesbians doing it, especially if "nigga" means field hand, crazy nigger, outsider, rebel, trickster, Ananci, or guerrilla. But if "nigga" means "unconscious, continuing self-hatred," as Jordan proffers in her 1976 *Ms.* article, "A Declaration of Independence I Would Just As Soon Not Have," reprinted in *Civil Wars,* "lesbian" is not the equivalent of it. It is hard to believe that Jordan has not edited out or recanted that whole passage in which she denigrates lesbians; even for 1976 the attitude was reactionary! Maybe June Jordan should have used "bulldagger" in the analogy if she wanted to evoke the negative of lesbian—at least the terms "nigga" and "bulldagger" are equivalent. And if she still really believes that "lecherous, exploitative, shallow, acting-out and pathological behavior" is synonymous with lesbian, then maybe June Jordan ought to find out more about lesbians. Get some balance, sister.

Who one sleeps with is important. It just is. Sexuality is not neutral, personal, or a private matter. Just because we can keep it private, personal, closeted, repressed, the world still revolves around who sleeps with whom and the power implicit in that. Whoever one is. Whom one sleeps with never does not matter. Folk constantly think about who sleeps with whom and where. If I, an avowed lesbian and feminist, were to say that I still sleep with men, what do you think would be the response from my lesbian-feminist sisters? If I come out as a lesbian in the various Black groups I find myself among, am I not buked? If I label myself "bisexual," then who would trust me? So, who one sleeps with is a key issue, because the act speaks to how far one might go in perpetuating or tearing down the empire. As a lesbian, a feminist, and a "nigga," I am about the radical restructuring of all systems—whomever I sleep with.

Economically, lesbians thwart capitalism—and the blacker the lesbian, the more she should attempt to thwart capitalism, and the more she does. Lesbians or women who are "lovers" do not wed themselves to the institution of exclusive heterosexuality, which expresses itself unabashedly and unashamedly at every turn in our daily existence as women. Of course, lesbians are victimized economically like all women in capitalism, but there are additional threats to the economic and emotional survival of women who are lesbians—whether we are "out" or not. We can lose jobs, our children, our lovers, our freedom, our lives because we are lesbians in a homophobic culture. Thus, many Black women who love women are loathe to identify themselves as lesbians. Some of us feel we don't need another "handicap," "strike against us . . . we already Black." Being a Black lesbian is not easy, and the more non-middle-class, nonbourgeois elite the lesbian, the harder it is. There are fewer mechanisms in everyday life and in the institutions that run our lives for dealing with homophobia than there are to deal with racism or sexism. People recognize racism and sexism as legitimate oppressions. Many folk still feel the best medicine for homosexuality is to string the "queer" up on the nearest tree.

I name myself "lesbian" because this culture oppresses, silences, and destroys lesbians, even lesbians who don't call themselves "lesbians." I name myself "lesbian" because I want to be visible to other Black lesbians. I name myself "lesbian" because I do not subscribe to predatory/institutionalized heterosexuality. I name myself "lesbian" because I want to be with women (and they don't all have to call themselves "lesbians"). I name myself "lesbian" because it is part of my vision. I name myself "lesbian" because being woman-identified has kept me sane. I call myself "Black," too, because Black is my perspective, my aesthetic, my politics, my vision, my sanity.

A woman does not have to be sleeping with a woman or women to cultivate a lesbian perspective. McDowell, hooks, and Jordan, for example, could cultivate a lesbian perspective. Such cultivation might be therapeutic for their antilesbian attitudes. Any self-determined woman can call herself a lesbian if she is about affirming herself and other women.

The issue of lesbianism, as politics, as a way of being in the world, as just plain life, needs talking about, not silence, not subterfuge, not coyness. Every rime I meet a Black woman who lives somewhere in the hinterlands of South Jersey, who has been making her way with a woman, in isolation, in the closet, cut off from community, and who thinks she's the only *"one,"* it becomes ever clearer how much self-determined Black women matter. Black lesbians, Black feminists, Black lesbian feminists need to do some naming and claiming regarding our tradition of woman-bonding, e.g., *lesbianism.*

Postscript 1995

At this writing, I remain firmly convinced that our "enemies" despise "women and women, the fucking, the eating, the smells, the juices, the vaginas," although today, our enemies are different. Some of the Black feminists of whom I was "sharply critical" (Kahn, letter, June 1995) in 1983 have sharply revised their thinking on Black lesbian feminism. I have revised my thinking, too—both on Black lesbian feminism and about Black feminists who do not claim a lesbian politics.

I count Alice Walker, Deborah McDowell, and June Jordan among my teachers, allies, and friends. Walker's *The Color Purple* was profoundly informed by Black lesbian feminism. McDowell's astounding article, "That Nameless . . . Shameful Impulse," on the lesbian subtext of Nella Larsen's 1929 novel *Passing,* opened a whole new area of inquiry in African-American literary studies, from which I have benefited.

Jordan has taken many affirmative stands on love between women in her writing since the 1976 *Ms.* article and the 1981 publication of *Civil Wars:* e.g., her poem "From Sea to Shining Sea" (*Living Room* 1985), her insightful essay "A New Politics of Sexuality" (*Technical Difficulties,* 1994), and her exquisite *Haruko/Love Poems* (1994), a whole series of which are devoted to love between women.

The positions of bell hooks (a.k.a. Gloria Watkins) baffles me more today than in 1983, despite her formal shift in "Reflections on Homophobia and Black Communities" (*Outlook,* 1988). In this essay, hooks admits to homophobia among Black people, albeit no worse than in any other community, without consciously implicating herself. She seems more nonplussed about Black lesbians who show up at parties or meetings with their white lovers than about homophobia and heterosexism in Black "communities."

Her "reflections" are, as usual, provocative. In a June 1995 interview in the *Chronicle of Higher Education,* hooks still manages *not* to implicate herself, as she fantasizes about someone else's desire: "[T]here are probably many more young women thinking, wouldn't it be great to have sex with bell hooks, than young men." See also "In Our Glory: Photography and Black Life," in *Art on My Mind* (New Press, 1995), for an update of her preoccupation with Black women and white women in lesbian relationships. Yet, I do not foreclose the possibility that bell hooks' thinking and writing on Black lesbian feminism will get beyond voyeurism. I look forward to the day.

Part Two
Living as a Lesbian:
1986–1990

14th street was gutted

14th Street was gutted in 1968.
Fire was started on one side of the street.
Flames licked a trail of gasoline to the other side.
For several blocks a gauntlet of flames.
For several days debris smoldered with the stench
of buildings we had known all our lives. Had known
all our lives. I recalled the death of Otis Redding.
My sense of place was cauterized.
Since that time the city has become a buffalo
nearly a dinosaur and,
as with everything else white men have wanted
for themselves,
endangered
or extinct.

The woman who raised me

The woman who raised me asks me
'Where is the hope here, where is the hope?'
The fruit here is rotten.
All the roots are excavated.
The sidewalks are cracked and in pieces
and the rain forms stagnant pools.
Children walk the night through the streets here
and men make every urge so public.
And who will hear me cry for help?
Will they want to climb all these flights
up here to save me? And what will you do
when you wake up
and find your good woman
gone?'

I come to the city

I come to the city for protection
and to witness the thick transactions
of women
and women
and dance with my head.
My turns are calculated
to end on the right foot
to subdue the hip movements.
The city fumes with expectations
and the smells of women
wanting women.
I been in love
six times in the last six months
and ain't done tryin yet.

no more encomiums

This anger so visceral I could shit it
and still be constipated.
My ass is sore with the politics
of understanding the best given the circumstances.
I could spit this anger
and still choke on the phlegm
of memories.
Afraid, jealous, or stuck in some foaming
funk I learned from her in the circumstances
of her loneliness, I push away from my lover.
This hotness, this coldness still
in her aging she tricks me.

Sweet words and warm this time—
not like the last time salty and frigid
over some money I owed her—
telling me she's missing me, of the old days,
the pta meetings, Atlantic City in summers.
My stomach turns every day at 4:30
remembering anticipation of the hammer sound
of her spikes on the front porch
when in spite of herself
she was my champion
my song, my soul, my beauty.

Given the circumstances of her crowded life
I can't publish this poem
She sits on her bed working her
crossword puzzle searching back over 64
years of words to fit the boxes
And me sulking over 33 years of anger
edited for the space of these lines.
Hounding anger like cunt hurts to fuck
carnal anger and dreams over too soon.

In the dry heave of Arizona, in a tent,
in the middle of the scarlet streaked day,
I had this dream of her: she cursed me and
I determined I'd tell her she hurt me. I
rehearsed it. Yes, in the very dream I
rehearsed the words I'd say to her—
in spite of the circumstances and fuck
the circumstances—
to finally stand up for myself, to say:
'You hurt me and you always hurt me.'

I can only write this poem, my bilious anger.
This third person, my anger.
Visceral
I could shit it

spit it
fuck it
Phlegmatic and choleric
she hurts my fucking
cunt
My champion
my song
my soul
my beauty.

Vicki and Daphne

Being given a lover's key is an intimate gesture: without it one can figure what course the relationship will take; with it, trust is a temptation.

Blood of the cut from a serrated knife blotted by a slice of cake frosted white and garnished with a sugar molded rose the same color red as her blood set Vicki to musing on the risk she'd taken coming from an office party without warning with half a cake to persuade Daphne.

No bandages in Daphne's medicine cabinet or night table. (Daphne never had what Vicki needed when she needed it. But Vicki was an ex-Marine and compensated by being relentlessly adaptable.) So, she scissored a sanitary pad down to the size of a Curad (to her amazement Daph did have pads) and taped it round her hemorrhaging finger with Daph's last bit of scotch tape.

Vicki's feet hurt in her business pumps. Her business suit pinched her waist and pressed her breasts. The scent of perfume and deodorant mixed with the odor emanating from her pits. She didn't want to get too comfortable. She preferred to await Daphne's pleasure. Her feet might swell or Daph might want her to book.

Vicki removes one shoe and slides the other off her burning heel. (She carries sneakers in her bag but can't really stand the way treads look with nylons.) All day she'd been driven by lust for Daphne. She'd left messages by everyone who might see or speak to Daph to tell her she wanted her.

Where is Daphne? Surely she'd be home soon so Vicki could take off her clothes and complain about her aching pussy.

Being in Daphne's apartment at 11 p.m. without warning and Daphne not home but imminent, fantasy o'ertakes Vicki.

The sound of Daph's
keys in both holes
turning noisily
the house dark
Daphne comes for Vicki where she sits
runs her hand along her nylons
and beyond
Vicki guides her hand

Her throbbing finger draws her back to the reality of her situation: fully clothed, horny, and without warning, and how would she be able to take Daph up the cunt with her middle finger bandaged bulkily? She couldn't even stand air on the wound. Could she Daphne's salty cunt? And her right hand was not so dextrous.

Does Daphne come? Vicki prepares an appropriately humble expression and the honest explanation: *Baby, I'm gonna keep on lovin you til the day I die, cuz I love the way you satisfy.*

No keys in holes.
No Daphne.
Only next door neighbor fumbling.

Without warning, Vicki feels cramps. Her ankles swell. Her finger bleeds every time she flexes. Her pussy is gamey with secretions. She wants to lie down. But Daph hates wrinkled bed clothes.

Vicki falls into a daze, limps to Daph's bed and pulls backs its comforter and top sheet limps then to an odd chest of drawers and removes a small object of comfort. After pulling her skirt to her crotch, lies face down on Daph's bed and applies it to her genital eleven times calling Daph a whore sweetly and being Daph calling herself a bitch roughly.

Vicki sleeps deeply in suit, nylons, and one pump, awaking at 6 a.m. without warning, without Daphne, returns the object to its place pulls top sheet and comforter over passion and menses stained sheets smooths her wrinkles brushes the lint.

Intimacy no luxury

Intimacy no luxury here.
Telephones cannot be left off the hook
or lines too long engaged
or conversations censored any longer.
No time to stare at our hands
afraid to extend them
or once held
afraid to let go.
We are here.
After years of separation
women take their time
dispose of old animosities.
Tribadism is an ancient panacea and cost efficient
an ancient panacea and cost efficient.

nothing

Nothing I wouldn't do for the woman I sleep with
when nobody satisfy me the way she do.

kiss her in public places
win the lottery
take her in the ass
in a train lavatory
sleep three in a single bed
have a baby
to keep her wanting me.

wear leather underwear
remember my dreams
make plans and schemes
go down on her in front of her
other lover
give my jewelry away
to keep her wanting me.

sell my car
tie her to the bed post and
spank her
lie to my mother

let her watch me fuck my other lover
miss my only sister's wedding
to keep her wanting me.

buy her cocaine
show her the pleasure in danger
bargain
let her dress me in colorful costumes
of low cleavage and slit to the crotch
giving easy access
to keep her wanting me.

Nothing I wouldn't do for the woman I sleep with
when nobody satisfy me the way she do.

the change

She used to smile, small talk, almost flirt
speaks only if I speak first, swells like cow
udder wanting a milking, acts real curt.
Her countenance is hard toward me now.
Speaks tersely to me, to you kowtows
when she meets us in the hallway.
Impertinent, rude, and untoward now,
your neighbor used to be more friendly.

Your cat died. She found you a kitten
before you'd grieved properly. That, I thought
nervy, but I'm prone to suspicion.
Her countenance is hard toward me now,
throwing smiles like flowers at you and frowns
like needles at me.
The mangy kitten's a cat now. I vow—
your neighbor used to be more friendly.

Who is this woman? Who is she to you?
Bringing tonics to quicken your prow-
ess. Try my chili seasoned high, hot, and true.
Her countenance is hard toward me now.
You smile, turn from me, lead me to the couch.

Not to worry, not to worry.
I go down on you and chew
your clit. She used to be more friendly.

Me on top of you on top of the couch.
Her countenance is hard toward me now.
You give her good cause to cut her eyes at me.
Your neighbor used to be more friendly.

We are everywhere

We are everywhere and white people still do not see us.
They force us from sidewalks.
Mistake us for men.
Expect us to give up our seats to them on the bus.
Challenge us with their faces.
Are afraid of us in groups.
Thus the brutal one on one.
Like a t.v. news script, every transaction frustrates
rage. Hand in hand with me
you admonish
not to let them come between us
not to let them come between us on the street.
We are struck by war crazy men
recording their gunfire on stereo cassette decks.

Since my lover left

Since my lover left the city without warning
for a less carcinogenic zone
some place in the desert
where she can stop hating her own people
my sister passes the night with me
who'd rather be drowning in the deep
blue sea. My lover having left the city without
warning, my sister passes the night with me
and speaks of the murders of Hampton and Silkwood
of the blood of Santiago and Soweto.
Stores her handgun in the night table
passes the night with me and plays the record
player loud. And I remember the words
of a lost slave song.

living as a lesbian underground: a futuristic fantasy

in basements
attics
alleyways
and tents
fugitive slaves
poets and griots
seminoles from Songhay
vodun queens—
all in drag,
stumbling over discarded fetuses
hitching
dodging state troopers behind shades
searching for safe houses
uptight but cool
    the tam
    the aviator frames
    the propped cigarette
    and singing
    'I was born in Georgia.
    My ways are underground
    It you mistreat me
    I'll hunt you like a hound.'
Lack of money produces such atavism

But . . . don't be taken in your sleep now.
Call your assassin's name now
Leave signs of struggle.
Leave signs of triumph.
And run
cept don't stop in Chicago
to give yourself up to a pimp
Leave signs.

And . . . don't be taken on the nod now.
The Arabs are only a temporary phobia.
It's a short trip from Nyack to the
shores of Tripoli and back
Thewitchhuntisbuildinghere
Where you gon be standin when it comes?
Leave signs.

And . . . don't get caught sleeping with
your shoes off
while women are forced back to the shelter
of homicidal husbands
rapists are forced to pay child support
children of lesbians orphaned
and blacks, browns, and tans
herded into wire fences somewhere

round Tucson.
Listen for footsteps
Leave signs.

Travel light
and don't wait til morning.
Qadaffi is only a fleeting distraction
radiating the 3rd world with his
macho, mercurial, maligned smile.
A scapegoat.
Uptight but cool
The terror is here somewhere
in Detroit.

And . . . don't sleep before midnight
And don't fret over the Poles.
We in the same fix
with the Pope's position on lust
and family protection
a storefront on every corner
in Manhattan.

Don't be no fool, now, cool.
Imperialism by any other name
is imperialism.
Even Vietnam was finally over.
It's all the same
a-rabs, gooks, wogs, queers . . .
a nigger by any other name . . .
Johannesburg is Jamesburg, New Jersey.
Apartheid is the board of education
in Canarsie.

So . . . don't be taken in your sleep now.
Call your assailant's name now
Leave the building empty
the doors unlocked
and raise the windows high
when they pass by.
Leave signs of struggle.
Leave signs of triumph.
And leave signs.

An exile I have loved

An exile I have loved tells me she's going home.
Smug I say
   'Back to the city?'
   'No. First to Zambia. Then Zimbabwe.
   Finally Transvaal. Home,' she answers sad.
We sleep and wake to voices of men in the hallway
asking through doors of faces that are changed
and names that have not been spoken since
I hold her to me
and remember the gold in my ears
ask for a way to stay in touch with her
tell her she's got a home long as I got mine.
Hold her to me until she must push away
and slip from the room.

living as a lesbian on the make

Straight bars ain't so bad
though filled with men
cigarette smoke
and juke noises.
A martini straight up and jazz
can take me beyond their static.
Alone she came in denim and a
magenta tee
hair cut to a duck tail
ordered Miller's and smoked two
kinds of cigarettes
sat at a table close but distant
was pretty and I was lonely
and knew she was looking for a woman.
All through the set I looked at her
until she split in the middle of it.
I almost followed her out but was too
horny to leave the easy man talking
loud shit to me for a seduction I'd
have to work at.
The music sounding tasty
saxophone flugelhorn bass and drums
hitting familiar riffs
the titles escaping me.

sexual preference

I'm a queer lesbian
Please don't go down on me yet.
I do not prefer cunnilingus.
(There's room for me in the movement.)

Your tongue does not have to prove its prowess
there
to me
now
or even on the first night.

Your mouth all over my body
then there.

Kittatinny

I wanna love and treat you, love and treat you right.
—Bob Marley

Kittatinny Tunnel in that holy place you let me hit.
I push on toward your darker part.
I'll take you there and mean it.

In my car, by the road, in a tent, in a pit
stop, and practice a funkier art.
Kittatinny Tunnel of that holy place you let me hit.

Shout, cry, promise, beg, cajole, go limp, or spit
on me with dirty words to test my heart.
I'll take you there and mean it.

Crawl from me, pitch a fit
stand, hug the wall, bend, and direct me part
and penetrate Kittatinny, that holy place you let me hit.

And take it, take it, take it.
Call it bitch, whore, slave, tart.
I'll take you there and mean it.

Tribad, dildo, lick your clit-
oris. Come, pee, shit, or fart.
I'll take you there and mean it.
Kittatinny Tunnel of that holy place you let me hit.

living as a lesbian at 35

in my car I am fishing in my pocketbook
eyes on the road
for my wallet
in my mind I am fishing in your drawers
eyes on the road
for your pussy.
high speeds evoke fucking.
depending on your mood you come.
it goes on:
I do too from you
over the wheel
hand between my thighs
eyes on the road
and the end of all: sex.

my mind:
a favored child has more freedom from her parents
a hippocampus more freedom from the horse and dolphin
a hippopotamus more freedom from her short legs
and muzzle
than my hypothalmus from lusting
and the end of all: sex.

my age?
the years I missed?

the women I had no opportunity with?
an old lover is sweet and good.
an old friend surprising and familiar.
all bodies possibilities.
any bodies.
lust, the cause of every tribute and transaction
for the end of all: sex.

to work to the end of day
to talk to the end of talk
to run to the end of dark
to have at the end of it all: sex.

the wish for forever
for more often
for more.

the promises
the absurdity
the histrionics
the loss of pride
the bargaining
the sadness after.

in wakefulness wanting
in wakefulness waiting.

The Space in Me Where
Baldwin Lives

The American idea of masculinity: There are few things under heaven
more difficult to understand or, when I was younger, to forgive . . .
On every street corner, I was called faggot . . .
—James Baldwin, "Here Be Dragons," 1985

JAMES BALDWIN WAS the first seriously black writer I read. I'd read Frank Yerby and discovered, like LeRoi Jones, that he was good for "at least one hard on." But Baldwin's writing said to me I could be black, gay, and live to tell about it. I've loved him all these manic years since I was 15 and first discovered novels. He showed me, in the stark loneliness of my Catholic adolescence, how to imagine those unspeakable experiences, feel those unutterable urges: for the same sex, the opposite race, and both at the same time. It was Baldwin, because he'd experienced himself as the love object of his own sex, who made me envision my own sexual possibilities in those early years. His work taught me that sexual passion and longing are rebel urges much as the slave's urge for freedom.

Through *The Fire Next Time, Notes of a Native Son, Go Tell It On The Mountain, Giovanni's Room,* and especially *Another*

Country, I felt the poetics of resistance in black literature at a visceral level for the first time—the next time would be when I would begin to read black women writers.

I began my preparation for lesbianism with the reading of *Another Country* in 1963. I would not know this for ten more years. I learned three lessons from that novel: people are eminently sexual creatures; they are capable of a multiplicity of relationships in spite of the complications and because of them; and words are powerful aphrodisiacs. But because I was the Taurus child of a working-class-aspiring-to-be-middle-class black American family growing up in Washington, D.C., the citadel of the black bourgeoisie, I was seduced into repressing the lessons of *Another Country*. I moved on to more rational pursuits like college.

Though suppressed, Baldwin lived in me. I wrote a long paper on *Another Country* in my freshman year at Howard University. But by 1966, at the dawn of the Black Power Movement, Baldwin had become suspect and unacceptable to those black people (men), like Eldridge Cleaver and LeRoi Jones, who were formulating the criteria of blackness and whose books had to be read or at least carried around if one did not want her blackness called into question. "Equality of the sexes," interracial love, non-monogamy, and certainly homosexuality were deemed antithetical to blackness. This was no time for novels—not Baldwin's anyway.

But the burden of having read *Another Country* and having absorbed its lessons had finally to be borne. *Another Country* was an act of courage we did not witness again until Morrison's *The Bluest Eye* and Walker's *The Third Life of Grange Copeland*. Most critics—black and white—unilaterally agreed that *Another Country* was a "bad" novel. Black critic Addison Gayle, a loud proponent of the black (male) aesthetic, accused Baldwin of "distortion" in his critical study *The Way of the New World*—not so very different from what many black male critics were to say of Walker's *The Color Purple*, which *Another Country* anticipates. Even my high school English teacher, a white nun, warned me that the characters of *Another Country* are not real: "Real people don't act like that." But it is this novel, this panoramic representation of existential grief that most unequivocally epitomizes Baldwin's truth that no one is innocent. James Baldwin is the first and only black American male writer to treat the issue of male homosexuality positively and realistically in fiction. Though his treatment of women in the novel is not particularly advanced—they are depicted mostly as groupies, band chicks, hangers-on, male-identified, or avenging angels—the book still lives in me. In re-reading *Another Country* recently, I discovered, more certainly than ever in this discomfiting time, that I am Rufus Scott* in all his pathology and rage as surely as Baldwin must have seen Ida Scott as himself, relentlessly stalking this society for its culpability in Rufus's death.

---

*The black male character of the novel around whose death the action of the novel resolves. Ida Scott is his younger sister.

The ugly-beautiful, bug-eyed black boy called faggot on every corner of the West Village until he migrated to Paris was always there to remind us of his pain and ours, his loneliness and ours. And he is *ours, our* native son. No matter who else claims him upon the safe and terrible occasion of his death, he is *ours*—in all his beautiful ambivalence over claiming *us* as his:

> all American categories of male and female, straight or not, black or white, were shattered, thank heaven, very early in my life. Not without anguish, certainly; but once you have discerned the meaning of a label, it may seem to define you for others, but it does not define you to yourself.[1]

I mourn him and I celebrate him—Jimmy.

Work Cited

James Baldwin, "Here Be Dragons," *The Pri\ce of the Ticket: Collected Nonfiction, 1948–1985*. St. Martin's/Marek: 1985, p. 681.

Silence and Invisibility:
Costly Metaphors

Why should the world be over-wise,

In counting all our tears and

sighs?

Nay, let them only see us, while

We wear the mask

—Paul Laurence Dunbar,

"We Wear the Mask," 1913

TONI CADE BAMBARA, writer, activist, and race woman, claims that Afro-Americans have given the world two "abiding metaphors, *silence* and *invisibility.* Black gay men and lesbians are double exemplars of these metaphors. In both the case of Afro-Americans in general and Afro-American lesbians and gays, the choices of silence and invisibility have been made in order to survive or to gain access to privilege in a hostile environment. Though black lesbians and gay men still pay a debt to "human guile" (Dunbar) because of our identities, at least we no longer—in most of the U.S.—have to suppress our black consciousness.

I know that in writing the following pages I am divulging the great secret of my life, the secret which for some years I have guarded far more carefully than any of my earthly possessions.

(James Weldon Johnson, 1912)

If one were asked what "great secret" Johnson is referring to in this passage from his famous novel *The Autobiography of an Ex-Colored Man,* the response would most likely be "homosexuality." The act or necessity of "passing for white" is almost unheard of today. However, the act of "passing" as heterosexual still reflects much of gay and lesbian life. While the act of "passing" as heterosexual is probably older than the act of "passing for white," the circumstances which cause gay men and lesbians to hide their identities still prevail. Not that racism has ended, but whiteness is not as compelling an ideal as it once was nor are the penalties for being black as severe or life-threatening—in most of the U.S.—as they once were. The consequences of divulging one's gayness are, in many cases, still severe and punitive. Thus, some people still try to take the *great secret* to the grave, e.g., Rock Hudson, Liberace; or some recant, e.g., Gladys Bentley, Little Richard; or some never claim a gay or lesbian community, e.g., James Baldwin; or some just remain in the closet. Walter White, who was a white-skinned Afro-American, passed for white while investigating lynchings in the South for the NAACP in the 1920s. Thousands of gay and lesbian people pass as straight just to get through the day. Black lesbians and gay men pass as straight in both the white and black communities.

Invisibility may be defined as the ability or will of the power group not to acknowledge the presence or influence of another group. Being invisible as a black person runs the gamut from the daily experience of entering a room full of white people and not being acknowledged to the other extreme of erasure from history. Where would Mick Jagger or David Bowie be without Little Richard? (Or even James Brown or Michael Jackson for that matter?) Silence may be defined as the act of subordinating the expression of one's needs to the will of the group in power. Sometimes the silence is strategic, as was Walter White's. Many times, it is a suppression of one's beliefs to accommodate what one has been told is the "greater good," the *this*-now-and-*that*-later philosophy. Many gay and lesbian people succumb to the oppression-ranking syndrome in groups whose politics are not anti-sexist, anti-heterosexist, or anti-hierarchical. We spend our lives, as gay and lesbian people, calculating the costs of silence.

Indeed, most of Afro-American literature reflects the struggle to be recognized, the struggle for a voice in a racist culture with genocidal tendencies. Much of our history on this continent has been the struggle to mark our existence—and much of our existence has been marked through the voice, a voice that many times has had to be duplicitous. The slave song was really a signal for escape, not just a sign of religion. The tales about trickster rabbits weren't children's stories or simply told to entertain white folk but were denunciations of white people. Many people forget that a crucial element of the Black Power movement was the struggle to stop the erasure of black people from history, the struggle to resurrect our heroes, to say, "Hey, you know a black person invented the paper bag, the stop light, the filament in the electric light bulb. . . ." And it was during this latter half of the 1960s that many Afro-Americans "came out" as black people, i.e., we articulated a black consciousness and a black agenda wherever we went.

This imposition of invisibility may be a Yankee tendency, as Baldwin seems to suggest in his essay, "Fifth Avenue Uptown":

> None of this is true for the Northerner. Negroes represent nothing to him, except, perhaps, the danger of carnality. He never sees Negroes. Southerners see them all the time. Northerners never think about them, whereas Southerners are never really thinking of anything else. Negroes are, therefore, ignored in the North and are under surveillance in the South, and suffer hideously in both places.
>
> (*Nobody Knows My Name*, 1960)

Afro-Americans created the politics of invisibility long before the publication of Ellison's *Invisible Man* (1953). The white Gay Liberation Movement appropriated this analysis, this way of seeing gay and lesbian oppression as erasure of existence, the understanding that unless gay and lesbian people "come out" publicly in defense of our lives, we would be destroyed. Black lesbians and gay men must re-appropriate this perspective to define our positions and predicaments within the context of the various political organizations and movements—and in U.S. culture as a whole. Black lesbians and gay men are strong enough to challenge the racial, gender, and sexual identity entitlements that have caused our issues to be excluded or absorbed, appropriated or sanitized. While we still must proceed strategically and cautiously with non-gay or non-lesbian people, proceed we must. Remember the Civil Rights Movement chant: "Move on over or we'll move on over you." Jesse Jackson, during his presidential campaign, was the first nationally known politician to speak to a gay and lesbian constituency and to take on advocating for our civil rights. Certainly, his action ought to be emulated by other politicos, politicians, and organizations.

Black lesbians have fared better in claiming visibility in the gay and lesbian community because of the women's movement. We certainly had become familiar with the practices of sexism and heterosexism via our experience in both black liberation movement organizations and white leftist and progressive organizations. We were also savvy enough to know that anti-sexist politics do not necessarily mean anti-racist politics just as anti-racist politics do not necessarily mean anti-sexist politics. We were emboldened by contemporary black women writers like Toni Cade, Toni Morrison, Alice Walker, whose writings were analyses of black women's oppression and were critical of the sacred institutions—marriage, heterosexuality, and the family. We found models of leadership in black lesbian writers like Audre Lorde and Barbara Smith, who were out there countering the imposed invisibility and silence of black lesbians.

Black gay men did not fare as well. Their models, e.g., the late James Baldwin and the late Bayard Rustin, had spent their lives subordinating their oppression as gay men to fighting for racial equality and/or struggling for artistic freedom. (Despite their silence, which is not to imply they were closeted, Rustin and Baldwin were still undermined and attacked because of their homosexuality.) Baldwin, whose work was always informed by male homoeroticism, made this surprising commentary on the homosexuality of writer Andre Gide:

> And Gide's homosexuality, I felt was his own affair which he ought to have kept hidden from us, or if he needed to be so explicit. . . . he ought, in a word, to have sounded a little less *disturbed.*
>
> ("The Male Prison," 1954)

I don't believe Baldwin would have said that in this decade, but, as was stated earlier, he never claimed a gay community, a community to whom his work was the world.

Though the black movement tried to keep him invisible, Rustin managed to always be in the thick, interceding for Martin Luther King, writing his speeches, preventing people from exploiting him, keeping the lid on the seamy escapades of King himself and his entourage (Garrow, *Bearing the Cross,* 1988). The 1963 March on Washington might not have happened had it not been for Rustin; but he had to be kept invisible because he was a gay man. And his identity as a gay black male elder could have been erased had it not been for the black gay male community embracing him late in his life. In an interview with the late Joseph Beam, anthologist, activist, and promoter of black gay male visibility and culture, Rustin said the following regarding "the closet:"

> [E]very Gay who is in the closet is ultimately a threat to the freedom of Gays. I don't want to seem intolerant. . . . and I think we have to say that to them with a great deal of affection, but remaining in the closet is the other side of prejudice against Gays. Because until you challenge it, you are not playing an active role in fighting.
>
> (*Black/Out,* 1987)

Rustin is certainly a model of gay leadership—for better and for worse. For better, because gay men and lesbians are tireless freedom fighters, organizers, facilitators, motivators. For worse, because in order to make our contributions to social change, gay men and lesbians have had to deny our lives. Gay men and lesbians have been able to contribute so much to social change movements, precisely because we have not been tethered to heterosexuality and heterosexistvalues.

The same style of leadership is apparent in the life of the late Ella Baker. I have often wondered if Baker was a lesbian and if her designation of herself as a "facilitator" as opposed to a "leader" was as much a tactic to protect a lesbian identity as it was reflective of her disdain for the "leader-centered" (Garrow) approach to organizing. Like her close friend Rustin, Baker was denied more visible leadership and greater influence in the black movement of the 1950s and 1960s because she was radical, a true grassroots organizer, didn't need heroes, especially male ones, and not least of all, because she was a woman. The fact that one has to wonder if Baker was a lesbian points to the more startling invisibility of black lesbians in the black movement. Why and how do we know that Rustin and Baldwin were gay men, and why and how don't we know whether a woman like Baker was a lesbian? Baker, who died in 1987, said this of her particular kind of leadership:

> I don't think I thought of myself largely as a *woman*. I thought of myself as an individual with a certain amount of sense of the need of people to participate in the movement. I have always thought what is needed is the development of people who are interested not in being leaders as much as in developing leadership among other people.
>
> (Lerner, *Black Women in White America,* 1971)

The Student Non-Violence Coordinating Committee (SNCC) would not have been organized without Baker. There is no conclusive proof that Baker was a lesbian. However, her autonomy and her preference for being in the background are often characteristics of the leadership style of lesbians working in straight organizations. Certainly, one can argue that this style is particularly female. Yet, I feel Baker's autonomy and unwillingness to be "enamored" of black male preachers and black male leadership set her apart and set her forth as a model of lesbian leadership—even if she was not a lesbian.

Both Rustin and Baker were excellent role models for anyone, and both were silenced because they did not fulfill conventional leadership expectations, i.e., neither wasted their energies adhering to heterosexual standards. Rustin was a gay man who did not pass as heterosexual; and Baker was a woman not dependent upon male approval. Black gay men and lesbians, like Rustin and Baker, have more energy and creativity in our own and other organizations, because we are not shackled to heterosexist models of leadership, even those of us who have chosen silence and invisibility.

The silence and invisibility are as costly as they are cautionary. I lose the opportunity to educate others and to speak up to protect my own integrity. Every time I don't come out, don't take a stand, don't protest erasure, the burden becomes heavier on someone else. And even though invisibility and silence have been abiding metaphors in the existential life of the race, the race can no longer impose them in order to suppress gay men and lesbians. The more black gay men and lesbians assert our identities as we assume leadership, the more support we create for others to come out. The black community, using Jesse Jackson as an example, has got to endorse gay and lesbian leadership. Black lesbians and gay men must be loud and flamboyant in transforming the black community toward that end. Happy gay and lesbian black history month.

Saying the Least Said, Telling the Least Told: The Voices of Black Lesbian Writers

The struggle for identity/ies:

> *Why should the world be over-wise*
> *In counting all our tears and sighs?*
> *Nay let them only see us, while*
> *We wear the mask.*
>
> —Dunbar, 1913

THE STRUGGLE TO be an "out" lesbian writer is simultaneous with the struggle to be a conscious, black identified (and anti-racist) black person. As a result of the female-oriented upbringing—with emphases on self-sufficiency and self-determination—and an undergraduate education at a historically black institution during the black consciousness era of the sixties, I found myself in pursuit of a "non-traditional" life and "non-traditional" relationships as well as in pursuit of role models—in life and in literature. I had taken up writing poetry as a way of entering into political dialogue with my peers, because other priorities prevented me from being a campus activist. After Baldwin, who I'd first read in 1963, the new black poets of the Black Arts Movement became my first literary role models. This protracted search first led me to graduate school in a very competitive program where there were few resources, no mentors, and little support for black women, especially those of us interested in things black.

During this time, 1970, I was thrown back upon my own devices and, so, I began to teach myself historic and contemporary black male literature. Baldwin was followed by Wright, Ellison, McKay, Hughes, and strange Jean Toomer. It was not until 1971 that I discovered the tradition of black women writers, when I saw *One Jump at the Sun,* a stage adaptation by black director Glenda Dickerson of Hurston's *Their Eyes Were Watching God,* in Washington, D.C. I rushed to find a copy of the novel, engaged myself in reading it, and began to teach myself the literature of black women novelists, whom I have read and been inspired by for the last nineteen years to the virtual exclusion of every other kind of writer, except for an occasional reading of a vintage black male writer. It is black women writers who became my primary literary role models. And I tried to write essays, criticism, and fiction as a way to enter into dialogue with those writers. These exercises in prose were as futile as the exercise in graduate school. I gave both up in 1974, a year after I had come out as a lesbian. I'd satisfied part of my quest. Choosing lesbianism was a process of affirming women and my love for women and of rejecting traditional and compulsory heterosexuality.

The struggle against silence and invisibility:

I know that in writing the following pages I'm divulging the great secret of my life, the secret which for some years I have guarded far more carefully than any of my earthly possessions.

—Johnson, 1912

If one were asked what "great secret" the narrator of James Weldon Johnson's *Autobiography of an Ex-Colored Man,* a novel not without homoeroticism, is referring to in the above passage, the answer would probably be "homosexuality." The act or necessity of "passing for white" is almost unheard of today. However, the act of "passing" as heterosexual, in a hostile, homophobic, and hetero-sexist world, still reflects much of gay and lesbian life. Not that racism has ended, but that whiteness is not as compelling an ideal as it once was nor are the penalties for being black as all-encompassing, severe, or life-threatening as they once were. The consequences of divulging one's gayness are, in many cases, still severe, punitive, and in many cases life-threatening. In either case, passing as "straight": or passing for white, the "passing" person must accept the twin albatross of silence and invisibility. Invisibility may be defined as the ability or will of the power group not to acknowledge the presence or influence of the "other." Being invisible as a black person runs the gamut from the daily experiences of entering a room full of white people and not being noticed to the other extreme of erasure from history. Where would Mick Jagger or

David Bowie (or James Brown and Michael Jackson for that matter) be without Little Richard? (No matter how much he recants, Little Richard is still gay.) Silence may be defined as the act of subordinating the expression of the other's needs to the will of the power group. Sometimes the silence is strategic, as in the case of Walter White, field secretary for the NAACP during the 1920's, who passed for white while he travelled through the South compiling statistics on lynchings; and sometimes it is a suppression of one's beliefs to accommodate what one has been told is the "greater good," as in the case of Bayard Rustin, socialist, black civil rights activist, and architect of the 1963 March on Washington, who was not allowed to assume visible leadership in the movement because he was homosexual.

Silence and invisibility, according to writer Toni Cade Bambara, are two of the greatest metaphors Afro-Americans have contributed to art in the western world—realistically and figuratively. But perhaps gays and women have contributed those metaphors also, perhaps all disenfranchised peoples have turned those metaphors into paradoxes and created ways for us and the world to understand our oppression. Thus, my sonnet:

We are everywhere and white people
    still do not see us.
They force us from sidewalks.
Mistake us for me.

Expect us to give up our seats to them
    on the bus.
Challenge us with their faces.
Are afraid of us in groups.
Thus the brutal one on one.
Like a t.v. news script, every
    transaction frustrates
rage. Hand in hand with me
you admonish
not to let them come between us
not to let them come between us on
    the street.
We are struck by war crazy men
recording their gunfire on stereo
cassette decks.

                        (*Living as a Lesbian,* 1986)

The challenge and difficulty have been in entering into dialogue with the black literary community and the white feminist literary community, who are willing, without irony, to impose silence and invisibility on black lesbian writers—either actively or unconsciously. Thus, a vigilance must be assumed to counter the sexism and racism of heterosexist black and feminist intellectuals and critics, who come between me and my audiences, who ignore and consign me to special interest categories—like the Gay and

Lesbian Caucus of the MLA—and exclude me from traditions that have nourished me. Make no mistake, I am here because you are here. And I thank you, again, for asking me to speak. But our voices have to be heard in the general body of sessions.

Barbara Smith's groundbreaking essay "Towards a Black Feminist Criticism" is a model of vigilance for all lesbian writers. Thus, I have used the essay for political expression and critical vigilance regarding issues of heterosexism and racism by commission and omission. The essay "Lesbianism: An Act of Resistance," in *This Bridge Called My Back: Writings by Radical Women of Color* (1981) was a way to enter into dialogue with other lesbian writers of color. This essay is used in many women's studies courses. Also my essay, "The Failure to Transform: Homophobia in the Black Community," in *Home Girls: A Black Feminist Anthology* (1983), was a way to enter into dialogue with many of the black literati who historically and currently exclude black lesbian and gay male writers, concerns, and perspectives from their black worldview. I consider essay writing a political responsibility, not a labor of love, rather a labor of labor. I became an active participant in the production of feminist and lesbian literature in 1981. I self-published my first book of poems, *Narratives: poems in the tradition of black women,* in 1982, and what an immense lesson that was, because I was very involved in the mental and physical acts of production. Producing a book is something I can always do, given certain resources. Also, I was invited to join the *Conditions* Magazine Collective, which is committed to new writing by women with an emphasis on writing by lesbians.

Understanding how books are made, understanding aspects of production, the politics of publishing and distribution, I came to see more clearly how much of an audience there is for lesbian writing, how committed women are to publishing women, and how many women are committed to telling women's stories. Joining feminist publishing, I also came to know the work of other lesbians of color: *She Had Some Horses, Zami, Abeng, Cuentos, A Gathering of Spirit,* as well as works written by my colleagues here today, Becky Birtha and Luz Maria Umpierre.

The feminist writing and publishing community, characterized by lesbian leadership, has enabled me not to be silent or invisible. Visibility and vigilance are integral to my everyday, nonwriting lesbian life.

So, as a writer, I have more than "moments of inspiration," I have whole movements of inspiration.

Poetry:

poets are among the first witches
so suffer none to live
or suffer none to be heard
and watch them burn before your eyes
less they recant and speak their verse
in latin

i'm a poet
i speaks in piglatin.
i eats pigs feet—a shonuff sign of
    satan
to those whose ears are trained to
dactyls and iambs
who resolve all conflicts in couplets . . .

                    (Living as a Lesbian)

I find the choices I have made regarding my identity are made more complex by my choice of poetry as my expressive art. This is a prose-oriented culture—commercially and in the scholarly realms. Certainly most of the critical paradigms have been constructed for the novel. What are the uses of poetry? I find, certainly, within the recent history of Afro-Americans, the Black Arts Movement is my mentoring movement. Yet, also, so was the black literary movement of the 1920's, which was propelled by poets. I find my life full of unconscious responses to traditions. Afro-American literary history begins with women poets, Lucy Terry and Phyllis Wheatley. For black people, poetry has been the great teacher of consciousness, of history, of self-love as well as duplicitousness, as expressed in Dunbar's poem "We Wear the Mask," with which I began this talk. And so has poetry been these things for women as an oppressed people and culture and no less for lesbians. I find my choice to be a poet consonant with this search-turned-journey I am engaged in for my life; it is consonant with choosing to be a lesbian, which is poetry, for both always were and neither have a beginning, middle, or end; it is also consonant with being African, which is the first become last.

My first book, *Narratives: poems in the tradition of black women*, was a self-published effort and served to tell some of the suppressed stories of black women regarding sexuality, age, empowerment, incest, development. All kinds of traditions helped me form these stories into poems: the prose poems of Toomer's *Cane*, the legends I grew up with in my family of origin, the early fiction of Alice Walker and Toni Morrison, the black lyric voice of Langston Hughes, and the telling irony of the blues:

If you got a good woman,
better tie her to your side.
Said, if you got a good woman,
better tie her to your side.
Cuz if she flag my train,
I'm sure gonna let her ride
    (*Narratives: poems in the tradition of black women,* 1982)

Living as a Lesbian, my second book of poetry, served to advance a lesbian aesthetic and perspective—politically, lyrically, and unequivocally. I plainly wanted to advance Audre Lorde's thesis in her piece "Uses of the Erotic," by promoting the concept of lesbian sex, which itself is poetry—it is and without beginning, middle, and end. It is the improvisational clarity of jazz that drove this book, and that, too, is lesbianism:

> the promises
> the absurdity
> the histrionics
> the loss of pride
> the bargaining
> the sadness after.
>
> in wakefulness wanting
> in wakefulness waiting.
>
> *(Living as a Lesbian)*

And *Humid Pitch* (1989), my new book of poems, returns me to the tradition of storytelling to once again unearth the untold or not told-enough tales of women of color, triumphant lesbians, ambivalent men, slave women, and the children who survive childhood, still moving language to the rhythms of black music, exploring my themes of love, sex, lesbianism, loss, and the open road:

> I'm a mean woman
> and don't need a man.
> I make my bed soft
> and take my lovin hard

drink my whiskey straight
and like my coffee sweet

(Humid Pitch)

Crossing the boundaries:
She dreamed of life beyond its
crumbling perimeters
and memorized the rarefied space
between lines of poetry.
Moby-Dick and the Bible whispered
their passages to her as she rode
the train downtown squeezed
between
Philistines.
She was a solitary dolphin.
Ilona of Hickory

. . . .

Ilona translated the language of
women,
did not fear men disguised in their
inventions.
She bonded with them both,
sometimes both at the same time.

(Humid Pitch)

I attempt to cross sexual boundaries, gender boundaries, and racial boundaries as a lesbian of color writer who is Afro-American. (I take issue with the term "Minority Writer.") Persons in academia have to begin to do this, if only in theory—i.e., use their imaginations, read between the lines, break the codes. Inclusiveness of writing by lesbians and gay men and lesbians and gay men of color, greater support of small and women's press books and journals in which much of our material appears, and more willingness to take risks with students are critical.

I want personally to thank all of you who have supported the work of gay and lesbian writers, especially those of us who publish in the small and feminist presses—because that is where most of us are thriving—in the small presses. You have bought our books, ordered them for your classes, included us in your bibliographies, made reference to us in your scholarship. Yet, you—we—cannot do it all. Your straight colleagues must now become "encouraged" to give more than tacit support to lesbian and gay studies. They have to do what you have done, take some risks. They must be more supportive of you, help create a safer environment for you to do your work as lesbian and gay scholars, take some stands.

As a black lesbian writer, my advice to myself, academicians, and other lesbian writers is: say the least said and tell the least told.

Knowing the Danger and Going There Anyway

We have no passion left to love the spring
who have suffered autumn as we did, alone
walking through dominions of a
browning laughter
carrying our loneliness, our loving and
our pain.

—"Second Spring," Audre Lorde, 1952*

WOMEN ARE NOT taken seriously as arbiters of history, nor are poets. And ironically, both the African and the European literary traditions in the United States begin with women poets, Phillis Wheatley and Anne Bradstreet—one a slave, the other a Puritan "housewife." Neither was legally permitted to learn reading and writing, and both wrote for their lives under varying degrees of privilege and duress. "So it is better to speak / remembering / we were never meant to survive," says Audre Lorde as she continues that Black woman poet's tradition of defiance and persistence. In the tradition of African-American woman writers (foremothers, foresisters, and contemporaries), Lorde accepts no dichotomy between the Black and human story and particularizes that story by placing Black women at the center of the action. She charts her orbits studiously, in parallel and in intertwining traditions of writing. Her nine books of poetry and four books of prose, including a self-styled "biomythography," mark her journey through this dangerous land. Hardworking. Serious. Undeterred.

Writing poetry for more than 40 years and actively publishing for more than a quarter of a century, Lorde has presented a truly exquisite body of work (which could bear more attention). She is a relentless exponent of the Black lesbian aesthetic. Year after year, she plumbs the interiors of her humanity as an African person, a woman, a mother, a lesbian and crafts her stunning poems. The poems are ancient legacies reborn in tightly woven, startling verse and imagery, haunting us in the urban madness of Manhattan, where still can be heard "the voice of a sparrow" ("A Poem for Women in Rage," *Chosen Poems*).

Audre Lorde found the first community for her voice in the late '60s with the New Black Poets whose mission was to liberate the Black soul from Western tutelage. Even then, refusing to be silenced by the conflicts between Black men and Black women, she wrote woman-centered poems of motherhood and childhood; poems of ambivalence and uncertainty; mythic and sorrowful poems:

How the young attempt and are broken
differs from age to age
We were brown free girls

love singing beneath our skin
sun in our hair in our eyes
sun our fortune
and the wind had made us golden
made us gay.

—"Generation," 1996

She has remained loyal to these themes, these parts of herself,
though there was, in that community of Blackness, no place for
her growing feminist and lesbian consciousness. Determined not
to be silenced or made invisible, she carried her lonely courage to
another part of earth, where she found and liberated us. But she
lamented, from her vantage point in Nedicks, as

the women rally before they march
discussing the problematic girls
they hire to make them free.
An almost white counterman passes
a waiting brother to serve them first
and ladies neither notice nor reject
the slighter pleasures of their slavery.
But I who am bound by my mirror
as well as my bed
see causes in color
as well as sex
and sit here wondering

which me will survive
all these liberations.

—"Who Said It Was Simple," 1970

And she had gone beyond survival.

In her useful article "Audre Lorde and Matrilineal Diaspora," in *Wildwomen in the Whirlwind,* Afra-centric scholar and critic Chinasole credits Lorde with tracing and creating a truly African-based woman-identification. *Using Zami, The Black Unicorn,* and the poem "Sisters in Arms" (*Our Dead Behind Us*) as points of reference, Chinasole says Lorde "develops a configuration of selves based on matrilineal diaspora. . . . [e]nabling us to experience distinct but related cultures while retaining a special sense of home as the locus of self-definition and power" in Harlem, Grenada, Dahomey. This particular vision is a lesbian vision, which sets Lorde apart from her literary foremothers, foresisters, and contemporaries. All too often Black women writers leave their Black women heroes isolated from the historical community of Black women. All too often they fail to tell the story of the women who called each other "Zami. A Carriacou name for women who work together as friends and lovers" (*Zami*).

And, indeed, for me, *The Black Unicorn,* with its spare and resonating lines, its reconciliation of imageries (African, Caribbean, Afro-American), its careful grandiosity and mythic sensuousness, is her most precious inscription of Black lesbianism, a vital revision of the story of the race. Refusing to "forget the warning of my woman's flesh / weeping at the new moon" ("Solstice," 1978), she continues to construct a revolutionary Black lesbian-feminist aesthetic.

Zami, Lorde's compelling prose piece, is autobiographical, fictive, poetic, didactic, and, above all else, erotic. It is, as Chinasole suggests, a key to *The Black Unicorn*. In *Zami*, Lorde tells us how she got to *The Black Unicorn*, her struggle for self-definition and autonomy, for sexuality, for lesbianism. In the scene of the adolescent Lorde liquefying the garlic and spices with mortar and pestle for her mother's souse, I hear Lorde writing *Zami*: "After all the ingredients were in the bowl of mortar, I fetched the pestle and placing it into the bowl, slowly rotated the shaft a few times, working it gently down through all the ingredients to mix them." As the term "Biomythography" suggests, *Zami* is the poet's use of her life to inscribe a woman-centered lineage as surely as it is the story of the women who have left "their footprints" on her, and in whose rooms she has grafted poems

> on the bathroom wall between the toilet and the bathtub,
> others in the window jambs and the floorboards under the
> flowered linoleum mixed up with the ghosts of rich food
> smells.

Lorde, like her contemporaries Adrienne Rich and June Jordan, has been loyal of poetry and to feminism. All three leave the chamber to reverie and foray into the arena of the essay to be heard. *The Cancer Journals, Sister Outsider, A Burst of Light* place Lorde in the tradition of essayists like Frances E.W. Harper, Ida B. Wells, Alice Dunbar Nelson, Mary Church Terrell, each of whom kept alive the dialogue on Black women's identity and duty, warned the race of its own pitfalls, and protested injustices done to the race and to the women of the race. However, Lorde goes further and deeper than her foremothers. She dissolves the visceral silence surrounding sexuality, death, illness, intimacy, and gives them a public voice—realizing the most basic feminist truth: the personal is political.

> And for the first time deeply and fleetingly a groundswell of sadness rolled up over me that filled my mouth and eyes almost to drowning. My right breast represented such an area of feeling and pleasure for me, how could I bear never to feel that again.
>
> —*Cancer Journals*

Her essays have transformed the way we live our lives and do our work as feminists and lesbians. Who else, before or since, has taught us that sex energy is life energy ("Uses of the Erotic," *Sister Outsider*)? Who else could have taken on, with such authority and humility, the antilesbian politics of progressive Black women, making them accountable for their repression of Black lesbians ("I Am Your Sister: Black Women Organizing Across Sexualities," *A Burst of Light*)? In

"Open Letter to Mary Daly" (*Sister Outsider*), Lorde, like many of her Black feminist foremothers, resorts to the immediacy of her prose to call white women to task for their racism: "The history of white women who are unable to hear Black women's words, or to maintain dialogue with us, is long and discouraging." She meditates on Daly's racism as she chants the names of African women—dieties, matriarchs, warriors, and communities—missing from Daly's book *Gynecology*. Despite its tone of condescension and presumption, her admonitions in "Eye to Eye: Black Women, Hatred, and Anger" (*Sister Outsider*) are useful to Black women as we continue to examine our internalization of racism. The poem "Between Ourselves" (*The Black Unicorn*), however, is a far more convincing lesson:

> if we do not stop killing
> the other
> in ourselves
> the self that we hate
> in others
> soon we shall all lie
> in the same direction
> and Eshidale's priests will be very busy
> they who alone can bury
> all those who seek their own death
> > —"Between Ourselves," *The Black Unicorn*

None of this has been easy. To be a Black lesbian activist in racist, heterosexist North America is not easy. To be a poet in a prose-privileging culture has not been easy either. Lorde continues to be where the danger is, to speak on it, and to reckon with it. We read her letters from St. Croix written by kerosene lamp after the devastation of Hurricane Hugo. We support her as she organizes with and for South African women against apartheid. We remember the times she read poetry for the liberation of Assata Shakur and other political prisoners and Black revolutionaries. She has entered many rooms and made it possible for others to enter those places and speak there also. All Black women have gained strength from Lorde's feminist work.

In her most recent book of poetry, *Our Dead Behind Us*, she shows, unequivocally, that war is not some distant, desolate land on a TV screen, where swaddled survivors run from bullets as they crouch to eat their supper. The horrors of "your fifteen-year-old daughter gut-sprung on police wheels" ("Sisters in Arms") or your "son bayonetted to the door in Santiago de Chile" ("Soho Cinema") hang at the edge of your Hollywood bed. The poems offer us vignettes of the wars we are in every day of our lives in America. The people of Beirut or Managua or Monrovia or Jerusalem, et al. know they are living in wars. In the West, our wars are hidden, and we think our lives "on this island easier safer / than the ones [we] rush home to peruse" ("Soho Cinema") on the evening news.

Haunting and visceral, *Our Dead Behind Us* is a cynical

acceptance of the inevitability of death and destruction. The poet sees the danger close at hand and is willing to bargain with it—every day.

In a review in *Gay Community News* (Dec. 11–17, 1988) of *A Burst of Light*, I said that Audre Lorde's work is "a neighbor I've grown up with, who can always be counted on for honest talk, to rescue me when I've forgotten the key to my own house, to go with me to a tenants' or town meeting, a community festival." I still feel this way and that she has more work to do. And so do we.

Finally, Audre Lorde is ever in search of her women's communities —from Staten Island to New Zealand. She finds us, always, and sings of us or reprimands us or helps us produce our own legends and legacies or leaves us:

There have been easier times
for loving different richness
if it were only the stars
we had wanted to conquer
I could turn from your dear face
into the prism light makes
along my line
we cast into the rapids
alone back to back
laboring the current
      —"Fishing the White Water," *Our Dead Behind Us*

We can enter the house she leaves open for us, "head for the source" of our own pain, and work with her to discover

Dark women clad in flat and functional
leather . . . whispering
sisterly advice. . . .

—"Beams," *Our Dead Behind Us*

. . .She Still Wrote Out the Word Kotex on a Torn Piece of Paper Wrapped Up in a Dollar Bill . . .

IN HER CRITICALLY responsible article "Black Women Poets from Wheatley to Walker," in *Sturdy Black Bridges* (Bell, Parker, Guy-Sheftall 1979), Gloria T. Hull assesses, for the first time in our history, the literary undertakings of black women poets prior to the Black Arts Movement of the 1960s. While her task is not to examine expressions of sexuality in the poetry of these women, she does engage in a process of criticism that bears on my efforts here: care, thoroughness, respect for the work, identification of woman-orientation, challenging of sexist notions and proscriptions, placing the poets in an historical context, formal and analytical approaches to evaluating the works' literary effectiveness.

In "Interstices: A Small Drama of Words," a dense and variously humorous paper delivered at the 1982 Scholar and the Feminist IX Conference at Barnard and subsequently published in *Pleasure and Danger: Exploring Female Sexuality* (Vance 1984), black feminist critic Hortense Spillers makes this observation about the language of black women's sexuality:

With the virtually sole exception of Calvin Hernton's *Sex and Racism in America* and less than a handful of very recent texts by black feminist and lesbian writers, black women are the beached whales of the sexual universe, unvoiced, misseen, not doing, awaiting *their* verb. (74)

Well, if not our verb, then at least more precise metaphors.

Through an examination of selected texts by black women poets since 1969, I will present an overview of various linguistic expressions of sexuality, sexual identity, and the erotic. I have chosen to focus on poetry published since 1969 because this juncture signifies a variety of expressions speaking to sexual experience, desire, identity, and gratification. I am defining "sexuality" as literal and metaphorical references to the sex act (with women, with men, with self), references to male and female genitals and body parts. By "sexual identity," I mean the language—coded and explicit—that defines the poetic persona's recognition of self as a sexual being whoever or whatever the object of her desire. And with respect to the "erotic," I will use a definition I find implicit in Audre Lorde's exploration in her published speech "The Uses of the Erotic: The Erotic as Power" (1978)—that is, any sensual connection of self to others, to work, to sex, to the here-and-now: a primordial energy, an enabling vision. And when I use the term "lesbian," in reference to the texts, as I will throughout, I am, like Barbara Christian (1985), limiting its definition to "women who find other women sexually attractive and gratifying" (189).

I hope my paper will raise questions about the role and function of black feminist criticism; will continue some of the dialogue opened by black feminist critics like Barbara Smith (1977), Barbara Christian (1980), Hortense Spillers (1979), Deborah McDowell (1980), Gloria Hull (1979), and others, on the subject of lesbian perspectives and lesbian criticism. (Here, I am using the term "lesbian" in the broader sense as a way of revisioning and envisioning emotional, sexual, political connections among women in explicitly lesbian as well as nonlesbian texts; and here also, the term "lesbian" implies "feminist."

Black women in the United States have constantly been in the position of proving or feeling we must prove our sexual morality due to racist, misogynist devaluation in the United States or in Western culture. Much like white women, who are either whores or virgins, black women are either passive-aggressive wet nurses or inarticulate belle sauvages. In Frances E. W. Harper's 1892 novel, *Iola Leroy*, the character Dr. Gresham, a white Yankee, in offering his hand in marriage, makes this presumptuous plea to the mulatto, ex-slave protagonist, Iola;

> "Iola. . . . You must not judge me by the worst of my race.
> Surely our country has produced a higher type of manhood
> than the men by whom you were tried and tempted." (115)

Iola responds, "as a deep flush overspread her face," in defense of her honor:

"Tried but not tempted. . . . I was never tempted."

Because of presumptions like that of the character Dr. Gresham and the corresponding projection of images of black women's sexual depravity, black women poets have avoided references to explicit sexuality, to genitals, to sexual acts or sexual gratification in our poetry until the late 1960s. And not to mention, United States' culture did not and does not sanction open discussions of sexuality from anyone or any group. Spurred on by the new philosophy of black self-determination, the era of the so-called "sexual revolution," and the later women's liberation movement, black women poets began to evince an explicit consciousness of ourselves as sexual beings, primarily heterosexual sexual beings except in rare cases.

As Spillers also states in the previously cited article, black women's

sexual experiences are depicted but not often by them and if and when by the subject herself, often in the guise of vocal music, often in the self-contained accent and sheer romance of the blues. (74)

The blues was not all "sheer romance," as we will discuss later.

In her discussion of black women singers in "Slave Codes and Liner Notes" (Hull, Scott, Smith 1982), Michele Russell says that

Bessie Smith "humanized sex for black women" (131) and "articulated how fundamental sex was to survival." Of course, I am not going to push a comparison of black women singers and black women poets, because many formalistic, audience-related, economic, class, and cultural issues differentiate the exponents of these two genres. But I do believe the blues *period,* as a form, is a great teacher for poets—in terms of its linguistic facility and directness.

In the songs of black women, particularly those of the classic or city blues form, we find brazen admissions of sexual desire and need, feelings about the uses and uselessness of men, money, sex/love relationships. Women spoke on when, how, who with and how long, and what one must do to get *"it"* (sex) with humor, bravada, and aplomb. There are plenty of songs that express loneliness and rejection, but just as many express the heroic, the independent, the in-control, tit-for-tat, out-there-on-the-make-with one-or-more-men woman.

> *Now let me tell you, baby,*
> *your mind is too full of sin.*
> *Now let me tell you, baby,*
> *your mind is too full of sin.*
> *Don't forget pretty daddy,*
> *that this world is full of other men.*
>
> ("Wise Woman Blues," sung by Dinah Washington,
> 1943–1945)

or

> *I'm crazy bout a good time*
> *like a dog is crazy bout his bone.*
> *So when you run out of money*
> *get a cab and send me home.*

("Good Time Mama," sung by Martha Copeland, 1927)

or

> *I will not sell it.*
> *I will not give it away.*
> *I will sit on it the rest of my days.*

("No Voot, No Boot," sung by Dinah Washington, 1943–1945)

Gloria Hull's (1979) historical, critical, and textual assessment of poet Angelina Weld Grimké's life, times, and work was an astonishing revelation as we learned of Grimké's "explicitly woman-identified poems" (17). Although we know and can imagine the constraints, isolation, and class imperative under which Grimké wrote about her lesbianism—much of it in secret— and the more public, bohemian, reputedly hedonistic lifestyle of her contemporary, Gertrude Malissa Pridgett, better known as Ma Rainey, we can compare the intents of Grimké's "A Mona Lisa," first published in Countee Cullen's *Caroling Dusk* (1927) and quoted by Hull in the context of Grimké's lesbianism and a few bars from Rainey's infamous "Prove It on Me," a bawdy and explicitly lesbian song recorded in 1928:

Grimké: *I should like to creep*
        Through the long brown grasses that are your lashes

Rainey: *I looked and to my surprise*
        the gal I was with was gone.
        Where she went I don't know.
        I mean to follow her everywhere she go.

Grimké's use of the pronoun "your" might still throw us off were it not for Hull's discovery of other lesbian poems—and I suppose it could still be argued that the object of the speaker's desire might be other than female—whereas Rainey identifies for us which gender the object of her pursuit is with specific female references. She also says things in the song like, "Yes, it's true I wear a collar and tie . . . talk to the women like any ole man. . . ." And, of course, the famous refrain: "I went out last night with a crowd of my friends. Musta been women cause I don't like no men." And one does not get the impression that the persona of "Prove It on Me" will be creeping in pursuit.

In addition to the repression, in a misogynist culture, of women's acknowledgment of our sexual-erotic energies, for many black women that repression has also functioned in the black community. So black women receive no encouragement anywhere to address ourselves as sexual beings. In her essay, "Uses of the Erotic: The Erotic as Power," black lesbian feminist poet Audre Lorde charges that women have been made to suppress "the erotic as a considered source of power and information within our lives" (1). Lorde responds similarly, in *Black Women Writers at Work* (Tate 1983), to interviewer Claudia Tate's self-observation about the jarring effect of realizing that the speaker in Lorde's poetry is a woman and that the "object of affection is likewise a woman" (110). Lorde says:

> Women have been taught . . . to suspect the erotic urge, the place that's uniquely female. . . . So just as we reject our blackness because it has been termed inferior as women we tend to reject our capacity for feeling, our ability to love, to touch the erotic because it has been devalued.

The 1970 anthology *The Black Woman* (Cade, ed.) created a public forum for black women to address each other and to criticize our second-class citizenship within the black political community. I was particularly struck by Cade's stunning proposal in her essay "On the Issue of Roles" for reconciling the gender politics therein:

> Perhaps we need to let go of manhood and femininity and
> concentrate on blackhood. . . . It perhaps takes less heart to
> pick up the gun than to face the task of creating a new iden-
> tity, a new self, perhaps an androgynous self, via commit-
> ment to the struggle. (103)

Clearly Cade saw this "androgynous self" as a means of eradicating
the unequal power relationships inherent in gender roles—at least
in Western culture. But whenever androgyny is put forth, there is
the implication of bisexuality and thus homosexuality. No wonder
this staggering proposal was met with silence and resentment.

The issue of the erotic as power, as creative force arises again in
Black Women Writers at Work from Tate's question to poet Sonia
Sanchez, "How do you fit writing into your life?" Sanchez
describes her process in a way that bears out her final analogy of
the act of writing and the sex act:

> I work in two or three notebooks. . . . I do everything long
> hand. I hate to see first drafts. I read them out loud. They're
> terrible, and then I read successive drafts. . . . All of a sudden
> there is a poem. I sometimes literally jump up and down. I
> might go cover up the kids and kiss them because I want to
> share my joy. It's a joy that has never been duplicated, per-
> haps the closest comparison is sex. (142)

Now, does the interviewer respond to this revelation with a question that might allow further exploration of this analogy; for example, does the poet consciously use her erotic power to craft her verse? Or, failing such a question, does Tate join with the poet to acknowledge that she's taken a risk? No, she plows right on to the next question, "For whom do you write?" The interviewer seems to fall into the same pattern of denial Lorde discusses in the statement cited earlier from the same work.

Gloria Wade-Gayles, in a recent book of black feminist criticism, *No Crystal Stair* (1985), charges that Gayl Jones' novel *Eva's Man*—a study of insanity—reads like "the script of an X-rated film" (175) because Jones uses graphic language and images to convey sexuality and sexual exploitation. Is the critic then relieved of evaluating the work? Would it were that the scripts of X-rated films were as well-written or written with as much truth! Though we can say that the previously cited critic's evaluation is symptomatic of the prudery, fear, and censoring of sexually explicit language—to say nothing of the acts themselves—it's also one of the ways black women are denied forums to discuss our sexuality, particularly if the discussion takes us outside the familiar realm of male-initiated sexual encounters, penile sex, or the cult of romance.

In an otherwise respectful and elucidatory article, entitled oddly "In the Name of the Father: The Poetry of Audre Lorde" (Evans 1983), Jerome Brooks dismisses Lorde's claiming, in *Cancer*

Journals, of her experience of breast cancer as "A Black Lesbian Experience." The perspective is only valid for Lorde, he says, postulating, "Her remarks are certainly of wider interest than the subtitle would indicate (275)." "Lesbian," like "sex" or the "erotic," is, in the words of Ntozake Shange's acolescent heroine Indigo, the word "Kotex" written "on a torn piece of paper wrapped up in a dollar bill" (1982) and sent to the drugstore via a child. Because Brooks does not wish to explore the meaning of Lorde's lesbian perspective, it's only valid for Lorde. And the rest of us can be left out here wondering about lesbianism like daughters are left wondering by their mothers what the meaning of menstrual blood is to the rest of life. So, I feel it is important to acknowledge that whenever black women express themselves sexually on paper or in the sack, we're taking the risk of being rejected, misunderstood, silenced. And the more non-male-oriented and women-centered, non-heterosexual and non-penile-oriented our expressions or acts, the greater the risk.

In my reading of the texts, I have noted four main types of sexual discourse in the poetry:

- *Wished-for sex,* which includes a variety of fantasy, wanting and not getting, and lack of gratification;
- *Hyperbolic expression,* which includes grand metaphors, conceits, and images of sex as something other than what it is; may include perverse, distorted, and violent images of sex;

- *Sexual loneliness,* which includes statements of unrequited love, fear of intimacy, betrayal, rejection, and lots of circumspection;
- *Sexual graphics and explicitness,* which includes concrete images of sexual encounters as sexual encounters; may also include perverse, distorted, sometimes violent images of sex.

Erotic language, images, and acts might appear in all four types. There is overlap. And admittedly, there are far fewer of the sexually graphic and explicit expressions than of the other three types. I am not using poems in which sex acts are vehicles for imagizing other events. In the poems I've chosen, sex is the subject of the comparison, and the poets may use a range of images to convey their concepts of sex.

At the beginning of the 1960s Black Arts Movement, black women poets as well as black men tended to mythologize and deify black women as nation builders, custodians of the revolution, and monolithic forces of regeneration, typified in Mari Evans' poem, "I Am a Black Woman," from her volume of poems of the same name.

> *. . . tall as a cypress*
> *strong*
> *beyond all definition still*

defying place
and time
and circumstance
   assailed
   impervious
   indestructible

Look
   on me and be
renewed.

Nikki Giovanni's poem "Ego Tripping" is another such example, with all its references to ancient African kingdoms. Hyperbole was needed, at that time, to create the larger-than-life archetype, the superwoman, the quintessential matriarch to offset the devaluing images of black women. However, since then we've discovered that queens like common women have physical needs that find us falling off the pedestals; consider, for example another poem by Evans, "I Who Would Encompass Millions," which expresses sexual loneliness in the image of the "single bed":

I
who would encompass
millions
am adrift on

this

my single bed. (17)

While we as poets have linguistic options aplenty and feel so deeply about so many things, our metaphors of sexuality, sexual desire, sexual need, sexual gratification are not often adventurous. We are usually tied to the values of heterosexual sex and sexual monogamy. Rarely are we as experimental in our pursuit of sex as the singers. We are not confident about and less direct in dealing in the here-and-now for conceit. We wish a lot for sex. In her poem, "Marrow of My Bone," Evans either wishes for or asks her lover to:

Fondle me
caress
me
with your lips
withdraw
the nectar from
me
teach me there is someone.

Nikki Giovanni, putative princess of the Black Arts Movement or, as Michele Wallace describes her, "a kind of nationalistic Rod McKuen" (1979, 166), gained popularity for her assertiveness in the sexual language of her poetry. In her poem "Seduction" (1970), she boldly fantasizes about initiating sex with her black nationalist warrior:

> *. . . i'll be taking your dashiki off*
> *. . . i'll be licking your arm*
> *. . . unbucklin your pants*
> *. . . taking your shorts off.* (38)

Giovanni usually reserves her more graphic sexual images for expressing criticism as in "No-Dick" from her poem "Nixon" (1970) or bitterness as in "Woman Poem"—her first and probably only feminist statement, which brings together black women's ambivalence about sexuality, the needing but not getting, the fear of appearing vulnerable. In a tight series of graphic descriptives, the poet posits the sexual roles black women deny ourselves:

> *gameswoman, romantic woman*
> *love-needer*
> *man-seeker*
> *dick-eater sweat-getter*
> *fuck-needing love-seeking woman.* (78)

In a poem called "Gray," published in *Callaloo's* special issue on (black) women poets, Alice Walker treats the theme of fear

of intimacy in a sequence of questions to and answers from a
woman friend, whom she "adore(s)," who is, perhaps, turning gray
from being "frantic and alone":

> *'How long does it take you to love someone?'*
> . . . .
> *'A hot second'* . . .
>
> *'And how long do you love them?'*
> *'Oh, anywhere up to several months.'*
> *'And how long does it take you to*
> *get over them?'*
> *'Three weeks . . . tops.'* (63)

This, I might add, could also be interpreted as a poem of latent les-
bian affection.

The wished-for, fantasy sentiment and expressions of sexual
loneliness appear in a poem by Sybil Dunbar, also in the *Callaloo*
issue, called "Words for Solitude's Pen":

> *wish i could light you candles*
> *at midnight*
> *and watch you glow*
> *in the deep blue haze*
> *of my wanting hours*

then i'd never again
turn my shivering body
beneath cold sheets
or part my legs
to dream figures
who beat their songs
on silent drums (110)

(Incidentally, there are no explicitly lesbian poems or poems by "out" lesbian poets in this issue of *Callaloo*.)

And Gayl Jones, in a poem called "Chance," also in this special issue on women poets, echoes the fear of intimacy, the danger of love and sexual relationships:

He reaches for her.
She kisses him with fear.
She's afraid to be tender,
afraid he'll think she wants something.

Sonia Sanchez has put forth a consistently sexual self in much of her poetry. Men (or *a* man) were and are the objects and subjects of her desire, lust, and her disappointment. She waits for black men ("To All Brothers," 1970); she extends her hand to them ("Poem at 30," 1970); they make her breathe ("Black Magic," 1970). A more recent poem, "I have Alked a Long Time"—also in *Callaloo*—makes one wonder if the persona has ever been gratified sexually. In a catalog of dense and exquisite images and metaphors, the persona's struggles and losses are tallied. She mourns the loss of sensuality, the erotic, and creativity:

ah, i have not loved
wid legs stretched like stalks
against sheets
wid stomachs drainen the piracy of
oceans
wid mouth discarden the gelatin
to shake the sharp self.
. . . .
between the yellow rain
and ash,
I have heard the rattle
of my seed.
so time, like some pearl necklace
embracen
a superior whore, converges
and the swift spider binds my breast. (19–20)

And, after this lush verse, the persona beseeches, characteristic of Sanchez:

You, man, will you remember
me when I die? (20)

In the poetry of many black women sex is fraught with danger, the threat of loss, fear of vulnerability, fear of objectification, and most of us have sworn at one time or another, like Silla Boyce in Marshall's *Brown Girl, Brownstones* (1959):

> *I wun let a Judas smile*
> *and Judas words in the night*
> *and* thing *turn me foolish.*
>
> (39, my emphasis)

In our silence and denial is the fear of betrayal and also the guardedness that comes with the objective knowledge of male dominance. Toi Derricotte, in her first volume of poetry, *The Empress of the Death House* (1978) presents graphic and explicit language with grotesque and perverse images of sex. In the hyperbolic poem, "Sleeping with Mr. Death," she opens this volume:

> *you go down on him*
> *he bursts in yr mouth*
> *a thousand stars*
> *flicker then die*
>
> *chalk dry, mr death* (13)

On her graphic references to genitals and use of gory, visceral images of an aggressive, vengeful female sexuality in the poem, "divorcee," spoken as a warning to men:

> *she has been bit so often*
> *in the cunt*
> *she has sewn it closed.*
>
> *she is teaching them [her daughters] to buy*
> *genealogy on time:*
> *on cunt hair a month. . . .*
>
> *she is teaching them that eating eating eating*
> *causes a woman to grow a penis*
>
> *She blasphemes teaches her daughter*
> *that the first man splintered off eve's pelvis*
> *& was born in a bag of pus*
>
> *she is teaching them to paint X's on the doors of*
> *churches*
> *in menstrual blood*

These images, as Audre Lorde says in her endorsement of *Empress,* are not easy. They make us uncomfortable.

Black lesbian poet Audre Lorde, whose work is always at the edge of pain and alienation and at the center of anger and hope, evokes the danger implicit in sex, especially for lesbians. Lorde has spoken often of her ostracism by the black literary community because of her explicit lesbianism. In her love poetry, Lorde is in the here-and-now and sees always the potential of pain, rejection, or destruction. Her metaphors are awesome for their sometime hermetic inaccessibility. In "love poem," an explicitly lesbian poem first published in 1974 in her volume *New York Head Shop and Museum,* and later reprinted in *Lesbian Poetry* (Bulkin and Larkin 1981) and *Chosen Poems: Old and New* (1982), earth is a conceit for the lover. The persona begins with an invocation to the earth that contains an hyperbole of her hips:

> *make sky flow honey out of my hips*
> *rigid as mountains*
> *spread over a valley*
> *carved out by the mouth of rain.*

And then she comes down to earth in a long stanza with a series of metaphorical and literal images of digital penetration, cunnilingus, female genitals, body parts, secretions, and erogenous zones. The voice is active and the tone reflects the awareness of risk:

> *And I knew when I entered her I was*

high wind in her forest hollow
fingers whispering sound
honey flowed
from the split cup
impaled on a lance of tongues
on the tips of her breasts on her navel
and my breath howling into her entrances
through lungs of pain.

(*Lesbian Poetry*, 23)

Lorde is more than anything sensual and explicit, even when her metaphors are inaccessible. Even lesbians suspend their guardedness in Lorde's wished-for poem, "woman," from *Black Unicorn* (1978):

I dream of a place between your breasts
to build my house like a haven
where I plant crops in your body
. . . .
and your night comes down upon me
like a nurturing rain. (82)

In "Fog Report" *(Black Unicorn)* she raises the issue of loss of self in intimate relationships. The sensual imagery, as usual, is unequivocal as are the desperation and humor:

I am tempted
to take you apart
and reconstruct your orifices
your tongue your truths your fleshy altars
into my own forgotten image
so when this fog lifts
I could be sure to find you
tethered like a goat
in my heart's yard.

And in the searingly beautiful "Meet," again Lorde returns to the store of images of common and exalted people and places she used throughout *Black Unicorn,* to talk to this dangerous love, replete with ingenious hyperbole, well-placed allusions, and explicit references to physical intimacy:

You shall get young as I lick
　　　your stomach
hot and at rest before
　　we move off again
you will be white heat in
　　my navel
I will be sweeping night
Mauwulisa foretells our bodies

. . . .

Taste my milk in the ditches of
Chile and Ouagadougou

. . . .

in the innermost rooms of moment
we must taste of each other's fruit
at least once
before we shall both be slain (34)

The inventive Ntozake Shange in *nappy edges* (1978) and *A Daughter's Geography* (1984) continues the style of love poetry which characterized the black poetry of the 1960s—replete with allusions to Africa, the South, black music and musicians, black historical figures, and metaphors of love and sex as natural wonders and ancient monuments and latter-day revolutionary movements and third-world landscapes. Shange is consistently male-identified in terms of her muses and sexual references in poetry, despite her flirtation with the theme of lesbianism in *Sassafrass, Cypress,* and *Indigo.* Her verse is not only free; it is wild. Her poetic diction is, what Alice Walker would call, a "black folk language" or what a friend of mine calls "Shange-ese."

i can't allow you to look
        at me
how you do so i am
    naked and wantin
to be explored like a

> *honeysuckle patch*
> *when you look at me how you do so*
> *i am all lips and thigh*
> *my cover is blown & the kisses*
> *run free/only to hover sulkin over*
> *yr cheek/while i pretend*
> *they are not mine*
> *cuz its happenin/but you don't know*
> *abt it.*

The same whimsicality and coyness express themselves in "Where the Amazon meets the Mississippi":

> *you fill me up so much*
> *when you touch me*
> *i can't stay here*
> *i haveta go to my space.* (28)

She uses animal imagery to convey the feeling of sexual gratification as in "You are such a fool," from *A Daughter's Geography*:

> *you make me feel like a*
> *cheetah*
> *a gazelle*
> *something fast and beautiful. . . .*

While Shange is an effective exponent of the hyperbolic style of sex poetry, I also believe poets are obligated to liberate our sexual discourse as well as our sexuality from the flowers, collard greens, and okra, from nights in Tamaris, from fierce animals, and some black male musician's tenor solo.

However, Shange is guarded about sex and can become quite graphic, like Giovanni, when she wishes to convey bitterness, fear, or anger. In "Improvisation," a nine-part poem with stanzas separated by treble and bass clefs and musical time notations, using choking as a metaphor, she is stifled by "this place"—a physical as well as emotional terrain. Not only are there "pollutants," drugs, desperate women, and decadence, but also:

some man/wants to kiss my thighs
roll his tongue around my navel
put his hands all up my ass
& this place is in my throat (14)

In an erotic poem, "Take the A Train," she transfers her sexual desire for men to a sensual connection with black people:

i could sleep with a man
but I'll lay with the souls of black folks
maybe i could grow me something
some azure flower that would smell
like life to me . . . (18)

In the imagistic play, *No,* a political, erotic-romantic, woman-identified poetic statement of *negritude,* Alexis DeVeaux offers this spare, direct, and celebratory recipe called "Cuntery":

I make a savannah of my
dreads

I will make an incense of my
pussy

I will make breadfruit of my
hands

I will make a fetish of your
love.
(also appearing in Blue Heat, a chapbook)

DeVeaux effectively mixes, like Lorde, a literal and figurative erotic language, and like Shange she expresses her work in a black folk language. Like Shange and Lorde, her work is replete with allusions to ancient African kingdoms, queens, goddesses. Where Lorde is filled with the sense of danger implicit in women being with women, DeVeaux is filled with the sense of infinite possibility. Except for her story "The Riddles of Egypt Brownstone," which also appeared in *Midnight Birds* (Washington 1980), *No* is rather other-worldly, seemingly set in some mythic zone.

Sometimes one wonders where these women are. They may be in
"The Land of Fa"; but wherever they are, the stuff of erotic dreams
is happening amidst "Musk oil and lapis lazuli . . . nipples . . .
tongue . . . and sassy blackness," "somewhere on the edge of
Brooklyn." Though quite often DeVeaux's work reveals a black
lesbian world, she does not choose to define her woman-centered
poetics as "lesbian." In fact, in the poem "Are there no more
prophets," she argues that:

> *the problem is still whatcolor/*
> *whichgender*
> *if is not sex*
> *or if you are what sex you*
> *   sleep with*
> *or when*
> *or how many ways*
> *   a week*
> *how many times an hour you can come.*

Another instance of an attempt to silence expressions of female
sexuality occurred during the production of *No* in New York City
at the Henry Street Settlement Mouse Theatre in 1981 in an
article that appeared in the *Amsterdam News,* a black publication
in New York City noted for its homophobic journalism. A black
male reviewer published an attack on DeVeaux for what he

defined as themes of "lesbianism" in the play, charging that homosexuality is not fit subject matter for black writers to be addressing. He admitted to leaving at the play's intermission.

Lastly, in a poem called "The Diver," using diving to convey the idea or act of sex, DeVeaux is at her inventive, loving, humorous best:

> *dives into me/tongue first*
> *into mouth suc culent*
> *breath like ethiopia supple*
> *Black girl*
> *swing among my poems and flaws*
> *swim diva: come, up for air*
> *swim against my tide(s)*
> *breast stroke the waves*
> *I'm watching on the sidelines, baby*
> *I'm rooting for you*

Summation

Sexually explicit language makes women uncomfortable, for it so often is the language of female sexual objectification, especially when used by men. As writers, particularly as feminists, we do not use language that depicts sex graphically for fear of being judged "politically incorrect" or irresponsible. When black women project our sexuality, we frequently use exalted language, or we're filled with ambivalence and circumspection, sometimes fatalism. This fatalism is consistent with the culture we live in that often likens sex to death or "sin"—for which the wages are death. But sex is dangerous for us—it has meant violation, vulnerability, loss of economic security, devaluation, loss of independence more than it has meant pleasure and gratification. While black women singers use material that is more direct and earthy about sexual need and desire, much of their material has been written by men—and white men at that—who are projecting a male view of women and a male view of black women. I believe the poets, when we do express sexual views, perhaps represent a more authentically female perspective of sex because we are the writers. Our visions have been repressed because of a coerced adherence to acceptable sexuality. Usually those models are heterosexual and monogamous. Recently, we've witnessed greater experimentation with themes of lesbian sexuality in our fiction and poetry, by lesbians and by women who aren't lesbians. And this is happening at a time of great pressure from the conservative and moral majority communities to censor sexually explicit and graphic language and images while at the same time they bombard us with television commercials, magazine ads, and billboards full of subliminal and not so subliminal and distorted images of male and female sexuality.

We have much to work against and for. We have to work against the custom of silence as well as our own fear of power as sexual beings.

The implications for feminist criticism are the responsibilities of both looking at the ways black women writers treat sexuality in their work, not glossing over its expression, and examining the language of sexuality, the absence of the language, and what the discourse means. Also more of us are beginning to break down the isolation of lesbians by looking at the work of lesbians, looking at what traditions lesbians have created within the literature, and beginning to adjust the heterosexist myopia through which we've viewed black women's sexuality (and literature).

I think black women writers—poets and fiction writers—could stand to lose some primness, some fatalism, and one-dimensional sexual perspective: one man (or woman), one body, one way, and fade out to flowers.

I say to throw away the Kotex, forget the tampon, and BLEED!

Note

This essay was first presented by Cheryl Clarke at the Black Women Writers in Diaspora Conference, East Lansing, Michigan, Oct. 27, 1985, as part of the panel "The Politics of Romance and Sexuality in Twentieth-Century Literature by Black Women." The title of the essay is from the novel *Sassafrass, Cypress and Indigo* by Mtozake Shange (New York: St. Martin's Press, 1982).

Works Cited

Brooks, Jerome. "In The Name of the Father: The Poetry of Audre Lorde," in Mari Evans, ed., *Black Women Writers 1950–80: A Critical Evaluation.* Anchor/Doubleday, Garden City, N.Y., 1984, pp. 269–276.

Cade, Toni, ed. *The Black Woman: An Anthology.* New American Library, New York, 1970, p. 103.

Christian, Barbara. *Black Feminist Criticism: Perspectives on Black Women Writers.* Pergamon Press, New York, p. 189.

Derricotte, Toi. *The Empress of the Death House.* Lotus Press, Detroit, 1978, pp. 13, 24–25.

Dunbar, Sybil. *Callaloo: A Black South Journal of Arts and Letters,* Vol. 2, Feb. 1979, p. 102.

Evans, Mari. *I Am A Black Woman.* William Morrow, New York, 1970, pp. 12, 17, 32.

Giovanni, Nikki. *Black Feeling Black Talk, Black Judgement.* William Morrow, New York, 1968, pp. 38, 78.

Grimké, Angelina W., in Countee Cullen, ed., *Caroling Dusk: An Anthology of Verse by Negro Poets.* Harper and Brothers, New York, 1927, p. 42.

Harper, Frances *Iola Leory.,* AMS Press, New York, 1971, p. 115.

Hull, Gloria T. "Black Women Poets from Wheatley to Walker," in Bell, Parker, Guy-Sheftall, eds., *Sturdy Black Bridges.* Anchor-Doubleday, New York, 1979, pp. 69–85.

——. " 'Under the Days': The Buried Life of Angelina Weld Grimké," in *Conditions: Five, The Black Women's Issue,* 1979, pp. 17–25.

Lorde, Audre, in Bulkin and Larkin, eds. *Lesbian Poetry.* Persephone Press (reissued by Gay Press Association, 1985), 1981, p. 23.

——. *The Black Unicorn.* W. W. Norton, New York, 1978, pp. 33, 70, 82.

——. *Uses of the Erotic: The Erotic As Power.* Out & Out Books, Trumansburq, N.Y., 1978.

Marshall, Paule, *Brown Girl, Brownstones.* The Feminist Press, Old Westbury, N.Y., 1981, p. 121.

Russell, Michele. "Slave Codes and Liner Notes," in Hull, Scott, and Smith eds., *All the Women Are White, All the Blacks Are Men, But Some of Us Are Brave: Black Women's Studies.* The Feminist Press, Old Westbury, N.Y., 1982.

Sanchez, Sonia, in Gwendolyn Brooks, ed. *A Broadside Treasury.* Broadside Press, Detroit, 1971, pp. 136, 137.

———. *Callaloo,* Vol. 2, Feb. 1979, pp. 19–20.

Shange, Ntozake. *Sassafrass, Cypress & Indigo.* St. Martin's Press, New York, 1982, p. 23.

———. *nappy edges.* St. Martin's Press, New York, 1978, pp. 26–28.

———. *A Daughter's Geography.* St. Martin's Press, N.Y., 1984, pp. 14, 18, 28.

Spillers, Hortense. "Interstices: A Small Drama of Words," in Carol Vance, ed. *Pleasure and Danger: Exploring Female Sexuality.* Routledge, Kegan-Paul, London, 1984, p. 74.

Tate, Claudia, ed. *Black Women Writers at Work.* Continuum, New York, 1983, pp. 109, 141–142.

Wade-Gayles, Gloria. *No Crystal Stair: Visions of Race and Sex in Black Women's Fiction.* Pilgrim Press, New York, 1985, p. 175.

Walker, Alice. *Callaloo,* Vol. 2, Feb. 1979, p. 63.

Wallace, Michele. *Black Macho and the Myth of the Superwoman.* The Dial Press, New York, 1979, p. 166.

Records

Washington, Dinah. Wise *Woman Blues: Rare and Early,* 1943–45 + 1. Rosetta Records, 115 West 16th Street, New York, 10011, 1984.

Rainey, Ma. *Ma Rainey.* Milestone Records. 10th & Parker, Berkeley, Calif. 94710, 1974.

Copeland, et al. *Mean Mothers: Independent Women's Blues, Vol. 1.* Rosetta Records, New York, 1980.

Part Three
Humid Pitch: 1991–1995

party pants

'Ain't nuthin but a house full of mamas and papas,
gal.
Tonight I'm a papa.
Sh-sh, don't ya tell nary soul.
Go to my closet.
Gimme them pants I caught you trying on
th'other day.
Yeah.
They fit you right good.
But, no, you ain't wearin em.
Not tonight.
I wears the pants when pants
got to be worn.
Gimme them suspenders . . .
Honey, now that pretty black bow tie
and the red shirt I stole from Foley . . .
Oh, baby, now my velvet jacket.'

A miracle stood before Star.
Hadn't seen the change herself she
wouldna believed it was Candy but some
exquisite form of man.
But didn't Jesus change water to wine?

Multiply the loaves and fishes?
Raise Lazrus from the dead?
Raise hisself?
Oh, Mary, don't ya weep
and Martha don't ya moan.

'Get yo hat—the one with the ostrich tail feather—
smooth yo dress and button yo coat.
I like that tight waist.
Take my arm, gal.
Tonight I wanna show you
what I took you out that field for.'

Bulletin

Disguising her vigilance with passive stance, she read the
bulletin stealthily, with some difficulty and great under-
standing.

*The General will esteem it as a singular favor if you can
apprehend a mulatto girl, servant and slave of Mrs. Wash-
ington, who eloped from this place yesterday. She may intend
to the enemy. Her name is Charlotte but in all probability
will change it. She is light-complected, about thirteen years of
age, pert, and dressed in brown cloth westcoat and petticoat.
Your falling upon some method of recovering her will accom-
modate Mrs. Washington and lay her under great obligation
to you. A gentle reward will be given to any soldier or other
who shall take her up.*

A spray of brown fluid splashed upon the publishing. She
tore it down from its post and ground it into the dirt.

'I bootblacked my face and hands
and any other parts that shows.
Ain't answerin to Charlotte, nigger,
nor no other name they give me.
I'm wearing a westcoat and pants,

left the petticoat in a cornfield.
I'm sixteen. Thirteen was a lie the owner told
the auctioneer.
I'm evil, mean, and will use my knife.
I dips snuff, chews tobacco, smokes a pipe.
Ain't no son of satan gon fall on me lessn
he want his tail curled.
Won't be intendin tward no white folk
—all of ems enemies.
I'm headed West.
I'll swim any river—maybe the Ohio—
follow any star.
And whoever try to take me up
may be ketchin his guts as he run.'

Stuck

where i am you may also be.

The Hermit

i laughed at that boy
a tropical bird trapped
in his fear of mounds of leaves
where he saw children hiding
and straight pins in his food
and driving by himself.
i laughed at him and roughly
pulled his pants and shorts down.
then, when he cried at how i
mocked him,
i pretended empathy,
so i could fuck him.
i did not want to know his demons
(or his angels).
i did not want to know my own.
i was full of appetites then
and quick poetry.
my menses flowed many days.
arrogance was my way.

i ate that boy.
i laughed so hard at that boy
placing his pleading personals
each week and waiting tables.
i was mean and capable of any
metaphor.
smoked a lot.
kept late hours.
(that boy's shower was so hot
i was scalded before i knew
the water wasn't cold.)
ego is numbing.

my blood last two days now.
and now i understand that boy's fear
if he drove in the country
in fall he might run over a child
hiding in a mound of leaves.
i tore through a heap myself
this year,
thought i heard the screams
of a bleeding child.
i laughed at myself
and saw the boy in my rearview
mirror crying.
for distraction

i bought a shirt
and removed seven of its eight
straight pins.
the eighth was mysteriously missing,
its hole gaping at me
fish eye.

i counted the odd number of pins.
it was missing.
i felt myself choking on it.
my lover calmed me, told me
i hadn't swallowed it.
looking askance, i laughed at
her desperate reassurances
and wore the shirt.
all day i felt it sticking me
but couldn't find it
though i undressed several times.
i was afraid to eat or drink.

that night i saw the boy
on my fire escape peeping in
my window, a toucan lighting
on his shoulder,
'the pin is in you,' he said,
'so is the bleeding child.'

Sisters Part

The men's clothing was a becoming fit
and Justina gave Gatsey the blue stone,
the dark of its matrix
would be diamond by now
in that far place they were forbidden to say.
Forbidden and nearly forgot
on the eve of Gatsey's getting-out time.
The rain would be an awesome shield.
Justina was stern and sharp-eyed.

'No time for that lost look.
Git out now.
Now while ole woman sick
and ole man fraid to leave her side.
Don't . . . he'll have his way with you
sho.
You think what he already done
bad.
Wait till he git a freer hand.
Don't think bout nuthin but leavin.'

The stone was the blue of an autumn noon
and the dark of its matrix would be

diamond by now.
Justina was hard and unchangeable.

   'Come famine, fire, flood, war.
   not goin nowhere.
   Ain't leavin my ghosts.
   You, ya ain't got that kind of comp'ny
   yet.
   You still sleep.
   Day ain't long enough for me . . .
   Go. Leave
   here.'

Justina smiled.

   'Don't come back for me.
   Neither send nobody.
   Only promise I want
   is you leavin.
   If ya caught,
   swallow what I give ya.'

Gatsey pulled on the hat
and gripped the stone.

Ella Takes Up the Slack

When others were trifling, Ella took up the slack
before they failed to do their parts.
She bore two children in the Great Depression,
locked out a wayward husband, held a gov't job
when others stood on soup lines and street corners,
took in her Mother—all with such tenacity.

Her Mother envied Ella's tenacity
and secretly blessed her own slack-
ing at not warning Ella of beckoning dark corners
and alleys where fast boys and girls took part
in acts older folk would pass up for a gov't job.
Ella was strong in spite of creeping depression.

Supporting two children was depression
enough and sure tested her tenacity.
But she took to them as she took to her gov't job
—a routine, something at which she would not slack.
She fed them, dressed them well, set them apart
from others' children, kept them off street corners.

Ella's daughter was the child of a dark corner,
the more protected, she outwitted depression.

Ella's son was the first mistake corrected, part
of and apart from Ella. Both had tenacity.
Neither cared about ambition nor the slack
nor aspired to a gov't job.

Ella resented both because their jobs
around the house were never done, cobwebs in corners,
dirty dishes, wrinkled linen. How dare they slack-
en. She evicted both in huffy depression
and took in boarders. Her tenacity
had always served her best of all her parts.

And what of daughter and son of neglected parts?
They read many books, took and left many jobs.
Daughter found protectors, sweet with tenacity.
Son saw the world to all its far corners
where quick promises stifled depression.
Neither sought recompense and neither slacked.

Ella still did her part: cleaned her corners,
fed her boarders, cursed her depression,
and boasted her tenacity would never slack-
en.

Kitchen Mechanics Sequence

i.

D.C. was where we went to find work.

Mama could cook anything from possum to pheasant.

She loved a good time and a loud laugh.

She laughed at everybody and herself.

We was partners

and worked everywhere together.

Never let me take no live-in job.

Times always rough for poor folk

and every Thursday off was a starchy gravy.

Thursday night we took to the streets

and our separate ways.

Did not look over our shoulders.

Away from white folks' houses

to the crowded, smoky, noisy joints

on U Street, the nigger strip.

Ran away with a gal one Thursday.

She got me a live-in job

out in Rosslyn

where she worked.

Me and her spent a whole month together

—late at night and real early.
Thursdays we took the streetcar
to her aunt's in Foggy Bottom
and onto evening
made our way to U Street.
It was on U Street Mama found me
and went up in my face and say:

   'You may have to be a stud,
     but you ain't gotta be no live-in slave.'

That was the last time I did live-in work
or left Mama.
Nineteen then.
Been working since I was eight.

ii.

Every Thursday 6 o'clock
Mercy took me and Pru to the York Theatre.
There the three of us saw everything Hollywood made
then.
I was three when I saw *Mogambo*.
All I remember is Ava Gardner in the jungle singin
'Comin Through the Rye.'
But Mercy . . .

her eyes froze to the screen
the minute the lights went out.
Thursday was her day
no matter what was showin.
Me and Pru sat through the double feature
trying to make our Jujy Fruits last.

Frances Michael

Sister Frances Michael was a black nun,
a black nun in a white order.
Not a missionary order or a cloistered
order but a teaching order.
When she wasn't teaching science
she coached basketball.
(Easier since shedding the habit.
Never regained her peripheral vision,
though. But compensation is a nun's way.)

When she wasn't in the gym
or wasn't in the lab,
Frances Michael roamed the halls
with a wide-legged gait and a chip
on her shoulder.
Only sister Alphonsus, the choir
directress, was bold enough to counsel
Frances Michael to tread more straightly
and narrowly, to act less arrogantly.
Mother Superior kept to her office
whenever she heard Frances Michael's
brown laughter.

Brainy, brawny, brash Sister Frances Michael.
The white flight girls with their make-up
and hair spray called her the *Ace of Spades.*
The model black girls who integrated the school
proffered the affectionate ridicule of *Mike.*
The rowdy, truant girls—a mixed, rag-tag bunch,
whose cigarettes and adult books she always took—
called Frances Michael *Dyke.*

Rabbit

Marquette was my uncle.
His mother my grandmother.
My mother his sister.
We even had the same father
who taught us to stone rabbits
and other treacherous games.
Two years younger than me,
Marquette learned faster and
was better.
I began to use a slingshot
and struck more.

Neighbors praised us for the rabbits.
The Mothers would take them from us,
singing to one another as they skinned
and fried them.
I'd sit watching
wishing my Mother's joyful noises
just once
were made to me.
She gave in to the Grandmother.
Favored Marquette.
Disciplined me.

A rock dispersed them running across
the narrow field like maggots
through rotten meat,
except one,
who hopped slower toward the thicket.
My cheek burned from the blow
and the blood was thrilling.
Marquette ran to me, cupped my face,
pressed his lips to the gash,
sucked at the wound,
and cried his guilt.

Marquette ate rabbit like it was chicken.
I kicked him under the table.
Wide and teary-eyed, he looked at me
over the little carcass.
My Grandmother warned me to have respect
and my Mother pinched me.
I hated Marquette and the taste of rabbit.

In the years to follow
I watched Marquette's petulance become
a craggy coastline the ocean
of the Mothers' seamless affection
tore against.

The Grandmother spent her days in bed.
My Mother turned to prayer.
I spent my days practicing my aim
my afternoons in the company of lovers.

Marquette and I went our ways
but celebrated our survival
once a year
matching skills in the woods,
at the shooting range,
on the dance floor.

One year, I pitied Iris of the sleepless eyes
over Marquette's campfire.
Star-gazing, crystal-gazing Iris,
doleful woman,
running to gather kindling
to Marquette's specifications
and him badgering her to light
the yellow lantern, his favorite toy
to swagger about with.

I fished with bow and arrow
in the shallow lake, bringing back
to the fire sufficient catch.

Iris scaled them and fried them.
Marquette praised me for my luck and
ate more than either of us,
picking the bones out of his mouth
as he chewed.
I choked on the bones.
Iris fed me bread and stroked my scar.
The yellow lantern flickering,
Marquette ordered her to add kerosene.

Stunned me like a rock, Iris.
Licked some innocent, sore place inside me.
I could go on a long hunt for you, baby.
Track you, baby. Show you my open wounds
and wait for the healing wet of your tongue.
Iris.
A long hunt, Iris.

After nights of violent passion between them,
afternoons would find Iris in my sunny
bungalow.
She always held her own.
I wanted Iris, wanted her at night,
yes. Iris in all her sleepless and
anxious desire.

You, baby, at night, yes.

I dreamed in colors and saw Marquette's
wide, teary eyes, afraid he'd scarred me
that day in the woods.
Taking my bloody cheek between his lips,
sucking and licking the gash,
tears mingling with blood,
the stunned rabbit hopping away.

One afternoon I kissed Iris's swollen eyes
and gave her my vision:

   'I see a beautiful place, baby,
   just waiting for you to plant yourself
   in.
   Spring's coming. Wild geese returning.
   Spring's coming. Wild geese returning.
   Get reborn, baby. Migrate.
   Reborn, baby. Migrate.'

Afraid of the sky, the open field, the pine-
laden land. Iris always kept close to the fire.

'He won't be able to live by
himself. He
needs
me.
He won't let me go.'

Patiently, I baited her:

'Slave.'

Lifting her skirt, she baited back:

'Your slave.'

Marquette:
his maroon Pontiac
circling my street,
tires spitting gravel,
the rabbit stunned but still hopping,
wide, teary eyes
through the tinted windshield.

Iris:
bruised and sore
a Friday afternoon
our favorite time,

packed her clothes.
her crystals,
and rolled her pallet.

   'He will have to get on without me.
   He'll have to get on,
   Marquette will.'

I dictated the leaving letter and stumbled
over the yellow lantern,
shattering its glass.
She stooped to gather it like a fallen child.
Her eyes welled with sadness:

   'Get reborn, baby.
   Migrate,'

I warned and sucked
her cut finger.

Iris of the sleepless eyes.
Star-gazing, crystal-gazing Iris,
waiting for the new moon to soak
her crystals
in honor of her new altar,
washing my blood from her pallet.

Maroon Pontiac still circled my street,
tires spitting gravel,
eyes wide and teary,
the rabbit stunned but still hopping.

'The room across the hall is empty,'

Iris tells me flatly.

A month passes. My paperwork is backlogged.
My coworkers complain. I am above censure
and oblivious to it. The vacant room is taken.

Flecks of glass glimmering in the gravel.
And no sign of the maroon Pontiac.
I fly to Iris's altar.
Her window is dark.
Her door is silent.
Across the hail, a brazen fire burns
in the yellow lantern,
its glass still missing.
The jagged edge of the rock
splits my cheek,
the dazed rabbit hopping
toward the thicket.

High School

Sister Elise Marie.
Ah, Daughter of Charity (of St. Vincent de Paul).
Vigilant and voluptuous in her habit.

The girls wore lipstick
the wrong color sweater
the wrong length of sock
hems too short
hair too long
too much jewelry
just to be told by Sister
to take it off
tie it back
roll em down
wash it off
to be kept after school
to clap her erasers
to discover her in the
cloakroom adorning her cinched
waist with some errant scarlet scarf
slipped from its hanger
to the floor.

Rigorous in the classroom as St. Ignatius
in a den of apostates
was Sister Elise Marie
and charismatic:

   'Girls, the serpent pride,
   the apple arrogance,
   the banishment punishment,
   the knowing of sin.'

Loved poetry. Hated Aquinas.
Quoted *Fleurs du Mal* regularly and languidly
for the wearing of perfume:

   'And from her clothes, of
   muslin or velvet.
   All redolent of her youth's purity
   There emanated the odor of furs. . . .
   Ah, girls, *What the devil does,*
   he does well.'

Then chastening herself after the vagaries
of poetry with lessons in Rome's manifest
destiny:

'Naked in the main
the natives of La Côte d'Ivoire.
Private parts exposed . . .
First the Church gave them clothes . . .'

On All Saints' Day
recounting the 400-year history
of her order,
evangelical was Sister Elise Marie:

   'Girls, though we were Vincent's idea,
   Louise, scrupulous widow, had a vision of us,
   trained and bound us
   to good works
   for the poor
   to charity
   humility
   later chastity . . .

Fondling her bodice, smoothing her skirt,
Sister Elise Marie
transfigured:

   'Girls, the many-layered gabardine
   and its undercloth

of

muslin

screening out lustful stares.

This mountainous cornette, white

guides my gaze heavenward

longing for sight of the beatific vision.

never to pander vain stares . . .

Girls, uncross your knees and close your legs.'

No Place

This ain't no place to love a woman.
Not a mother.
Surely not a daughter.
Not even some stray mule of a girlchild
whose mama died cursing her pale sire.

The men sang softly and clapped
as we danced.
I withdrew from the circle of women
to also marvel at her supple movement
her wide feet marking rhythm.
I fancied:

She dances for me
and she will lay with me
in this place.

The men clapped for me to dance again.
The women called me back to the circle.

The Homoerotic Other

EUROPEANS HAVE MANUFACTURED a predatory image of African sexuality to justify our enslavement. But the real erotic life and imagination of black folks are still behind the veil—covert, suppressed, and subverted. African Americans do not talk often enough or openly enough about pleasure except in the direct lyrics of the blues.

To bolster their respectability and try to get out from under, the black bourgeoisie tries to uphold marriage, monogamy, and the nuclear family. Much as I detest racists like Daniel Patrick Moynihan, who continues to appear on talk shows espousing the pathology of the black family, it scares me that so many of the black bourgeoisie believe that compulsory heterosexuality and white definitions of what constitutes a family will solve our most pressing problems as a race.

We have but to consider Spike Lee's films. Everybody, or at least the main characters, must always prove his or her ability to be heterosexual. No matter what happens—a brother murdered by a white cop, one's place of employment destroyed, one's neighborhood looted and burned, women raped—everything's cool, 'cuz we still be heterosexual.

Black lesbians and gay men are not exempt from the racist corruption of African sexuality. We are silenced and sometimes too grateful for images like those of the "snap queens" on the television show *In Living Color.*

These "spoofs" on gay black life may be comforting to some, but we need more than the freedom to be disparaged. Black lesbians are, of course, still invisible, still behind the veil.

Working against the mainstream culture, black women (lesbian and nonlesbian) and black gay men have created a homoerotic traditio —openly, as in the novels of James Baldwin and the poems and prose of Audre Lorde, or between the lines, as in Nella Larsen's *Passing* or James Weldon Johnson's *Autobiography of an Ex-Colored Man.*

As we begin to discover that many of the well-known writers of the Harlem Renaissance may have been gay or lesbian, it's interesting to read Countee Cullen's famous poem "Yet Do I Marvel" as the poet's sadness at not being able to sing the song of a black man loving other black men.

The African-American literati today refuses to acknowledge the positive existence of gay men and lesbians in their own work. The straight black man still finds himself on the horns of a sexual dilemma. His sexuality is defined by his devaluation of black women's sexuality, as illustrated in the opening lines of Charles Johnson's *Middle Passage,* winner of the National Book Award for fiction in 1990: "Of all the things that drive men to sea, the most common disaster, I've learned, is women. . . ."

White people (gay, lesbian, straight) have simply the task of rejecting their legacy of debasing African sexuality—in life, literature, and the flesh.

But whoever we are—European or African—Black History Month compels us all to celebrate the black homoerotic.

The Everyday Life of Black Lesbian Sexuality

to work to the end of day
to talk to the end of talk
to run to the end of dark
to have at the end of it all: sex

the wish for forever
for more often
for more.

the promises
the absurdity
the histrionics
the loss of pride
the bargaining
the sadness after.

in wakefulness wanting

in wakefulness waiting.

from "living as a lesbian at 35"

in *Living as a Lesbian*[1]

HOW DOES THE writer make use of the energy of the erotic? How much a part of everyday life is it for the poet, even as she denies it, even as she resolves to be monogamous or celibate because of its danger? The erotic has always been risky for Black women, and poets no less. Promising to reject the lurid uses it is put to by capitalism or masturbating while writing becomes boring. What is its source in my life? Where do I go for it?

I first learned my sexuality is an endangered sexuality as a child growing up in a lower-middle-class Black family with a secret. I learned there was a secret when no one would tell me why my older sister and brother had a different surname than my younger sister and I. My mother's sexuality was the secret—she was married previously and pregnant before she married. Later I learned that this secret was subterfuge for another more compelling secret—she killed a jealous admirer in self-defense before she married my father and before she divorced her first husband. So, the messages I received about my sexual self were: above all else, suppress it, control it, confine it. Besides, "Love," as the character Nanny says in Zora Neale Hurston's *Their Eyes Were Watching God,* "is the very prong the colored woman gets hung on." The secrets and the pretending not to know them made me risk the ironies of poetry.

I learned early that "love" (read *sex*) was something I had best not mess with. Love was best left to Hollywood and television. My mother consumed movies, television, and books. She let me have plenty of all three, hoping to distract me from the inevitable urge, which, of course, she presumed would be heterosexual. My earliest concept of how I wanted my sexual self to be was free from obligation to a partner, namely a husband. My father secretly advised me not to get married, "You see how much trouble *it* can cause. Make your own living before you get into *it*." The *it* was not marriage but sex. According to my mother, neither was supposed to happen before I was ready to commit myself to monogamy and permanency, even though this equation has produced nothing but contradictions in her life.

The suppressed erotic intrigued me as well as all the secrets hiding it. In spite of how she denied its importance and denied it in herself and tried to turn me against it, my mother's erotic was all over the place: in how she made herself up, in the way she dressed—the high heels, the fitted suits, and tight, low-cut evening clothes. And then there were the reactions of men on the street. My mother's best friends were women and they were the recipients of her erotic energy, her infinite versatility. Women filled our house one Sunday a month. I grew used to women, their ways, their stories, their excitement over one another's infrequent victories, their denials, and their ambivalences. They were pretty in my mother's dining room. If not pretty, they were talkative and always full of wit. Each had her forte. They wore wide skirts and colorful blouses, always high heels. They relied on one another. I longed for those Sundays once a month. I wanted their devotion and had my favorites.

Though she taught me how to suppress my erotic, my mother taught me that the enjoyment of female friendships is the enjoyment of female sensuality. And from a very early age, I decided I wanted to be in the company of women. Then began my dreams of being the lover of women, and those dreams would become poetry.

My mother and her women friends taught me an unsparing and sexual humor, a hallmark of the oral tradition of African-American women. African-American women's humor holds everyone and everything up to scrutiny and contempt, and self is never exempt. They allowed themselves the tutelage of the blues and the advice songs of Dinah Washington, popularly tagged, during the fifties, queen of the blues:

I've got a secret way of loving
and I own the copyright.
I'm gonna put it on the market
and do all my business right.
Yes, I'll thrill you, baby,
I can really satisfy your soul.
I can really thrill you, baby,
because I can satisfy your soul.

I've got a secret way of loving
that never has been told.

from "Mellow Mama Blues"[2]

My mother and her friends talked mainly politics, money, and day-to-day race relations. Sexuality was addressed in asides. Because I began to grow breasts early, someone would occasionally forget and speak directly about somebody's man's infidelity. I overheard one of them commiserating with my mother once over the fact that I would soon be pressured into having sex (with men), because I was "big for my age." And she was correct. Compulsory heterosexuality.

My mother did not push heterosexuality on me any more than she denied homosexuality. Her message, delivered anecdotally, was, it's safer just not to be sexual. Once you realize how pleasurable lust can be, you won't be able to control yourself. Or the other. Then, after the lust, there's pregnancy; then, the baby; and possibly a coerced marriage or giving the baby up for adoption or a guilt-ridden single-parenthood. If not that script, then a worse script: an illegal abortion, continued promiscuity, venereal disease, cigarettes, alcohol and other drugs, or coming to any number of other bad ends. Much better to be in school or working, and a virgin in either case.

I will not sell it,
I will not give it away.
I will sit on it the rest of my days.[3]

My older sister inherited my mother's erotic and she, too, was unmarried when she became pregnant. This pregnancy and my sister's ostracism from our family were major events in my life, emblems of the danger of the erotic. I believed my mother's admonitions. These events inform the fiction of several poems: "fathers" and "Ruby the runaway" in *Narratives: poems in the tradition of black women,* "funeral thoughts" in *Living as a Lesbian,* and "Ella Takes Up The Slack" in *Humid Pitch.* My father had no decision-making power in our family, but he was a buffer between us and my mother's overwhelming authority.

In my article "The Failure to Transform: Homophobia in the Black Community," in *Home Girls: A Black Feminist Anthology,* I tell of the first time I saw Black lesbians:

I was walking down the street with my best friend, Kathy. I saw two young women walking together in the opposite direction. One wore a doo-rag, a Banlon button down, and high-top sneakers. The other wore pink brush rollers, spit curls plastered with geech, an Oxford tailored shirt, a mohair sweater, fitted skirt with kick pleat . . . I asked Kathy, "Who are they?" "Bulldaggers," she answered. "What's that," I asked again. "You know, they *go* with each other," Kathy tried to explain. "Why?" I asked still confused. "Protection," Kathy said casually. "Protection?" I repeated. "Yeah, at least they won't get pregnant," Kathy ended the querying.

I was given a Roman Catholic education, which placed on my shoulders the burden of keeping the secret of my mother's erotic. Premarital sex (fornication) and divorce are major sins and lust is a cardinal sin. My adolescent relationships abounded with girlfriends who became pregnant and whose lives changed radically; and others who were having sex, using birth control pills, and living with quantities of guilt. I was reading James Baldwin's *Another Country,* which introduced me to the homoerotic. And women were my best friends. I began to wonder why I was expected to give up, avoid, trivialize the acceptance I felt from women in order to pursue the tenuous business of getting a man. Could I resist the draft?

I did suppress the erotic and the lesbian in me until I was twenty-six and four years away from Washington, D.C., the mecca of predatory heterosexuality and the place of my birth. Heterosexuality never inspired a single poem in me, not even when I was practicing it.

That other black lesbians existed and were willing to be out made me embrace lesbianism as a politic. For many years, I said that lesbianism is a political identity not *just* a sexual identity. I was part of a generation of lesbians who struggled against the past stigma of sexual perversion/inversion and, in so doing, discarded some of the pleasure along with the dominance-subordinance of compulsory heterosexual relationships. With the publication of my second volume of poetry, *Living as a Lesbian,* I quarreled with this dismissal of sex. As long as my freedom to be sexual with women is endangered and under attack, as long as lesbian sexuality is the most invisible sexuality, politically, my poetry must be a medium for the sexual politics of lesbianism:

> bump the supreme court and edwin meese
> i'll read anything, do anything to be sexually aroused
> i'll be a lesbian, queer, whore, a sleaze
> and it won't be a peep show i ain't caroused.
>
>   from "committed sex," *Conditions* 16

My everyday life as a Black lesbian writer is marked by the struggle to be a (sexual) black lesbian, the struggle for the language of sexuality, and the struggle not to be the "beached whale of the sexual universe."[4] So, I created several black lesbian archetypes in my poetry that I might have a mythology, among them the women of "Of Althea and Flaxie" and "The moon in cancer" in *Narratives,* "Vicki and Daphne" in *Living as a Lesbian,* and "The Day Sam Cooke Died" and "Bulletin" in my most recent work, *Humid Pitch.*

Bulletin

Disguising her vigilance with passive stance, she read the bulletin stealthily, with some difficulty and great understanding.

The General will esteem it as a singular favor if you can apprehend a mulatto girl, servant and slave of Mrs. Washington, who eloped from this place yesterday. She may intend to the enemy.

Her name is Charlotte but in all probability will change it. She is light-complected, about thirteen years of age, pert, and dressed in brown cloth westcoat and petticoat. Your falling upon some method of recovering her will accommodate Mrs. Washington and lay her under great obligation to you. A gentle reward will be given to any soldier or other who shall take

A spray of brown fluid splashed upon the publishing. She tore it down from its post and ground it into the dirt.

"I bootblacked my face and hands
and any other parts that shows.
Ain't answerin to Charlotte, nigger,
nor no other name they give me.
I'm wearing a westcoat and pants,
left the petticoat in a cornfield.
I'm sixteen. Thirteen was a lie the owner told
the auctioneer.
I'm evil, mean, and will use my knife.
I dips snuff, chews tobacco, smokes a pipe.
Ain't no son of satan gon fall on me lessn
he want his tail curled.
Won't be intendin toward no white folk
—all of ems enemies.
I'm headed West.
I'll swim any river—maybe the Ohio—

follow any star.

And whoever try to take me up

may be ketchin his guts as he run."

Black women's sexuality is still an endangered sexuality. The experience of slavery and the sadistic practices of that institution as it was applied to Africans in North America still mark us in the expression of our sexuality and the erotic. Our sexuality is further endangered by AIDS, compulsory heterosexuality, racism, class oppression, and the ever-present threat of rape. While I am privileged to write openly as a lesbian and to have my work appreciated and to sleep with a woman, I am reminded daily that this ain't no place to love a woman.

Notes

1. I titled this paper after a panel I spoke on in 1984 at the National Women's Studies Association Conference which was entitled "The Everyday Life of Lesbian Sexuality." The title gives sexuality a dailiness and seeks to extend Audre Lorde's essential speech and article "The Uses of the Erotic," which encouraged women, especially lesbians, to allow their sexuality, their erotic selves to exist in life.

2. "Mellow Mama Blues." *Wise Woman Blues: Dinah Washington, 1943–1945*. Rosetta Records, 155 W. 6th Street, New York, N.Y. 10011, 1984.

3. Ibid.

4. Hortense Spillers, "Interstices: A Small Drama of Words," in *Pleasure and Danger: Exploring Female Sexuality*, edited by Carol Vance (Boston: Routledge and Kegan Paul, 1984).

Selected Publications
Books

Narratives: Poems in the Tradition of Black Women. Latham, N.Y.: Kitchen Table: Women of Color Press, 1983.

Living as a Lesbian. Ithaca, N.Y.: Firebrand Books, 1986.

Humid Pitch. Ithaca, N.Y.: Firebrand Books, 1989.

Co-Edited Journals

Co-editor of *Conditions,* a feminist magazine of writing by women, with an emphasis on writing by lesbians.

Anthologies

"Lesbianism: An Act of Resistance." In *This Bridge Called My Back: Writings by Radical Women of Color,* edited by Cherrie Moraga and Gloria Anzaldúa. Watertown, Mass.: Persephone Press, 1981; Latham, N.Y.: Kitchen Table: Women of Color Press, 1984.

"The Failure to Transform: Homophobia in the Black Community" and "Women of Summer" (short story). In *Home Girls: A Black Feminist Anthology,* edited by Barbara Smith. Latham, N.Y.: Kitchen Table: Women of Color Press, 1983.

"palm leaf of Mary Magdalene" (poem). In *The Leading Edge: Anthology of Lesbian Sexual Fiction,* edited by Lady Winston, 141. Denver: Lace Publications, 1987.

"Living as a Lesbian Underground" and other poems. In *Serious Pleasure: Lesbian Erotic Stories and Poetry,* edited by the Sheba Collective. London: Sheba Feminist Publishers, 1989; Pittsburgh: Cleis Press, 1991.

"Of Althea and Flaxie" and other poems. In *Bluestones and Salt Hay: An Anthology of Contemporary New Jersey Poets,* edited by Joel Lewis. New Brunswick, N.J.: Rutgers Univ. Press, 1990.

Journal Publications

"Black Women on Black Women Writers: Conversations and Questions" (a five-woman discussion with Jewelle Gomez, Evelynn Hammonds, Bonnie Johnson, Linda Powell). *Conditions* 9 (1983).

"Leavings" (short story). *13th Moon* "Narrative" issue (1984): 133–141.

"Indira" (poem). *American Voice.* (Summer 1986): 20–22.

"The Homoerotic Other/Gay Voices, Black Voices." *The Advocate* (February 1991): 42.

"Making Face, Making Soul/Haciendo Caras, edited by Gloria Anzaldúa" (book review essay). *Bridges: A Journal for Jewish Feminists and Our Friends* 2, no. 1 (Spring 1991/5791): 128–133.

Articles and Reviews

Calvin Hernton. "The Tradition." *Parnassus* (1986): 518–550.

Barbara A. Caruso. "Book Review of *Living as a Lesbian.*" *Obsidian II: Black Literature in Review 2,* no. 1 (Spring 1987): 94–100.

Margaret Randall. "Lesbian Poet Has Many Voices." Review of *Living as a Lesbian. Guardian Book Review Supplement* (Summer 1987).

Gary Indiana. "1988: Some Thoughts from 15 Artists." *Village Voice* 33, no. 3 (1988): 95.

Stephanie Byrd. "The Outer Limits of Commitment." Review of *Humid Pitch. Lambda Rising Book Report* (October/November 1989).

Two Rich and Rounding
Experiences

To create! To create! To bend with tight intentness
over neat detail, come to
a terrified standstill of the heart, then shiver,
at that rebuking thing, that obstinate and
recalcitrant little beast, the phrase![1]

IN THE SUMMER of 1968, in a course entitled "Negro Literature in the United States," taught by Arthur P. Davis at Howard University, I first read Gwendolyn Brooks. I did not understand or appreciate Brooks's prosodic virtuosity. At that time, her narrative voice and authority and her allegiance to the race captivated me. For me, the poems "hunchback girl: she thinks of heaven," "a song in the front yard," "the ballad of chocolate Mabbie," "Sadie and Maud," "Mrs. Small," "The Ballad of Rudolph Reed" were memorable experiences. I loved their language—which I thought a bit quaint in that time of sixties' bombastic verse; and I could recognize the subjects. Brooks was urban—at that time I regarded the urban sensibility as superior to any other regional sensibility—black or white.

A Street in Bronzeville (1945), *Annie Allen* (1949), for which in 1950 she became the first black to win a Pulitzer Prize, *Maud Martha* (1953), *The Bean Eaters* (1960), and *In the Mecca* (1968) became my narrative models. I continued to buy her books when I could find them. After the publication of the now out of print *The World of Gwendolyn Brooks* (1971), Brooks ended a twenty-seven year relationship with Harper and Row, thereby ending mainstream access to and control of her work. Brooks thereafter became a full participant in building black institutions and published her next four books of poetry, *Riot* (1969), *Family Pictures* (1970), *Aloneness* (1971), a children's book, *Beckonings* (1975), and her autobiography, *Report from Part One* (1972), with Broadside Press. Broadside was for ten years the most important black small press publisher. Since that time, she has self-published two manuals for young poets (1980, 1983), *Primer for Blacks* (1980), and *Near-Johannesburg Boy and Other Poems* (1986). *To Disembark* (1981), a collection of her poems from the sixties to 1980, was published by Third World Press of Chicago, a thriving black press established by Haki Madhubuti (don l. lee). She has also published numerous "broadsides," and occasional poems.

Brooks has contributed greatly to the Afro-American and American literary canon for over forty years. "Yet," as critic and scholar D. H. Melhem states in the "Introduction" to *Gwendolyn Brooks: Poetry and the Heroic Voice* (hereafter abbreviated to PHV), "despite honors and esteem, it is mainly black scholars and critics who have accorded her poetry its due" (1). After establishing the criteria for a major poet and pronouncing the limitations of "historical considerations" as an evaluative means, Melhem sets out on the open sea of Brooks's *oeuvre* to "measure the vital distance into the heart of composition," to analyze "poetic structures." And she does so with painstaking line-by-line elucidation of virtually every poem Brooks has published, with the exception of her most recent volume. Brooks's development of the "heroic voice," that is, of the prophetic and the bardic, the mythic and the real, the historic and the quotidian, rivets Melhem's study. For Melhem, Brooks is "the Homeric bard, the Anglo-Saxon scop, the African griot, the balladeer" (238), "grand" and "plain."

In terms of format, Melhem reviews Brooks's work chronologically from 1945 to 1980. She begins with a description of the particular volume; close readings of individual poems follow; sometimes poems are categorized according to theme or form; and finally the work is summarized in terms of its organic elements, its meaning, and its place in the poet's development of the heroic voice. Not dismissing historical considerations entirely, Melhem interpolates references to Brooks's correspondence with her Harper editor, as well as discussions of the impact of World War II on her early works and the impact of the Civil Rights and Black Power movements on the later works, including the Broadside publications.

While Melhem analyzes later works respectfully, her discussions of the work from 1945 to 1968 are more exhaustive. Her reading of the much over-looked metaphysical sequence "A Catch of Shy Fish," from the "New Poems" section of *Selected Poems* (1963), is engaging and delightful. Her discussion of "In Montgomery," a poem commissioned by *Ebony* magazine in 1971, which Melhem says is Brooks's "most serious and sustained effort" (214) since "In the Mecca," is a thoughtful contribution to Brooks criticism. Melhem is concerned with presenting the close relationship of Brooks's form to her content, and also with Brooks's expressions of race consciousness and universal love, "caritas." And we are made to see, through Melhem's attentive and focused lens, that no *thing* escapes Brooks's poetic empathy.

In *A Life Distilled: Gwendolyn Brooks, Her Poetry and Fiction* (hereafter abbreviated to ALD), Maria K. Mootry and Gary Smith have collected eighteen articles by scholars, black and white, on Brooks's work. Well-known essays by such critics as Houston Baker, George Kent, and Hortense Spillers are reprinted here along with ten original pieces. This collection, says Mootry, presents analyses of the range of Brooks's work, of better known but least understood works, and of neglected works. The contributors, including the two editors, offer a cornucopia of evidence of the poet's multidimensionality, her "tripartite base of regionalism, race, and gender" (4), and her modern/metaphysical, black/white consciousness.

Take, for example, Brooks's second volume, *Annie Allen;* it is perhaps the poet's most self-conscious attempt to deconstruct language and revise forms to tell the bleak, parodic, antiromantic and antiheroic story of a black woman. Claudia Tate states in her essay that *Annie Allen,* lauded by critics because of its "complicated techniques," has, for seemingly the same reason, been allotted less critical attention than other works. Tate sets out to prove that it is the "structural formats for the poems, in and of themselves" (ALD141), which communicate Annie's story, particularly the format of the mock epic "The Anniad." For Tate, Annie is the embodiment of suppressed anger. According to Tate, in "The Anniad" Brooks also incites the reader's anger at the satirized conventions which restrict Annie's imagination and her life.

Hortense Spillers's article "Gwendolyn the Terrible: Propositions on Eleven Poems" is full of wit and power, astonishingly penetrating and quick-paced. In addition to ten other poems, Spillers analyzes "The Anniad" as "one of the liveliest demonstrations of the uses to which irony can be put" (ALD 226). Spillers notes that no modern poet before Brooks addresses the psychic and spiritual distress caused to black women by the light skin/dark skin conflict, which is a "crucial aspect" of "The Anniad" and much of Brooks's poetry.

Brooks's vignetting technique is finely displayed in her fourth work, *Maud Martha,* which the poet has called an "autobiographical novel." Melhem seems to forsake her careful literary analysis for plot summary in the section devoted to *Maud Martha* and declares it a "little appreciated masterpiece of classic simplicity and poetic precision" (94). Barbara Christian talks more about the poetic precision of the work in a lively article, "Nuance and Novella: A Study of Gwendolyn Brooks's *Maud Martha*," reprinted in the Mootry and Smith collection.

Christian, who never dismisses historical and political considerations, reads *Maud Martha* technically as a novella, for it does not project the "grand or heroic and broad social sweep of the novel" (243). Further, Christian claims *Maud Martha* has not been given serious critical consideration because its protagonist is an ordinary black woman captivated by her intense inner life without the "dramatic rises and falls" of the " 'character in a conflict' motif" (247), such as that which characterizes the novels of Brooks's contemporaries, Baldwin and Ellison. Like Melhem, most of the contributors to *A Life Distilled* speak at length about Brooks's literary influences; Christian is the only critic who alludes to Brooks's literary godchildren. For Christian, *Maud Martha* prefigures the 1960s and 1970s novels by black women writers like Toni Morrison, Paule Marshall, and Alice Walker.

In an energetic article, " 'Tell It Slant': Disguise and Discovery as Revisionist Poetic Discourse in *The Bean Eaters*," Maria K. Mootry presents stunning close readings of four poems from Brooks's third volume of poetry: "Jessie Mitchell's Mother," "A Bronzeville Mother Loiters in Mississippi. Meanwhile, A Mississippi Mother Burns Bacon," "Mrs. Small," and "A Lovely Love." Her analysis is feminist and deconstructionist. Mootry interprets these poems as subverting and revising common stereotypes of the quotidian female world as well as enriching and expanding "the dominant American poetic discourse" (180).

The Mecca of *In the Mecca* was an "actual structure built in 1891" in Chicago for rich white families, which degenerated into a slum dwelling for dispossessed blacks, according to Kenny J. Williams in her literary/historical article "The World of Satin Legs Smith, Mrs. Sallie, and the Blackstone Rangers: The Restricted Chicago of Gwendolyn Brooks." And it is against this backdrop that the protagonist, Mrs. Sallie, searches for the youngest of her eight children, Pepita. "In the Mecca," Brooks's epic narrative from her fourth volume of poetry, *In the Mecca,* is a visual, "horizontal," and "vertical" experience Mrs. Sallie asks Pepita's whereabouts of a plethora of indifferent neighbors. None have seen her, most don't know who she is, and all are too preoccupied with the vagaries of life to care. "In the Mecca" culminates in Mrs. Sallie's discovery of the murdered Pepita in the apartment of one of the Mecca's tenants.

In the Mecca, as a whole, shows the subtle causal relationship between the tragic lives of the Mecca's tenants and national tragedies such as the assassination of Malcolm X and the murder of Medgar Evers, the deeds of Chicago's Blackstone Rangers, and the street bombast of the disciples of black revolution. And for Melhem, *In the Mecca* signifies Brooks's achievement of her grand heroic style and a political/spiritual turning point.

In the Mecca is a prelude to the poet's so-called spiritual revision of her black consciousness—which was to become more evident in her Broadside publications, *Riot* and *Family Pictures.* Kenny J. Williams offers the following insight into Brooks's "conversion":

> Much, of course, has been made of the alleged 'conversion' of Gwendolyn Brooks to black nationalism. . . . From the beginning of her work, Brooks was well aware that racism was a powerful consideration in the American experience and protest has served as a cornerstone of her poetic world.

I agree. Yet, after *In the Mecca,* poems about heroic black men, of the "grand" and "plain" varieties, become more emphasized and her female personae seem to recede. In fact, though Brooks's work is rich in realistic black female portraiture, mostly of the "plain" heroic type, she has published no poems which celebrate or even eulogize "grand" heroic black women. One wonders why the poet, with such a gifted black woman's sensibility, has not penned a sonnet or a ballad to Phillis Wheatley, Harriet Tubman, Ida B. Wells Barnett, Fannie Lou Hamer, Ella Baker, Angela Davis, or Joann Little.

The only shortcoming of the Mootry and Smith collection is that none of the articles deals with the poetry of Brooks's Broadside era. However, both books are rich and rounding experiences, like the spiralling genius of their subject. As I read both, I was exuberant. We need these and so does Brooks. I hope, as a result of these critical works, Brooks's poetry will become more available to us. Melhem says Brooks is writing a sequel to *Maud Martha.* Melhem also lists in the "Bibliography of Works by Gwendolyn Brooks" a collection in progress which will comprise all of her poetry since 1945. *Poetry and the Heroic Voice* and *A Life Distilled* are invaluable to students of Gwendolyn Brooks and to most students of poetry. Their most important achievement is the creation of a desire to immerse oneself in the poetry of Gwendolyn Brooks.

Note

1. Gwendolyn Brooks, "In the Mecca," in *In the Mecca* (New York: Harper and Row, 1968), 6–7.

Living the Texts *Out*

Lesbians and the Uses of Black Women's Traditions

I am a mannish dyke, muffidiver, bulldagger, butch, feminist, femme,
and PROUD.

Political poster, New Brunswick, NJ, November 1991

TO RETHINK BECOMING a Black lesbian writer and reader of
Black women writers provokes feelings of pleasure and trepida-
tion. To reflect on any one of the three subversive identities—
lesbian, Black, poet—that fill my work and days is to reflect on the
expectation I place on the writing and the writer to be useful.
Black and lesbian have always been bolder identities for me,
threatening always to subsume the poet. I dreamed of writing years
before I was sleeping/being with women, years before I craved
literacy of my blackness. Blackness—my own and others'—
contextualizes the dangerous parts of myself, gives them voice
and visibility. I do not give up *Black* for "African-American." I
remain connected to what the term signifies for me as a participant
in the late 1960s Black consciousness movement in the USA.
Blackness—that reclaiming of culture, that will to revolution;

embracing the remarkable and violated past, the very tenuous present, and the unpromised future as an African in diaspora, an ex-slave, lesbian, poet.

The first serious work of fiction I read by a black writer was Baldwin's *Another Country* in 1963, and it was the first novel I read that treated homosexuality, albeit male. *Another Country* made me imagine freedom from traditional monogamous heterosexuality and set me to thinking about the possibility of a "variant" life. There is nothing, however, in the novel to recommend lesbianism, only an inelegant put-down of Jane, an unkempt older white woman and lover of Vivaldo, who Rufus, the tragic Black character, says "dresses like a bulldagger" (Baldwin, 1962: 31). *Another Country* unsettled me forever and made me see the complexity of living as a sexual person.

The dialectic of Blackness and homosexuality was too subversive in the heterosexist Black consciousness movement of the late 1960s. Eldridge Cleaver, among others, attacked Baldwin for his homosexuality in *Soul on Ice,* which became the sacred (male) text during the Black Power movement. Poets abounded then: Sonia Sanchez, Nikki Giovanni, Carolyn Rodgers, Mari Evans, LeRoi Jones, Don L. Lee, Audre Lorde, joined by the distinguished Gwendolyn Brooks. All obligatorily espoused heterosexuality—except for Lorde and Brooks. They taught me how to make use of anger and gave me a rhetoric and the beginnings of a poetics. Blackness and Black people—ancestors and contemporaries—have been a self-replenishing store of poetry and knowing.

FINDING WORDS TO LIVE BY

I'm not one of those who believes
That an act of valor, for a woman
Need take place inside her.

(Lindsay, 1970)

Never far away. Always within reach. The anthologies. The novels. The journals. The broadsides. The pamphlets. Toni Cade Bambara's *The Black Woman: An Anthology* (1970) was the first autonomous collection of writings with feminist leanings published by Black women or any women of color in response to the resurgence of feminism in the late 1960s. Though I was not a lesbian in 1970, I was nonetheless struck by Bambara's stunning proposal for the resolution of antagonisms between Black women and Black men in her essay "On the Issue of Roles":

> Perhaps we [black people] need to let go of manhood and femininity and concentrate on blackhood. . . . It perhaps takes less heart to pick up the gun than to face the task of creating a new identity, a new self, perhaps an *androgynous* self, via commitment to struggle.
>
> (Cade Bambara, 1970: 103; emphasis added)

Though Bambara was not a lesbian either and none of the articles in her anthology dealt with lesbianism, she and the other contributors—among them Alice Walker, Sherley Anne

Williams (Shirley Williams), Audre Lorde, Frances Beale, Nikki Giovanni—were clearly preoccupied, as was I, with gender role expectations and male domination in the Black community/movement. These preoccupations were a precursor and a model for many other women of color, primarily lesbians, in the USA to examine nearly a decade later the intersections of race, gender, class and (hetero)sexuality in our lives and to write about them.

Before 1973, I had no conception of Black lesbians except as exotic subjects of curiosity and an adolescent memory which I was to recount in a 1983 essay entitled "The Failure to Transform: Homophobia in the Black Community":

I can recall being about 12 years old when I first saw a black lesbian couple. I was walking down the street with my best friend, Kathy. I saw two young women [in their early 20s] walking together in the opposite direction. One wore a doo-rag, a Banlon button-down, and high-top sneakers. The other woman wore pink brush rollers, spit curls plastered with geech, an Oxford-tailored shirt, a mohair sweater, fitted skirt with a kick pleat, black stockings, and the famous I. Miller flat, sling-back shoe, the most prestigious pair of kicks any Dee cee black girl could own. I asked Kathy, "Who are they?" "Bulldaggers," she answered. "What's that?" I asked again. "You know, they go with each other," Kathy responded. "Why?" I continued. "Protection," Kathy said casually. "Protection?" I repeated. "Yeah, at least they won't get pregnant," Kathy explained.

(Clarke, 1983b: 206)

I was studying at Rutgers University right after Stonewall[1] and saw the beginning of the gay liberation movement there, led by Black gay activist Lionel Cuffie. Cuffie's anti-sexist and anti-heterosexist politics helped me see the connections among oppressions of Black people, women, and gay men and lesbians. In 1973, at one of the early gay[2] conferences at Rutgers University—trying to resolve the confusion of a Black identity and lesbian desire—I witnessed a contingent of *out* Black lesbians from New York City. When I heard those women—one of whom had been a classmate of mine at Howard University—talk boldly about the intersections of race, class, gender and their impact on Black women who were lesbians and our accountability to be struggling against and organizing around our oppression as well as celebrating our liberation from traditional and boring gender role expectations, I was transformed and asked myself the question: *With these women out here, why am I in the closet?* I realized that the major contradictions between Blackness and lesbianism were the sexist and heterosexist postures of the Afro-American (bourgeois) community. Witnessing a political Black lesbian community in the flesh was indispensable to this reconciliation of identities/cultures and saved me from wasting years in the closet of false consciousness.

I had already realized the potency of a rebellious literature and orality and would not have been able to nourish myself on feminist and lesbian-feminist writing had I not first found my anger in the poetry of the previously named writers of the Black Arts Movement. Later, I would connect with my feminist roots by reading the fiction of Black women, whose texts I live and write by: *Their Eyes Were Watching God* (Hurston, 1937), *Quicksand* and *Passing* (Larsen, 1928, 1929), *The Street* (Petry, 1943), *Lady Sings the Blues* (Holiday, 1956), *The Bluest Eye* and *Sula* (Morrison, 1971, 1973), *The Third Life of Grange Copeland, In Love and Trouble* and *Meridian* (Walker, 1970, 1973, 1976), Alexis Deveaux's surreal *Spirits in the Street* (1974), *Gorilla My Love* and *The Salt Eaters* (Bambara, 1972, 1980), Paule Marshall's tragedic *Brown Girl, Brownstones* (1959) and her homophobic *Chosen Place, Timeless People* (1969), and all the Ladies in Red, Blue, Green in Ntozake Shange's *for colored girls who have considered suicide when the rainbow is enuff* (1975). I stored the language of all their relentless, outrageous, angry and protective ghosts. I learned well to be the Black woman who turned up and "with a single glance from eyes that burned away their own lashes . . . discredited your elements" (Morrison, 1981: 39).

And when I used pretenders (drugs, cigarettes, food) to distract myself, I could feel them pulling me to poetry as patient and relentless as Hannah Kemhuff in Walker's "The Revenge of Hannah Kemhuff" (1973): "I can survive as long as I need with the bitterness that has laid every day in my soul" (67). And when

I questioned their faith, I heard Eva Peace in Morrison's *Sula* (1974: 69) berating her daughter Hannah:

> [W]hat you talkin' 'bout did I love you girl
> I stayed alive for you can't you get that through
> your thick head or what is that between your ears, heifer.

In 1975, speaking at the Socialist Feminist Conference at Antioch College in Yellow Springs, Ohio, Charlotte Bunch, "still, in part, a separatist," sternly educated the 1,100 women who attended—more than half of whom were intensely anti-lesbian, 200 of whom were out dykes and the rest were closeted dykes and bisexuals—about lesbian-feminism:

> Lesbianism is more than a question of civil rights and culture. . . . It is an extension of the analysis of sexuality itself as an institution. It is a commitment to women as a political group, which is the basis of a political/economic strategy leading to power for women, not just an "alternative community."
>
> (Bunch, 1987: 175)

The Socialist Feminist Conference was a left nightmare. However, I was fortunate to have been there. I met another Black lesbian feminist, Barbara Smith, whose life and work have remained crucial to me as a lesbian writer since 1975. In addition to the fact that she was/is a strong reader of Black women's literature, Barbara Smith was central in the USA to building a Black lesbian-feminist movement as well as a radical Black feminist consciousness, all of which have been inspired and motivated by Black women novelists, as the writers, in turn, have been inspired and motivated by the Black and women's political movements. Smith wrote her groundbreaking essay, "Toward a Black Feminist Criticism" (1977), which appeared in the lesbian-feminist journal *Conditions: Two*.[3] Smith made four important moves in this article: challenged white feminist critics on their literary elitism and erasure of Black women writers, developed Black feminist criteria for the evaluation of works by Black women writers, called our attention to Black women writers' subjectivity, and *read* Toni Morrison's *Sula* as a lesbian novel. This caused no end of controversy among the (heterosexist) Black literati who expressed themselves vituperatively when she delivered a talk based on the article at a Black Writers' Conference at Howard in 1978. Smith also organized four Black feminist retreats between 1977 and 1980. Most of us who participated were lesbians, others were bisexual and straight, all of us were progressive and radical, middle class and college-educated. These gatherings served to break down the isolation of being Black and feminist, and gave us the courage, if not the confidence, to do our anti-sexist, anti-heterosexist, and anti-racist feminist work. They helped me particularly to recognize historical Black women's leadership.

During that time Smith participated in the writing of "The

Combahee River Collective Statement,"[4] which defined Black feminist politics, practice, issues, and organizing, and was particularly distinguished by the concept that there is a simultaneity and no hierarchy of oppressions.

In 1979, Smith and co-editor Lorraine Bethel guest-edited *Conditions: Five,* "The Black Women's Issue." *Conditions: Five* was the first text to enunciate a pronounced Black feminist politic since Cade's *The Black Woman* (1970). However, its signal importance rests on the fact that the editors included the writings and perspectives of *out* Black lesbians. I might add, though Audre Lorde's poetry appeared in *The Black Woman,* she could not be out in that work, though she was a lesbian then; and though she had been out in her writing a number of years by 1979, *Conditions: Five* gave Audre Lorde a visible community. Bethel and Smith stated, "We placed a priority on writing concerning itself with the issues of feminism and lesbianism as they related to black women." Smith and Bethel called for all women of color to produce "autonomous publications that embody their particular identity." It was in this special issue that I came out as a writer—not as a poet, though. Two years later, I came out as a poet in an anthology simply, bluntly, beautifully titled, *Lesbian Poetry* (1981), edited by Elly Bulkin and Joan Larkin for the now defunct Persephone Press. (Bulkin also edited a companion volume, *Lesbian Fiction,* that same year for Persephone.)

Following upon the success of *Conditions: Five* in 1979 and the initiatives of diverse feminists of color in the USA, other feminist journals and presses took up Smith's and Bethel's challenge and published writings by other culturally marginalized women within the feminist community. The 1980s was a watershed of multicultural feminist publishing and all of it either self-published or published by independent feminist presses, which challenged the racism, anti-Semitism, class biases of the lesbian-feminist movement: the self-published *Top Ranking: Articles on Racism and Classism in the Lesbian Community* (Gibbs and Bennett, 1980), *This Bridge Called My Back: Writings by Radical Women of Color* (Anzaldua and Moraga, 1981); *All the Women are White, All the Blacks are Men, But Some of Us are Brave: Black Women's Studies* (Hull, Bell-Scott and Smith, 1981), *Nice Jewish Girls* (Beck, 1982), *Home Girls: A Black Feminist Anthology* (Smith, 1983); *Sinister Wisdom's A Gathering of Spirit: North American Women's Issue* (Brant, 1983); *Calyx's Bearing Witness/Sobreviviendo: An Anthology of Writing and Art by Native American/Latina Women* (Cochran, 1984). And while these various publications published writing by all women, lesbian leadership, i.e., editors, publishers, booksellers, reviewers, across all lines of race, culture, class, and education, made these publications possible, caused them to be read, have kept me going, and have made it possible for writers like myself to be useful. In 1981, I became a member of the editorial collective of *Conditions,* where my primary task was to facilitate the growth of writing by lesbians.

When asked in an interview for Gerda Lerner's *Black Women in White America: A Documentary History,* Ella Baker defined herself as a "facilitator" rather than a "leader" (Baker, 1973). She further elaborated that she saw herself as someone who made it possible for other people, who wanted to, to take leadership in their communities. Lesbian-feminists are facilitators. Our movement was buttressed by the publication of writing by women, most of whom were lesbians or women for whom relationships with women were an integral part of their lives, whose writing—in diverse forms and genres—would not have seen print were it not for our network. The network is worldwide and necessary.

Jewelle Gomez (1983) and SDiane Bogus (1990)—both Black lesbians—historicize the Black lesbian image in literature. Gomez does so from a critical perspective and Bogus attempts to be more theoretical, though is less careful about some of her facts.[5] Both agree that, in terms of the works written from the 1920s to the 1980s by white women and Black men in which there are Black lesbian characters, none is an authentic portrayal. They disagree, however, in terms of their perceptions of the authenticity of the images of Black lesbians in books by Black women writers—lesbian and straight. And they differ most decidedly in their assessments of the influence and value of Black lesbian fiction writer Ann Allen Shockley, about whom there has always been a great deal of ambivalence among feminist and lesbian readers, reviewers and critics—Black and white. Gomez, in "A Cultural Legacy

Denied and Discovered: Black Lesbians in Fiction by Women," states that the main flaws of Shockley's *Loving Her* (1974) and *Say Jesus and Come To Me* (1982), both of which depict dubious images of Black lesbians, are "not dissimilar from that of her white counterparts: the inability to place a Black Lesbian in a believable cultural context in an artful way" (Gomez, 1983: 114). Gomez goes on to cite Walker's *The Color Purple* and Lorde's *Zami* as exemplary texts which do not divorce "women-loving-women" from the Black community. Bogus, in "The 'Queen B' Figure in Black Literature," explores the etymology of the term "bulldagger" (i.e., "Queen *B*") and the bulldagger's presence in a larger range of texts than Gomez, takes Gomez and other critics to task for not recognizing "the import" of *Loving Her,* "that 'first' published black lesbian portrait drawn by a black woman" (Bogus, 1990: 277), suggests that Walker would not have been able to create Shug Avery had it not been for Shockley, and does not situate *Zami* within the "Queen B" legacy.

Historically important as it is, *Loving Her,* which I read after being out for only a year, did not satisfy my need for models. Looking for lesbians in fiction and most poetry was an unsatisfying quest back in the 1970s. Judy Grahn's *Common Woman Poems* (1969), narrative poems presenting images of working-class white women among whom were lesbians, intruded upon my store of images and preserved themselves there among the Hannahs, Scylla and Selina, Ruby, Janey, Helga, the Ladies in Green, Red, Blue. I was not to encounter positive Black lesbian images until Audre Lorde's *Zami* in 1982 and Walker's *The Color Purple* in 1983. However, despite and because of Lorde's lush, evocative prose, the narrator of *Zami* was too mythic and Shug and Celie were too unselfconscious as lesbians; Barbara Smith cites this as a lack of "verisimilitude" in the novel and questions whether Celie and Shug should be identified as lesbians at all (1990: 237).

Looking for Lesbians: Finding Anger . . .

Anger has been a critical trope for me, a black woman, ex-slave, poet, lesbian trafficking among enemies. During the early days of the 1980s I felt myself and other Black lesbians many times being "cancelled out" (Lorde, 1988) as feminists—our contributions and our status as women unacknowledged by other Black feminists. Frustrated by the Black Movement's treatment of Black women, the jewelry-maker and cultural worker, Ruby, in Toni Cade Bambara's *The Salt Eaters* (1980) expresses well the anger of Black lesbians:

I'm sick of leaflets and T-shirts and moufy causes and nothing changing. All I want is a good blowtorch and some paying customers for a change. And if one more rat-tooth mutha-fucka strolls into my shop asking to trade some cockeyed painting looking like a portable toilet for one of my master-piece bracelets, I'm gonna run amuck in the streets, I swear.

Following in the tradition of militancy established in the 1960s
Black consciousness movement, I took my first foray into what
had been the domain of Black men—the essay—and wrote the
manifesto-style "Lesbianism: an Act of Resistance," which
appeared in *This Bridge* (1981). As I reread this article today, I am
amazed at how much it reads like a revision of the writings of the
Furies Collective.[6] However, my model for this essay is the homo-
phobic father I wanted to "kill"—LeRoi Jones (aka Amiri Baraka).
"Lesbianism: an Act of Resistance" attempted to talk about who
lesbians are and the domain of our politics and struggle as well as
to locate Black lesbians within that world. It is loud and uncom-
promising in its criticism of the homophobia/heterosexism of the
Black community and ends with an incomplete critique of the
silence and hostility among lesbians of color and white lesbians
regarding interracial lesbian relationships. It cautions that political
alliances must be made on the basis of politics "not the specious
basis of skin color."

Sometimes the murkiness of my anger caused me to slay mem-
bers of my own family for the "murder" of my lesbian sisters. "The
Failure to Transform: Homophobia in the Black Community," in
Home Girls, attempted to be a critique of anti-gay and anti-lesbian
postures on the part of Black intellectuals. So, everybody from
Baraka to bell hooks caught hell in that piece. The "Pentalog,"
"Conversations and Questions: Black Women on Black Women
Writers"—a five-person conversation participated in by Jewelle L.

Gomez, Evelynn Hammonds, Linda Powell, Bonnie Johnson, and myself, which I edited for *Conditions: Nine* in 1983 was another platform for critiquing our extended family for its heterosexism, for exploring what it means to be a Black woman writing about Black women writers, and advancing a Black lesbian aesthetics/ politics. We *read* everybody in this—Black feminist critics, white feminist editors of feminist publications, Black lesbian writers, and some of our best friends. A particularly controversial concept was Linda Powell's revision of Samuel Johnson's metaphor of the "dancing dog,"[7] which she applied to the false praise by white women of the mediocre writing of Black women. After providing the parable of the "dancing dog," Powell continues:

> Now, the truth is this dog didn't do anything that remotely resembled dancing. However, it wasn't bad for a dog. So, it's been my experience that what's been operating in the women's community is that whole thing that if a black woman speaks the language and is nice around white folk, the "dancing dog" is in operation. She can speak at conferences. She can write reviews. And even if she's mediocre, it's not bad for a negro. Occasionally, they hit pay dirt. . . . They'll get something that's higher quality than much of the material they print. But it's not because they met [you], or they spoke to [you], or they knew [your] work or [your] involvement in women's issues. No, but because they saw

[you] at a party, [you were] dressed nice, [you're] black, and [you] went to Sarah Lawrence.

(Clarke et al., 1983: 102)

The "Pentalog" was laced with acerbic and caustic commentary. No Black feminist writer, scholar, or critic was spared our wit—not Alice Walker, not June Jordan, not Deborah McDowell, not bell hooks, not Ann Allen Shockley, not Pat Parker, not Barbara Smith, not Mary Helen Washington. As I rethink this experience, the most problematic question the "Pentalog" raises, as a piece of literature and as an historical document, is audience. How appropriate was it for us to give such public vent (and venom) to issues of conflict among Black women—lesbian-feminist to lesbian-feminist, lesbian-feminist to straight feminist—in a publication like *Conditions,* whose readership was largely white women, or so it was said. We were asked the proverbial question by both white women and other women of color: "Why did you air your dirty laundry in public?" Having seen that argument played out for more than a decade by that time, I had come to regard the question as a form of censorship. Can dirty laundry be aired any other place than outside? Really?

I do not apologize for the murders but echo the sparse words of Electra in the adaptation of Euripides' play by Black playwright Adrienne Kennedy:

I am guilty too. I burned with desperate rage against you, yet . . . I loved you . . . although I hated you.

(Kennedy, 1988: 138)

So, finally, I come to myself, my own blank page, where I had to speak the love that cannot call its name, to sing the thing not named, and give a body to that "nameless . . . shameful impulse"[8] in poetry. With all this and the memory of Baldwin's *Another Country,* I set out in 1982 to negotiate my own Black lesbian subjectivity.

Narratives: Poems in the Tradition of Black Women is my first negotiation. I went to the Afro-American narrative tradition— written and oral—for language, directness, lyricism, terseness, and pathos. *Cane* and *Maud Martha* insinuated a framework for these fifteen poems—each telling a different Black woman's story. *In Love and Trouble* and *The Bluest Eye* helped me see the violations and the triumphs of the souls of Black women. *Narratives* was a way for me, as a Black lesbian poet, to enter into dialogue with all the Black writers I had been reading since I was 17.

My everyday life as a Black lesbian poet is marked by the struggle to be a sexual Black lesbian, the struggle for the language of sexuality, and the struggle not to be the "beached whale of the sexual universe" (Spillers, 1984: 74). For many years, I said, along with many lesbians, that lesbianism is a political identity— *more* than *just* a sexual identity. What is this "more than"? *In addition to* or *better?* And "not just who you sleep with"? *Not just* meaning *merely* or just *not only?* And "more than who you sleep with"? Meaning *greater* or *in addition* to? Too much minimizing and dismissing of a major component of lesbian oppression—heterosexist repression of our sexuality. After the virulent antagonisms between anti-pornography feminists and anti-censorship feminists (among whom I count myself) in the early 1980s, I used poetry to reclaim lesbian sexuality and desire—in its diverse poetic and real forms. *Living as a Lesbian,* my second book of poetry, in 1986, quarreled with this dismissal of sex and served to advance another Black lesbian aesthetic and politic. Audre Lorde gave us the first and most searing in *The Black Unicorn.*

Sarah Vaughn singing "Lullabye of Birdland" to the trumpet interpolations of Clifford Brown (1954) was a driving counterpoint for these poems. I plainly wanted to advance Audre Lorde's thesis in her 1978 piece "Uses of the Erotic," by promoting the concept of lesbian sexuality, a poetry of itself in all its irony and paradox. Lorde's words:

When I speak of the erotic, then, I speak of it as an assertion of the lifeforce of women; of that creative energy empowered, the knowledge and use of which we are now reclaiming in our language, our history, our dancing, our loving, our work, our lives. Within the celebration of the erotic in all our endeavors, my work becomes a conscious decision—a longed-for bed which I enter gratefully and from which I rise empowered.

(1984, 55)

The lyric genre predominates here and all the Black women's vocal music I had listened to since my childhood. A disconnected morose seven-part sonnet sequence demarcates each section of this book and tracks a narrative consciousness from the deaths of Martin Luther King and Otis Redding to the return of a friend to the struggle in southern Africa. The poems of each section enunciate the themes of sex, death, and loss. In addition to sonnets, there is a sestina, two villanelles, and one ballade. The poems address local, national, and global issues, e.g., the assassination of Indira Gandhi, the murder of Kimako Baraka, the Miami riots of 1980. Out of forty-five poems, twenty-three address lesbianism and explicit lesbian sexuality; and five poems bear the phrase "Living as a Lesbian" in their titles to signify the lesbian subjectivity of this book. Lesbians like this book. I was trying to please lesbians.

In 1989, I returned to the tradition of narrative poetry in my last book, *Humid Pitch*. Lesbianism is in sharp relief. *Humid Pitch* attempts something heretical for a lesbian-feminist poet: male homosexuality and female bisexuality. This may account for the low number of reviews it received in the feminist presses. *Humid Pitch* unearths the untold or not told-enough tales of Black women, triumphant lesbians, ambivalent men, slave women, and the children who survive childhood. Pivotal to this work is the poem "Epic of Song," a 60-page narrative poem based loosely on the legend of the relationship between Ma Rainey and Bessie Smith.[9] Also I try to tell a triumphant story, to say that a "lady" can sing the blues and live to tell about it. Black women's vocal music is vital to all Black women—poets, novelists, critics, theorists, scholars—writing about Black women. "Epic of Song" pays tribute to Black women artists, who were often autonomous and sexually independent. The book attempts to evoke the language and color of the blues, of Black women's talk, the history of R&B. Several of my readers have criticized me for returning to the safety of the narrative form after the boldness of the lyrics in *Living as a Lesbian*. I don't agree or disagree. Each book has its own risks.

In my next book, *experimental love,* there is sex but a less invincible, less certain sex—a sex which gives itself sparingly. Nothing is promised here and everything could be finally destroyed as the old woman looks out on the rubble of what was her backyard after a Smart bomb or a nuclear holocaust. Lesbians are not virtuous here. They travel with latex. The sonnets return as well as a satirical pantoum; the lesbian living underground returns aboveground. Slavery is revisited, as always. There is no relentless pulling here and no ease of discovery.

My work has been to imagine an historical Black woman-to-woman eroticism and living—overt, discrete, coded, or latent as it might be. To imagine Black women's sexuality as a polymorphous erotic that does not exclude desire for men but also does not privilege it. To imagine, without apology, voluptuous Black women's sexualities. Audience is never an amorphous or theoretical concept for me. Long before I published, I was reading my poetry and witnessing the transformative power of orality. Orality helps me mediate the silence of the blank page and the relentless din of memory. The poem's power is not only the poet's working of her craft but how that working connects with people's experience of the poet saying out loud what has been distorted, suppressed, forbidden.

Audre Lorde, Judy Grahn, and Pat Parker are my foresisters and made it possible for me and many other lesbian poets to do our work during the 1980s. I was among a sisterhood of lesbian poets who interpreted the love that had finally begun to shout its name and its complexity in tongues of images and viscerally, writing a new cultural history. Our words were interstitial galaxies among the stories, letters, conversations, journal entries, and diverse prose forms in all the journals and anthologies mentioned previously. Joy Harjo, Chrystos, Irena Klepfisz, Sapphire, Dorothy Allison, Gloria Anzaldua, Paula Gunn Allen, Minnie Bruce Pratt, Jewelle L. Gomez, Terri L. Jewell,[10] and others whose names and words reverberate in the memory of those welcome audiences. Finally, lesbians and the lesbian community have made it possible for me to call myself a poet. While I am privileged to write openly as a lesbian and to have my work appreciated, I am still reminded that this ain't no place to love a woman.

Notes

1. The Stonewall Riots occurred the weekend of June 28, 1969, on Christopher Street in New York City as police stormed the Stonewall, a gay male bar, and gay men—mostly Black and Latino—fought back for three days. These riots caused gays and lesbians around the country to come out of their closets and fight against heterosexist oppression.

2. In 1973, men and women were identifying as "gay." Women reclaimed the term "lesbian" soon after as they began to leave male-dominated gay liberation organizations and establish their own lesbian-feminist or lesbian-separatist organizations and enterprises.

3 *Conditions,* founded in 1976 in Brooklyn, NY, was, along with *Sinister Wisdom,* one of the first lesbian-feminist literary journals, preceded by *Quest* and *13th Moon. Conditions* called itself "a magazine of writing by women, with an emphasis on writing by lesbians" and called for any "women for whom relationships with women are an integral part of their lives" to submit their writing. Elly Bulkin, Rima Shore, Irena Klepfisz, and Jan Clausen were the original editorial collective. In 1981, three of the four founding editors took action to make the collective a multicultural, multiracial, multi-ethnic, and class-diverse group. Throughout its history *Conditions* maintained an all-lesbian collective. The year 1990 was the last in which it published as a journal.

4. "The Combahee River Collective Statement" was prepared by a Black feminist group in Boston of which Smith was a member, and originally appeared in *Capitalist Patriarchy: The Case for Socialist Feminism,* edited by Zillah Eisenstein (New York: Monthly Review Press, 1978). The statement was later reprinted in *Home Girls: A Black Feminist Anthology,* edited by Barbara Smith (Latham, NY: Kitchen Table, Women of Color Press, 1983).

5. *Clara's Ole Man* (1967), by Black and male chauvinist Ed Bullins, was a play *not a novel,*

as Bogus says, which depicted a stereotypic Black lesbian relationship. While many feel Shockley cannot depict an authentic Black lesbian character, Shockley is a lesbian and not a "nonlesbian" as Bogus states in her article.

6. In 1971, Charlotte Bunch and Rita Mae Brown left the organized straight feminist movement and formed a separate lesbian political group called the Furies Collective. According to Bunch, "The Furies . . . committed ourselves to developing a lesbian-feminist political analysis, culture, and movement. . . . [F]ollowing the path of other oppressed groups, we concluded that we could influence it [the women's movement] best by building our own power base and politics first" (Bunch, 1987: 9).

7. See Mary Ellman, *Thinking About Women* (New York: Harvest Book, 1968), 31, for a similar discussion of (white) women writers and male critics.

8. This phrase from Nella Larsen's novel *Passing* was used by Deborah McDowell as part of the title for her 1988 essay " 'That nameless . . . shameful impulse': Sexuality in Nella Larsen's *Quicksand* and *Passing"* (in *Studies in Black American Literature,* Vol. 3, *Black Feminist Criticism and Critical Theory,* ed. Joe Weixlman and Houston Baker, Greenwood, Fla: Penkevill, 1988). Its use in my text is appropriate, for McDowell reads the phrase as a reference to Irene Redfield's suppressed homoerotic desire for Clare Kendry.

9. According to Chris Albertson, in *Bessie,* his 1972 biography of Bessie Smith (*c.* 1894–1937), the legend that Ma Rainey (1886–1939) and her husband kidnaped young Bessie Smith and taught her how to sing is merely a "colorful story." By 1916, when Bessie joined the Raineys, she had been on her own for several years. Though Albertson looks at both Ma's and Bessie's bisexuality and their relationships and sexual exploits with women, he cautions against believing that Ma Rainey "initiated [Bessie to embrace her own sex] . . . a theory supported by no more evidence than the improbable story of Bessie's 'kidnaping'." Chris Albertson, Bessie (New York: Stein & Day, 1972), 104, 117.

10. Terri L. Jewell died in 1995.

Works Cited

Baker, Ella (1973). "Developing Leadership," in Gerda Lerner (ed.) *Black Women in White America: A Documentary History,* New York: Vintage Books: 345–52.

Baldwin, James (1962). *Another Country,* New York: Dial Press.

Bambara, Toni Cade (1970). "On the Issue of Roles," in *The Black Woman: An Anthology,* New York: New American Library: 101–10.

—— (1980). *The Salt Eaters,* New York: Random House.

Bogus, SDiane (1990). "The 'Queen B' Figure in Black Literature," in K. Jay and J. Glasgow (eds) *Lesbian Texts and Contexts: Radical Revisions,* New York: New York University Press: 275–90.

Bunch, Charlotte (1987). "Not For Lesbians Only," in *Passionate Politics: Essays 1968 to 1986, Feminist Theory in Action,* New York: St Martin's Press: 174–81.

Clarke, Cheryl (1983a). "Lesbianism: an Act of Resistance," in G. Anzaldua and C. Moraga (eds.) *This Bridge Called My Back: Writings by Radical Women of Color,* Latham, NY: Kitchen Table, Women of Color Press: 128–37.

—— (1983b). "The Failure to Transform: Homophobia in the Black Community," in Barbara Smith (ed.) *Home Girls: A Black Feminist Anthology,* Latham, NY: Kitchen Table, Women of Color Press: 197–208.

—— *et al.* (1983). "Conversations and Questions: Black Women on Black Women Writers," *Conditions: Nine:* 88–140.

Gomez, Jewelle L. (1983). "A Cultural Legacy Denied and Discovered: Black Lesbians in Fiction by Women," in Barbara Smith (ed.) *Home Girls: A Black Feminist Anthology,* Latham, NY: Kitchen Table, Women of Color Press: 110–23.

Kennedy, Adrienne (1988). *Electra,* in *Adrienne Kennedy in One Act,* Minneapolis, MN: University of Minnesota Press.

Lindsay, Kay (1970). "Poem," in Toni Cade Bambara (ed.) *The Black Woman: An Anthology,* New York: New American Library: 17.

Lorde, Audre (1983). "Uses of the Erotic," in *Sister Outsider: Essays and Speeches,* Trumansburg, NY: Crossing Press: 53–9.

—— (1988). "To the Poet Who Happens to Be Black and the Black Poet Who Happens to Be a Woman," in *Our Dead Behind Us,* New York: W. W. Norton: 7.

Morrison, Toni (1974) *Sula,* New York: Knopf.

—— (1981). *Tarbaby,* New York: New American Library.

Smith, Barbara (1977). "Toward a Black Feminist Criticism," *Conditions: Two:* 25–44.

—— and Bethel, Lorraine (eds.) (1979). "Introduction," *Conditions: Five:* 11–14.

Spillers, Hortense (1984). "Interstices: A Small Drama of Words," in Carol Vance (ed.) *Pleasure and Danger: Exploring Female Sexuality,* New York: Routledge & Kegan Paul.

Walker, Alice (1973). "The Revenge of Hannah Kemhuff," in *In Love and Trouble,* New York: Harvest/HBJ Book: 60–80.

Part Four
Experimental Love: 1996–1999

A Great Angel

Oh soul, a great angel moves deep as th'Atlantic
gorged with tongues.

Today she let me see two hundred shades of green.

A great angel, oh my soul.
Oh my moon and coal black sea.

Living as a lesbian underground, ii

A faggot historian friend—once noted
now hunted—smuggled me the latest
in dyke fiction from Fiji.
I had to eat the manuscript
before I could finish it.

I was on my way underground when
uniformed children blondish forcing
my door nearly seized my journal.
I bribed them with adult books.
In a park a mustachioed gent in
trench coat no hat balding flashing
chased me for it.
(He recognized me from a photo in some old
literary review. It was a stunning photo.)
I outran him
and he yelled at me shaking his fists:

    "Hey, *poeta*, hope you have a good memory.
    Memory is your only redemption."

Hell I'm lucky.
I could be hiding some place

where I'm kidnapped
tortured on metal tables
fingers broken.
As it is my reveries have been confiscated
but my obsessions do me just as well.
Harder to manage and sexier.

An off-the-shelf mercenary counsels me:

"Detention is like solitude, and
don't poets need that? They'll let you
have a western classic or two,
a Norton anthology."

"Hell, what about a Portuguese-English dictionary?"

I ask as he pulls a leisure suit over his bush fatigues.

Around the time little Stevie Wonder's songs
were banned in the bantustans, a harried editor looked
up at me from my grazed manuscript,
shaking his head, said:

"Maybe in thirty years we can anthologize
an excerpt."

(Hell, I mimeographed the thing myself and gave it out in
    the quarantine we used to call Park Slope.)

But hell I still don't know what it's like
to be blocked by bayonets and frisked for
The Color Purple or be forced to dance
around a bonfire while my favorite passage
from Pushkin burns before my eyes.

A whore who'd been detained and raped every day
for a month escaped to the red hills where
she encountered me and showed me a word
from a book
not my own:

    "This word can get you violated,"

she said.

I'd never written the word.
But it was a good word.
It called me.
I had to write it or it would write me.
The pages of my journal were all written up
with words censored years before

they stopped selling blank paper,
pens, pencils, diskettes
(a few defectors had monitors).
I sneaked back into an old safe house
raided during the bombing of Tripoli.
I loosened a brick and pulled out
a suppressed manuscript
a tasty little piece
of interracial erotica
I'd written in the early days
of the emergency.
I wrote the word over and over
large and small on the back of every sheet
in cursive and in roman, in bold and fine.
I wrote it with my left hand
as well as my right.
I recited it every time I wrote it.
Played with my sex
as I wrote it
over and over.
And said it as I came
over and over

"Hey, *poeta,* memory is your only redemption."

Greta Garbo

Easter Sunday, April 15, 1990

I imagine you left Hollywood at thirty-six
because you had enough money to live as a lesbian
and didn't have to buy into heterosexuality
after Christina.

I imagine you overlooking the East River
or in Saks in fur coat
and sensible shoes asking,
"Please, do you have men's pajamas?"
A life of guarded anonymity, autonomy, alcoholism
all over Switzerland, the French Riviera,
and Italy wearing pants, flats, floppy hats,
dark glasses, and
toasting whiskey with an Alsace baroness
who liked it in the ass
yearly on the Rhine.

Movement

i.

I was a brown ball of a chap
when a small light-skinned Negro working woman
refused to give up her seat to a white bus rider.
Three months after, my father took me to our new church.
Surveying from a distance, I said, "How pretty,"
to those pastel dots of white people.
My father said, "Hush, girl."
I'd been taught the *Baltimore Catechism*
by cinnamon-faced Oblates of St. Thomas the Moor.
This would be my first mission.

ii.

His first mission was Alabama.
The cotton bolls sway in the gentle dusk breeze
Soft is the welcome darkening.
The evening star signals a tenuous freedom and workers
sing toward the Wednesday prayer meeting
eager for the spirits.
A woman with one breast and thick plaits is overcome
by the refrain, *Walk, children, don't you get weary.*

iii.

Walk, children, and don't get weary

before you get to Mississippi.

It was rough, Mississippi.

People got killed

and maimed regular.

We learned to drive fast at night.

One night not fast enough.

Three of us.

Driver didn't die though shot in the neck.

The two of us got him to a hospital

and sent a telegram to the President.

iv.

The President never understood the Civil War

that year I played alone at recess.

Boys on one side of the yard.

Girls on the other.

A nun at either end.

The boys' nun was five feet tall,

solid, and swarthy.

She spun like a top on her

thick black heels

when the boys tugged at her veil.

She was aloof from them though. And stern.

We surveilled one another the whole hour of
blue-grey play.

The girls' nun was giraffelike
and moved her brown lashes up and down
in blue-eyed laughter at
the girls gathering around her
for a touch, a word, a favor.
Her eyes sought mine every day
just above their heads of flowing hair
always just before the bell rang.

v.
Always just before the almsgiving
he was overcome by the burden of the love
people gave back to him.
He spoke from a familiar text that extraordinary night,
handkerchiefs signaling the anticipation,
the joy of victory.
Finally, he fell back from the pulpit
full with it
into the arms of his angel.

vi.

No guardian angel could protect
this light-skinned black boy
in our school that had the last name of Nixon.
His light-skinned black father, my dentist,
was voting for Nixon the first time
D.C. voted for a President.
The nuns pushed Democrats.
Kennedy called Coretta King
and every Negro in D.C. voted for him,
except Nixon's father.

vii.

Nixon's father was Edna Dockings' dentist, too. Edna Dock-
ings was our piano teacher. A birdish woman with bony,
veiny, rubbery fingers from years of abusive practice. Mrs.
Dockings was full of uplift stories, a graduate of Oberlin,
and a Yankee. While she drilled us in her basement studio on
Schirmer's Library, she read us her grandmother's letter from
a great-aunt who drove off slave catchers regularly with
stones. She called all three of us "Baby Sister."

Mr. Dockings, "Daddy," practiced a monotonous cello from
the third floor and smoked a dirty pipe. He called Mrs.
Dockings, "Edgy." While my two sisters received their les-
sons in the basement, I was made to practice exercises on the

faulty but sumptuous grand upstairs. Daddy would stop his
practice come down, and ask me to play Mozart.

viii.
Ask me to play Mozart and
imagine me being beaten in my face by a white man
until my eyes are lopsided
because I used a restroom
or sat at a counter
or drank from a water fountain.
Symbols are leaden.
Somewhere in Mississippi,
a black man is made to beat you until he tires.
A white man beats you some more.
You laying on your stomach,
trying to keep your dress down,
screaming.
The white man whispering close to your ear,
"Black bitch, big ass, you better shet up and be still."

ix.
I couldn't shut up and be still
whenever I was near Xavier,
my best friend.
I dreamed of sleeping with her before

the relentless pressure.

Her father, Pinky, let her drive his Dodge.

Xavier was a self-hating mulatto,

always trying to pass,

but her nose was too broad.

I loved her.

The memory shames me.

x.

That memory shames me, but then I remember

how my mother and her light-skinned lady friends loved

books and politics.

They read *Lady Chatterley's Lover,*

Tropic of Cancer,

Pinktoes,

Light in August,

Another Country.

The Negro in American Culture was the subject of a hot
    discussion

over a Pokeno game one Sunday.

xi. The Interview
"Even on Sunday slaves didn't deserve rest, sir.
Rather unworthy, slaves.
Not adequate.
No real powers of discernment
No souls.

 "A slave could be sick
her water breaking
feeble-minded
or six years old,
yet made to do unrelenting hard work
any time night or day,
sir.

"Though I was never treated cruelly,
I saw dastardly things done to others
for the slightest lack of measure.
A slave could be triced up to a tree and get
a hundred lashes and then be washed with brine;
or made to drink a strong medicine,
put in stocks, foul on himself, and be left
there for up to two days.
I saw a woman once. She cooked in the house.
Her mouth was locked with an iron muzzle."

xii.

The image of the iron muzzle stays with me. We should have stayed in Manhattan. But we let the nuns persuade us to return to D.C. with the rest of the class. It was a cold day and cops on horses were all about as surges of people covered Fifth Avenue. Scorned by the Movement, he walked at the head of the march. The sadness of the bus ride back and the loss of freedom. Then: married and caught in the quicksand; then out with barely the clothes on our backs. The year of my divorce I slept with an ex-nun wearing men's underwear.

passing

i'll pass as a man today and take up public space with my
urges in the casual way he does in three-piece suit and gucci
pumps big pants and large sneakers tight jeans and steel-
tipped boots read my newspapers spread-eagled across a
whole row of seats make my briefcase-boombox-backpack
into an ottoman on the seat across from me on the l.i.r.r.;
and spread my legs from here to far rockaway on the mighty
i.n.d.; and when i get sleepy or bored spreading the brim of
my blue fedora on the bus to queens hunch down cross my
fat feet into the aisle and lean forward with my arms folded
into the great press of rush hour flesh, hawking, spitting, and
pissing all the way.

Buttons

I wanted to unbutton every piece of your clothing
which was all buttons
from that silk shirt
down to the crotch of that gaberdine skirt.
My buttons too:
my jeans brass-button up,
my shirt has six shell buttons,
my camisole has three tiny ones.
This restaurant is in my way
when I want to be unbuttoned
and unbuttoning.
Can't you tell?
To do it now.
To reach across the bread.
To start unbuttoning.
My arms so long.
My fingers faster than the eye and omnidextrous.
Now, ain't that loving you?

interlude

late drinks
late talk
and a perfectly timed split
opening against
sheer blue-sheathed calf
denim desire
rough   tight
ass against crotch
seamhard.
oh, clothes and the clothes you cover
till skin
till hands vanilla as can be
motion toward all zippers
among the xerographic
and foolscap
untutored   groping light switch
and moving consensually
to undo frontal closures,
proud to be easy.

Rondeau

They are bodies left unburied.
Instead of roaming the underworld, they've tarried
to bring their nomadic anxiety
to my world with little propriety.
I'd rather them waylaid in Staten Island, unferried.

Sit next to this one here, pass her, there's that one there.
This one's pretty, that one tall.
Her there, she's fair.
Haunt my solitude, hurt my silence, make me crazy.
They are bodies.

I try to act modern, but still I'm worried.
We sleep together every night and still I'm worried
that she or she loves you more expertly sexually
than me obsessed by her or her like voices of insanity.
Provocative and sexy nonmonogamy in theory.
But they are bodies.

Remember the Voyage

for Noel DaCosta

Remember the voyage,
the leaving, the theft of mangoes.
The poorly tuned but graceful fiddle
haunting Harlem school days.
The small parlor.

Remember the breadfruit and ancient marketwomen
marking their places,
gapped-tooth women of the calabash,
whose hands were always busy
even after purple dusk cooled equatorial sun.
Remember mountains singing in the Caribbean,
and the blue twilight of Harlem melting into bawdy moon.
The blood.
Remember the Etruscan ruin
and fingers seasoning unplucked strings.
Remember the calabash.

Dykes Are Hard

Dykes are hard
to date.
A dyke wants commitment,
romance without abatement,
and unrelenting virtue—
all before the first show of flesh.
While you, a dyke too (and also hard
to date),
may only want to fuck her,
tell her she's got a nice
back, touch her pussy, talk dirty,
she's got another whole agenda.

Dykes should break loose and put off
monogamy, pregnancy, permanency.
Pack your rubber, latex, and leather,
and go on the make.
I know we'll hook up somewhere.

living as a lesbian at 45

Oh, it's a frequent dream:

He (He?) *comes home hot and*
wanting too.
You're in your room and wanting too
but wanting to control and orchestrate
so you can get it without really
acknowledging it will have a past
this
one way or another
in concert or in solitude
late
your juices built up from the day
odors sanguine
in the mood to take yourself
you set your works and toys out
and him
even though he knows you're a lesbian
there are those times
he still loses his crotch
in the part of your ass through your dress.

And that's how it happens

and it doesn't happen just once

and you may have work like poetry

to do like now and it starts

making you

pay it

some attention

and you run

and get your accoutrements

in excessive solitude

and space ephemeral with wetness.

Najeeb

(1974–1989)

The last Sunday
I saw you,
you were so brilliant with light
I could not see your face.
You'd grown taller than me
and were clumsy in your new height
choosing to wear your denim jacket indoors.
Loving your new adolescence, excited by the prospect
of years of growth ahead:
Would you care for me in my old age?
Did I have a right to expect that,
being only an aunt?

Instead I should have held you until you broke away
and even as you broke away.
As it is I cannot remember if I
even touched you as you left
that last Sunday.
You were so brilliant with light
I could not see your face.

Elegy

for Donald Woods

December 18, 1957–June 25, 1992

I loved your brown grace and mauve words
from the first night I heard you through
the mist in a Manhattan auditorium.
So like the young redwood, growth inevitable,
its passionate powers,
a poet whose comeliness
I will no longer be able to wrap my arms around.
I fall to pieces and still want your promise
and the sound of your slant voice.
I am not resigned.
You were too quiet.
You sang too low.
How prized if not known?
What would I have done had I known?

an old woman muses from her basement

there's absolutely no reason (in the world)
nor no need
to go outside again.

i've kinda hoped for this
leveling
to nobody and nothing.
it seems the only honesty possible
without heroes.
rather shabby.
tacky.

no reason (on earth) to go out
unless any of them that's left
outside
comes in here.
ain't likely.
but lord knows i got enough down here
to stock a hotel for a month.
but i'll miss the little runs
papa took me on in the sedandeville
to the safeway.

least i'm beginning to pick up static
on the tv

and papa just went the first thing.
i sewed his easy body in the sheet,
dragged it out to what was his garden,
i look out on him
the sheet more shrunken each day.

me—divorced, two children, the depression,
roosevelt's death.
the death of billie holiday.
no electricity to no electricity.
i always knew it was all a bum steer.

down here
and old bicycles squeaking.
the sudden death of a child
is an awful fact.
good thing i did my big shopping early.
my timing was always perfect.

A House of Difference

Audre Lorde's Legacy to Lesbian and Gay Writers

I THANK YOU very much for your exceedingly warm welcome. It is my honour to come before you at this necessary gathering— "Outwrite." It is also my honour to be speaking in a space that commemorates Audre Lorde, one of the most brilliant poets of the twentieth century, one among an illustrious sorority of contemporary black women and radical lesbian writers and thinkers who have changed literature and the world, and one of the first feminists to insist that integration of identities is crucial to politics, culture, activism, and "feeling deeply." All of our selves (and some of *his* tools) are needed to replace the master's house with houses of liberation, and writing is one of the tools the so-called master tried to keep from us that we have used tirelessly to sustain our revolution. So we need to be writers at least as much as we ever did. We need our bookstores, publishers, and movement to keep us writing, for we write and live in the dangerous imaginary that the world wants our writing.

I welcome the chance to rediscover with you Lorde's exquisite language and her lifelong preoccupations with geographies—of relationships, of political moments and movements, of identities, of cities. I will read from the poetry that is charted in sharp relief on *my* everyday life as a *fin de siècle* black lesbian poet.

We are familiar with the uses to which Lorde put writing: critique, instruction, exhortation, incitement, self-reflection. As the speaker sharply questions the manchild in this sequence of her stately elegy "On My Way Out I Passed Over You and the Verranzano Bridge":

> I am writing these words as a route map
> an artifact for survival
> a chronicle of buried treasure
> a mourning
> for this place we are about to be leaving
> a rudder for my children your children
> our lovers our hopes braided
> from the dull wharves of Tompkinsville
> to Zimbabwe Chad Azania
> oh, Willie sweet little brother with the snap in your eyes
> what walls are you covering now
> with your visions of revolution
> the precise needs of our mother earth
> the cost of false bread
> and have you learned to nourish your sisters at last
> as well as to treasure them?[1]

The question was put to all of us—not just "Willie sweet little brother"—who think we got our minds set on freedom and won't be turned around and before we be slaves we be buried in our graves, who undervalue our contradictions, or who are immobilized by difference, or who refuse mutuality, or who are not mindful of our own contamination by the systems we seek to overthrow.

Certainly, we have been irrevocably changed by Lorde's essays: "Feminism and Black Liberation: The Great American Disease,"[2] "Breast Cancer: A Black Lesbian Feminist Experience,"[3] "Uses of the Erotic," "Uses of the Anger," "Poetry is not a Luxury,"[4] "Black Women Organizing Across Differences."[5] Like two of her contemporaries, Adrienne Rich and June Jordan, Lorde is loyal to poetry and to feminism. All three poets leave the chamber of reverie to foray into the arena of the essay. *The Cancer Journals, Sister Outsider, A Burst of Light,* place Audre Lorde in the tradition of essayists like Frances E. W. Harper, Ida B Wells, Alice Dunbar Nelson, Mary Church Terrell, each of whom kept alive the dialogue on black women's identity and duty, warned the race of its own pitfalls, and protested injustices done to the race and to the women of that race. However, Lorde goes further and deeper, dissolving the visceral silence surrounding sexuality, death, illness, intimacy, giving them public voice.

Yet for twenty-five years we lived also with a poet whose poetry bespeaks an inveterate traveller for whom no place or emotion is too far to go the distance. As lesbian poet and fiction writer Becky Birtha commented at an Audre Lorde memorial service in 1993 at the University of Pennsylvania: "Audre was *out* there—reading, meeting people, travelling. . . ." That so many people, including many young people, across differences and generations encountered Audre personally—had not only read her work and met her, but had also talked deeply with her, shared their work with her, partied intensely with her, had been encouraged by her, driven by her—always amazes me. She was *out* there. She considered herself a "travelling cultural worker," going and reading her poetry, dropping "seeds" and then leaving—hoping they would spring into something, finding out they did, sometimes never finding out, having "faith and fun along the way."[6] In the poem "Touring" she offers a somewhat more racy and overly determined conceit of the travelling cultural worker whose good intentions are mediated by endings and the temporal failure to make deep connections:

> Coming in and out of cities
> where I spend one or two days
> selling myself. . . .
> I leave poems behind me
> dropping them like dark seeds that
> I will never harvest
> that I will never mourn
> if they are destroyed
> they pay for a gift
> I have not accepted.

Coming in and out of cities
untouched by their magic
I think without feeling
this is what men do
who try for some connection
and fail
and leave
five dollars on the table.[7]

What are we bequeathed—as lesbian, gay, bi, trans, black, white, young, coloured, old, men, women, queer, and multiply challenged writers—in the poetry of Audre Lorde, that "strong" reader of the world, that transgressive public intellectual? In this space devoted to our thoughts and feelings on Audre Lorde, is it appropriate—and perhaps, indeed, *urgent*—for us to recommit ourselves to her legacy, the study of her life, the example of her work, as we prepare to take our work and words into the twenty-first century?

How do we use Audre Lorde's poetry to live, act, think? How do we resist pedestalizing and canonizing Audre Lorde, resist immobilising ourselves by false comparisons, resist not acting and not feeling? In "Diaspora" she gives us a compelling metaphor: "Afraid is a country with no exit visas."[8]

Lorde's poetry has never been as transparent as her prose, in which she faithfully enunciates her "Black lesbian feminist socialist mother of two" subjectivities.[9] Also, as in the sequence just read, she is more prone to enunciate and to analyze her diaspora identity, her black Atlantic heritage, her Pan-Africanist consciousness. There is the legend that, after hearing Lorde read a poem in workshop, the late John O. Killens, said, "Yeah, you're a poet. I don't know what you're saying, sweetheart, but you're a poet."(Imagine calling Audre Lorde "sweetheart"?) For many years, I was critical of what I called her "hermetic inaccessibility." The realm of the literal is not a place Lorde visits long. One can construct of her poetry narratives of instability, uncertainty, and possibility—always possibility:

> you cannot make love to concrete
> if you cannot pretend
> concrete needs your loving[10]

Relationships are rather like concrete sometimes—and so is the muse. A great deal of performance is necessary.

Pain, alienation, travail hover always at the margins of Lorde's poems, vying for prominence with anger, hope, and rectitude/righteousness. The poems are most often effected in short, tight lines. Frequently, the line bounds the idea, image, insight; just as often, however, the thought is running or fragmented or disappearing and turning up later in the same or another poem or book. There is hardly any punctuation, except the occasional, well-placed period. The "spatial pauses"[11] between words and lines, the imagined spaces after lines, the appositives, are some of the more obvious stylistic practices which characterised her poetry from its earliest soundings. For one whose "So it is better to speak / remembering / we were never meant to survive" is so often quoted and lived by, the uses of silence are as powerful as repetition. Lorde's prosodic efficiency is as evident in *The First Cities*[12], her first book of poems, as it is in *The Marvellous Arithmetics of Distance,*[13] her last voyage, where her lifelong themes, concerns, and rhetorical brilliance are reprised. She refuses us the comfort and inevitability of the vamp, of rhyme, of the blues, the sonnet, the ballad, the spiritual, iambic pentameter; gives us instead the sparing refrain of some forgotten R&B song and the bridge of some lost percussion solo. The angry, spare refrain in the poem "Moving Out or the End of Cooperative Living"[14] is an example:

> I am so glad to be moving
> away from this prison for black and white faces
> assaulting each other with our joint oppression
> competing for who pays the highest price for this privilege
> *I am so glad I am moving*[14]

Audre Lorde found the first community for her voice in the late sixties with the New Black Poets, whose mission was to liberate the black mind from Western tutelage. Even then and before then, refusing to be silenced by the conflicts between black men and black women, she wrote woman-centered, mythic, and sorrowful poems of motherhood and childhood, poems of failed love relationships, of ambivalence and uncertainty. Lorde is unparalleled in her concern for children and young people, except by her sister poet, Gwendolyn Brooks, whose poetics and poetic concerns diverge so sharply from Lorde's. In "Generation," published in 1968, the speaker elegizes innocence before the onset of experience:

> How the young attempt and are broken
> differs from age to age
> We were brown free girls
> loved singing beneath our skin.[15]

And again the popular "For Each of You," a poem published four years later, in which the speaker exhorts the imagined black community to take pride in its matrilineal and slave heritage. In a parenthetical phrase, the speaker also makes that imagined black community accountable to children—not just those we parent:

> Speak proudly to your children
> where ever you may find them
> tell them

you are the offspring of slaves
and your mother was

a princess
in darkness.[16]

Audre Lorde leaves us a sexual legacy as blatant and as subtle as we ourselves want to be in our own "uses of the erotic." The poems never doubt the body or the body's desire, only the objects of its desire. How can we use the poems to teach us about sex? Sex energy is life energy. The love object/subject of desire is either ungendered or gendered female—enunciating possibilities other than but grounded in the specificity of love between women (perhaps I should say "among"):

When you love, you love. It only depends on how you do it, how committed you are, how many mistakes you make. . . . But I do believe that the love expressed between women is particular and powerful because we have had to love ourselves in order to live; love has been our means of survival, and having been in love with both men and women, I want to resist the temptation to gloss over the differences.

I don't think these differences between men and women are rigidly defined with respect to gender, though the Western input has been to divide these differences into male and female *characteristics*. We all have the ability to feel deeply and to move upon our feelings and see where they lead us.[17]

Sex is spectacular, oracular, primal and dangerous, especially for women, especially for lesbians. The poems are in the here-and-now, always prophesying the potential for rejection and destruction. Her metaphors are awesome as much for their exquisiteness as for their earthy explicitness—as in this series of metaphorical and literal images of digital penetration, cunnilingus, female genitals, body parts, secretions, and erogenous zones in "love poem." The speaker's voice is active—and rather butch:

And I knew when I entered her I was
high wind in her forest hollow
fingers whispering sound
honey flowed
from the split cup
impaled on a lance of tongues
on the tips of her breasts on her navel
and my breath howling into her entrances
through lungs of pain.[18]

And even lesbians suspend their guardedness in the transcendent "woman."

> I dream of a place between your breasts
> to build my house like a haven
> where I plant crops in your body
> ....
> and your night comes down upon me
> like a nurturing rain.[19]

In "Sisters in Arms," from *Our Dead,* the mythic and real instability of the erotic is displayed and sex and death coalesce shamelessly in the context of a dangerous and violent world:

> I could not return with you to bury the body
> reconstruct your nightly cardboards
> against the seeping Transvaal cold
> ....
> so I bought you a ticket to Durban
> on my American Express
> and we lay together
> in the first light of a new season [20]
> ....

"Smelling the Wind," from *The Marvelous Arithmetics,* is a compressed love lyric that encapsulates the intentions of this posthumous volume and the intentionality with which Lorde lived her life as an artist, lesbian, and African in diaspora:

> rushing headlong
> into new silence
> your face
> dips on my horizon
> the name
> of a cherished dream
> riding my anchor

Gloria Hull argues in "Living on the Line"—which is a model of how Audre Lorde's poetry should be written about—that, while she "spent her entire career as a black lesbian feminist poet writing against hegemonic, phallocentric whiteness," that "Black/lesbian/ mother/woman are no simple fixed terms." These terms represent "ceaseless negotiations of a positionality from which she can speak":

> Almost as soon as she achieves a place of connection, she becomes uneasy at the comfortableness (which is, to her, a signal that something critical is being glossed over) and proceeds to rub athwart the smooth grain to the roughness and

the slant she needs to maintain her difference-defined, complexly constructed self.[21]

I think surely Lorde leaves us this legacy of uneasiness and the refusal to be consoled.

On my way up and down the New Jersey Turnpike in the weeks (well, actually, the day, maybe the hour) preceding this necessary conference—Outwrite—I have tried to figure a conclusion: some horatory remarks of my own. Read one of my poems? Write a new poem for this important occasion. Read from one of Audre's? Thunder the poem "Sacrifice" at you, which warns us that even with all our righteous precautions, "pleasure will betray us," that "unless we refuse to sleep / even one night in houses of marble [We better get out of there, then] / "the sight of our children's false pleasure / will undo us," and "learning all / we can / use / only what is vital / The only sacrifice of worth/is the sacrifice of desire."[22] Perhaps I can read from "Oshun's Table," a simple lyric in which lovely food is a temporary bond for the unstable:

A short hard rain
and the moon came up
before we lay down together
we toasted each other
descendants of poets

and woodcutters
handsome
untrustworthy
and brave[23]

Perhaps from "Blackstudies," her enraged admonition to those Africans in diaspora, who hold too fast to notions of "real blackness," yet we can read all of us in the subtext, all of us who are opiated by the sacred cow identity, who have become dogmatic, doctrinaire, and fixed in our politics and visions of revolution:

Now all the words in my legend come garbled
except anguish.
Visions of chitterlings I never ate
strangle me in a nightmare of leaders
at crowded meetings to study our problems
I move awkward and ladylike
. . . I worry on nationalist holidays[24]

. . . it is better to speak
remembering we were never meant to survive.[25]

Or:

I have been woman
for a long time
beware my smile
I am treacherous with old magic[26]

Or:

I do not believe our wants
have made all our lies
holy[27]

Or:

But I who am bound by my mirror
as well as my bed
see causes in color
as well as sex

and sit here wondering
which me will survive
all these liberations.[28]

Or:

I cannot recall the words of my first poem
but I remember a promise
I made my pen
never to leave it
lying
in somebody else's blood.[29]

I wish to give no advice about what in Audre Lorde's life and legacy we must emulate and carry forward—only that we must do something. I find my own answer in the poem with which I began, "On My Way I Passed Over You and the Verranzano Bridge":

And I dream of our coming together
encircled driven
not only by love
but a lust for a working tomorrow
and the flights of this journey
mapless and uncertain
and necessary as water.[30]

(I owe a great deal to Gloria Hull's magnificent essay, "Living on the Line," one of the only works of criticism to plumb the layers of Lorde's poetry.)

Delivered at Outwrite '96: the Audre Lorde Memorial Lecture, February 24

Notes

1. Audre Lorde, *Our Dead Behind Us* (New York: W.W. Norton, 1986), p. 55.

2. See *The Black Scholar* 1979.

3. Audre Lorde, *The Cancer Journal,* Argyle, NY: Spinsters Inc., 1980).

4. Audre Lorde, *Sister Outsider* (Trumansburg, NY: Crossing Press, 1984).

5. Audre Lorde, *A Burst of Light* (Ithaca, NY: Firebrand Books, 1988).

6. See the conversation with Lorde in Claudia Tate, ed., *Black Women Writers at Work: Conversations* (New York: Continuum, 1983).

7. Audre Lorde, *Black Unicorn* (New York: W.W Norton, 1978), p. 36.

8. *Our Dead Behind Us,* p. 32.

9. *Sister Outsider,* p. 114.

10. See "Making Love to Concrete," in Audre Lorde, *The Marvelous Arithmetics of Distance* (New York: W.W. Norton, 1993), p. 5.

11. See Gloria T. Hull, "Living on the Line," in Cheryl A. Wall, ed., *Changing Our Own Words* (New Brunswick, NJ.: Rutgers University Press, 1990).

12. Audre Lorde, *The First Cities* (New York: Poets Press, 1966).

13. *The Marvellous Arithmetics of Distance* (New York: W.W. Norton, 1983).

14. In Audre Lorde, *From a Land Where Other People Live* (Detroit: Broadside Press, 1973).

15. In *The First Cities.*

16. In *From a Land Where Other People Live.*

17. In Tate, *Black Women Writers at Work.*

18. Audre Lorde, *Undersong* (New York: W.W. Norton, 1993), p. 141. *Undersong* was originally published in *New York Head Shop and Museum* (Detroit: Broadside Press, 1976).

19. From *Black Unicorn.*

20. From *Our Dead Behind Us.*

21. Hull, "Living on the Line," in *Changing Our Own Words.*

22. From *Undersong.*

23. From *The Marvellous Arithmetics of Distance,* p. 37.

24. From *Undersong.*

25. "A Litany for Survival," in *Black Unicorn,* p. 32.

26. From "A Woman Speaks Out" in *Chosen Poems* (New York: Columbia University Press, 1982), p. 5.

27. From "Between Ourselves," in *Making Face, Making Soul,* Gloria Anzaldua, ed. (San Francisco, California: An Aunt Lute Foundation Book, 1980), p. 113.

28. "Who Said it Was Simple," in *From a Land Where Other People Live,* p. 39.

29. From "To the Poet . . ." in *Our Dead Behind Us,* p. 7.

31. In *Our Dead Behind Us,* p. 55.

Transferences and Confluences: The Impact of the Black Arts Movement on the Literacies of Black Lesbian Feminism[*]

The history of participation by poets in American social and political movements of this country has been important to the feminist poetry movement. . . . [I]t has provided examples of women poets, some of them early feminists, to whom we have been able to look for inspiration and encouragement. The Harlem Renaissance, a chapter of the Black struggle that was a social as well as a cultural movement, was led by poets. . . . Gwendolyn Brooks, Nikki Giovanni, and Sonia Sanchez were closely identified with the Black Power movement.

—Jan Clausen, *A Movement of Poets*

The fact of music was the black poet's basis for creation. And those of us in the Black Arts movement were drenched in black music and wanted our poetry to be black music. Not only that, we wanted that poetry to

* This essay appears in an expanded form in *After Mecca: Woman Poet and The Black Arts Movement* (Rutgers Press, 2005).

be armed with the spirit of black revolution. An art that could not commit itself to black revolution was not relevant to us. And if the poet that created such art was colored we mocked him and his inspiration as brainwashed artifacts to please our beast oppressors!

—Amiri Baraka, *The Autobiography of LeRoi Jones*

IN 1968, THE assassinations of Martin Luther King and Robert Kennedy within two months of one another are only two of the weighty and salient deaths on the North American landscape since the 1953 *Brown v. Board of Education,* Topeka, Kansas, decision. Media spectacles of violence against black citizens in the African American freedom struggle became major signifiers of oppression and liberation. State-sanctioned police violence was inscribed over every major urban center, from L.A. to Detroit to New York City. And the urban rebellions that punctuated the decade from 1965 to 1968 were only the most expressive gestures of despair and rage. African Americans—from integrationists to nationalists—were intensely alienated from white people, American institutions, and American so-called values. The Black Arts Movement articulated the alienation. The Black Arts Movement interpreted the varied longings for community among African Americans. Poetry became a discursive repository for the Black Power Movement—as spirituals and gospel music were to the earlier Black Civil Rights Movement.

In his 1969 antimodernist tour de force "Black Art," Amiri Baraka radically redefines poetry as visceral life, "Poems are bullshit unless they are / teeth or trees"[1] This redefinition of poetry is also a redefinition of blackness in which the death of whiteness is explicit. Baraka theorizes further:

> We want poems that kill. Assassin poems. Poems that shoot guns. Poems that wrestle cops into alleys and take their weapons leaving them dead with tongues pulled out and sent to Ireland.[2]

Baraka here exemplifies a critical piece of black arts literacy: the enunciation of a violent rhetoric.

Audre Lorde's 1977 essay "Poetry Is Not a Luxury," meditates on poetry as the language of women's deepest emotion, power, and creativity. Written in the same vein as her later essay "The Uses of the Erotic" (1978), this essay reifies poetry (and women) as the source of "true knowledge" and "lasting action." Baraka's less essentialist work externalizes the potential of poetry as a force of destruction and regeneration. Lorde sees poetry as a "dark" and "hidden" resource—much like the erotic—women carry within themselves that will ultimately enable them to take action:

> For women, then, poetry is not a luxury. It is a vital necessity of our existence. It forms the quality of light within which we predicate our hopes and dreams toward survival and change, first made into language, then into idea, then into more tangible action.[3]

Similar to developments in jazz and black theater, black poetry of the late '60s became instrumental to advancing black nationalism, a radical revisioning of the place of black people in the mind and body politic of "wite America." The work of Black Arts poets and black lesbian feminist poets signified a decided rupture with the "West / a grey hideous space."[4] Both paid homage to black consciousness and black culture. Black arts deferred to the new music, exemplified in the work of John Coltrane, Eric Dolphy, and Sun Ra, to name a very few. Black lesbian feminists—as many black feminists—reclaimed past black women writers such as Zora Neale Hurston, Nella Larsen, Alice Dunbar Nelson, and exalted contemporary black women writers, especially Alice Walker and Toni Morrison. According to Larry Neal, in his crucial article of the same name, "The Black Arts Movement is the aesthetic and spiritual sister of the Black Power concept," and called for a "cultural revolution in art and ideas" opposed to the "Western aesthetic . . . which must either be radicalized or destroyed."[5] The ritual of rejection of all manner of white patriarchal narratives was as crucial to black lesbian feminists as rejection of the "Western [white] aesthetic" was crucial to black arts literacy. Such rejections made a counter narrative, that is, change, imperative.

Black lesbian feminists struggled with white lesbian feminists for reallocations of resources within their communities, and—along with other women of color—opened spaces within lesbian-feminist organizations for more diverse representation and participation. By the time black lesbian feminists became visible and active, the black power phase of the African American freedom struggle had waned; and J. Edgar Hoover's Counter Intelligence Program[6] had destroyed or disabled most black nationalist and revolutionary organizations. Black lesbian feminists, while critical of racism and class oppression within the lesbian feminist movement, rejected black nationalism and lesbian separatism, and warily participated in multiracial enterprises and alliances that included white lesbians.

Instrumentality of Poetry

Longings for a militant literacy, sexual autonomy, and a poetics uncircumscribed by whiteness and maleness fomented black lesbian feminist production circa 1973–1979. By the early seventies lesbian feminists—mostly white, some black—were forming and joining autonomous women's organizations, institutions, businesses, and communities—some as separatists. They shared a desire for "women-identified-women's" culture and politics. U.S. black, Latina, Native American, and Asian lesbians embraced feminism more visibly in the seventies.

> San Francisco was inundated with women poets, women's readings, & a multilingual woman presence, new to all of us & desperately appreciated. . . . During the same period, Shameless Hussy Press & The Oakland Women's Press

Collective were also reading anywhere & everywhere they could. In a single season, Susan Griffin, Judy Grahn, Barbara Gravelle, & Alta, were promoting the poetry & presence of women in a legendary male-poet's environment. This is the energy & part of the style that nurtured *for colored girls.* . . .

In the summer of 1974 I had begun a series of seven poems, modeled on Judy Grahn's The Common Woman . . .[7]

In the passage above, Ntozake Shange describes her witness of the ways women's literary culture changed women's lives in the 1970s. That Shange cites the work of lesbian feminist poet Judy Grahn and the West Coast women's independent press movement as having enabled and influenced *for colored girls who have considered suicide when the rainbow is enuff* is striking. In 1976, citing an allegiance to feminism and lesbianism was still risky for ostensibly straight black women writers. Even more striking is the poet's omission of her debt to the Black Arts Movement. Shange was deeply influenced by the movement's vernacular poetics and politics, its theater, and its reverence for the new music. Like her older black lesbian poet sisters, Pat Parker and Audre Lorde, Shange had lived through the Black Power Movement and carried its lessons to the nascent feminist projects in which she became involved. The lessons of the Black Arts Movement internalized by black lesbian feminists were internalized by white lesbian feminists. Perhaps in citing Grahn as an influence,

Shange pays tribute to her Black Arts influence. (Rather like knowing that behind every Jerry Lee Lewis there's a Little Richard.)

This article focuses primarily on how Black Arts strategies were deployed by black lesbian feminist writers to advance a "cultural revolution of art and ideas" about women. The texts of black women writers, mostly poets, will be used to read the "racial" and cultural strategies applied by proponents of Black Arts and black lesbian feminism. It will illuminate tensions, ruptures, erasures, elisions, and intertextualities. It is hoped that there will be some illumination of the theory that "Black Aesthetic theorizing [which] opened up exciting new possibilities of artistic experimentation . . . and sought to redefine the relationship between writer and audience" created spaces for lesbian feminists to do the same thing.[8]

Despite its antifeminism, homophobia, and heterosexism, the uncompromising assertion of identity politics practiced by Black Arts exponents served black lesbian-feminist writers well—as it did much of the multicultural lesbian feminist movement. The counter-historical narrative, the rejection of the "West," the reverence for same ("race" and/or sex), the embrace of revolution, the taking of public space, the establishment of alternative institutions and venues were the literacies many lesbian feminists appropriated and reappropriated from the Black Arts Movement. This paper will privilege black lesbian feminist appropriations.

Black Arts, Sexism, and Homophobia

I am not a lesbian but I would like to have a real experience with a
girl who is. What should I do?

—June Jordan, "The Talking Back of Miss Valentine Jones"

From Montgomery, Alabama in 1955 to the San Francisco Bay Area in 1970,[9] black women were key organizers, theorists, revolutionists, and artists and coexisted with subtle and overt forms of sexism, male chauvinism, and male dominance in the black freedom struggle. According to Paula Giddings, "when the [civil rights] movement began to deteriorate after 1964, the intensity of that chauvinism increased."[10] In her 1974 autobiography, Angela Davis speaks of her firsthand experiences with male domination. Giddings uses this example in *When and Where I Enter.* As Davis tells it, she was organizing speakers for a political rally in San Diego in coalition with several other groups, among them Ron Karenga's U.S. organization, when she "ran headlong into a situation . . . to become a constant in my political life," that is, the dread male jealousy of competent women:

I was criticized very heavily, especially by male members of Karenga's organization, for doing "a man's job." Women should not play leadership roles, they insisted. A woman was supposed to "inspire" her man and educate his children.[11]

From 1975 to 1979, Ntozake Shange and Michele Wallace were censured roundly by the black intellectual community for their unsparing critiques of black male-female relationships in *for colored girls who have considered suicide when the rainbow is enuff* and *Black Macho and the Myth of the Superwoman* (1977). Robert Staples's long opinion piece in the then-influential journal *The Black Scholar* captures the curious defensiveness of black men over black women writing about the funky sexual politics in the black community. Staples, also an editor of *The Black Scholar,* stops short of calling black feminists an instrument in a white women's conspiracy to destroy black men:

> Since white feminists could not marshal an all out attack on black males, and well-known black female activists such as Joyce Ladner and Angela Davis would not, how could they be put in their place? Enter Ntozake Shange and Michele Wallace. While other black writers have trouble finding a forum to discuss the persistence of racist conditions, Ms. Shange's play, 'For Colored Girls Who Have Considered Suicide When the Rainbow Is Enuff' [sic] is on Broadway and road shows have drawn sell-out audiences throughout the United States. . . . Michele Wallace's new book, *Black Macho and the Myth of the Super-woman,* has been heralded as the most publicized book since *Roots.* . . . Watching a performance [of *for colored girls* . . .] one sees a collective appetite for black male blood.[12]

Whither sexism goes, heterosexism does not lag far behind, if lag at all. In the passage quoted at the beginning of this section, June Jordan's questioner is seeking advice from Miss Valentine Jones regarding her desire to "sleep with a girl who is" a lesbian.[13] Talking back, Miss Jones counsels, "Jesus is the answer. Join the church. The Lord will keep you busy on weekends." Jordan's poem exposes the hazards of lesbian desire "within the circle" of blackness.[14]

Some, however, braved the hazards. Using as a guide Alice Walker's singular 1974 essay "In Search of Our Mother's Gardens," black lesbian feminist critic Barbara Smith visited the gardens of black literary foremothers and ushered in the watershed era of contemporary black feminist writing with her provocative essay "Towards a Black Feminist Criticism."[15] Her theory of reading black women's texts generated unparalleled conversations that more than twenty years later enrich the soil of black feminist thinking.[16] Smith asserted that lesbianism was a broad intellectual bed: "[Toni] Morrison's work poses both lesbian and feminist questions about black women's autonomy and their impact upon each other's lives."[17] Not content to keep herself busy on weekends with "the Lord," Smith proposed the same theory at a Black Writers Conference at Howard University in 1978. Smith thought herself on the solid ground of a beloved black text when she made her claim that Morrison's "*Sula* is an exceedingly lesbian novel in the emotions expressed," hastening to add not that she meant Morrison is a lesbian and "[n]ot because the women are 'lovers,' but because they are the central figures, are positively portrayed and have pivotal relationships with one another." Interestingly, June Jordan was the moderator of the panel in which Smith participated, which also included Acklyn Lynch and Sonia Sanchez. Jordan had gone out on her own limb when she introduced the panel by telling the audience that she had been raped the fall before and, on a very primal level, understood why she needed feminism. Howard's Cramton Auditorium, which at that time held approximately 500 people, was filled to capacity. Audre Lorde was in the audience, along with twelve or thirteen other black lesbian feminists, including this writer, who had come to see and support Smith (and Jordan). A visceral collective groan resonated throughout the room when Smith said the words "lesbian novel." We witnessed extreme reactions from a number of well-known figures of the black cultural world—nationalists and non-nationalists—in response to Smith's lesbian reading. The emphatic hostility astounded both Smith and Jordan. In the midst of the contention both Lynch and Sanchez fled the stage to be other places, leaving Jordan and Smith to field all the questions, comments, sermons, and ravings. Jordan held the stage and Smith held her position. The audience was finally subdued enough for Stephen Henderson, Howard professor, literary critic, and conference organizer, to come onto the stage to close the session. Many people stayed to talk through and argue through the vexed questions of sexuality—lesbianism at that—with Smith, Jordan, and many of Smith's lesbian supporters. Why was this racial confluence disrupted? Smith's article deploys signal traits of Black Arts signifyin(g): critique of white cultural dominance and affirmation of black cultural traditions. However, their deployment in the interest of a lesbian reading, albeit black, did not make for a happy nexus with the black literary public, hell-bent on having its literature be heterosexual.

In 1979, Smith and Lorraine Bethel coedited *Conditions: Five, the Black Women's Issue.*[18] *Conditions: Five* featured for the first time in the history of African American literary strivings the work of self-identified black lesbian writers. However, Toni Cade Bambara's 1970 work *The Black Woman: An Anthology,* the first collection of writings by black women with feminist leanings, gave impetus to *Conditions: Five.* In their introduction to the issue the coeditors cite the perils of writing as a feminist or a lesbian "within the circle:"

> In choosing from the work that was submitted we placed a priority on writing concerning itself with the issues of feminism and lesbianism as they related to Black women. Our major reason for this standard comes from the belief that anti-feminism and homophobia in the Black community make it difficult, if not impossible, for Black women to publish lesbian/feminist writing in the traditional Black media.[19]

Newspapers, journals, anthologies, presses, and bookstores were established in the 1970s primarily by white women. Jan Clausen, in her little-known monograph, *A Movement of Poets,* discusses the enabling power of these independent ventures.

> By the mid-1970s, Diana Press and Daughters, Inc. had emerged as relatively powerful, well-organized lesbian controlled publishing efforts. Out & Out Books issued its first titles in 1975, among them *Amazon Poetry: An Anthology,* the largest collection of lesbian poetry then available, and the most comprehensive through the end of the decade. . . . Audre Lorde subsequently became poetry editor of *Chrysalis,* begun in 1976—as was the more explicitly lesbian-focused *Sinister Wisdom. Azalea,* a magazine by and for Third World Lesbians, and *Conditions,* a magazine of women's writing with an emphasis on writing by lesbians, began publication in 1977. Throughout the mid-1970s, most feminist presses and periodicals published substantial amounts of poetry . . . [and were] extremely important to lesbian poets because of their role in the development of a specifically lesbian-feminist literary culture and community.[20]

Despite the fact that most of the lesbian-run publications, bookstores, and presses were established by white women, women of color, including black women, were integral to this "lesbian-feminist literary culture and community."

Parallel Longings

If "I am a woman" had been the central proposition focusing the poetic explorations of early-'70's feminists, then "I am a lesbian" was by mid-decade the resounding theme . . . interpreted not merely in a sexual sense but as self-affirmation, proclamation of independence from patriarchy, and assertion of the primacy of emotional bonding among women, was indeed at the heart of their work.

—Clausen, *A Movement of Poets*

Much lesbian feminist poetry rejected heterosexual conventions just as the black arts poems rejected any sexuality but heterosexuality. Black Arts women poets proclaimed, "I am a black woman," privileging race as precedent and the primary category of struggle. Open heterosexuality was also the only sexual option for women (and men) in the circle of the black arts movement, as Sonia Sanchez's 1966 poem "to all sisters" proclaims:

> there ain't
> no MAN like a
> black man.
> he puts it where it is
> and makes u
> turn in/side out.[21]

Gender, because of the entire uppercasing of "man," seems to take precedence over race in this poem. Or perhaps it is heterosexuality that is primary in this early Sanchez poem, as she signifies sexual intercourse?

In Nikki Giovanni's "Seduction,"[22] the speaker announces a step-by-step process of how she will seduce/objectify her correct revolutionary brother. All the while she imagines him more intent on making revolution than on her *making* him: "I'll be taking your dashiki off . . . licking your arm . . . and unbuckling your . . . pants."[23] Cleverly Giovanni inserts herself into the narrative, heralding her heterosexuality—at least in the context of the poem. She imagines the object of her desire will question the revolutionary appropriateness of her move. "Nikki/isn't this counterrevolutionary . . . ?" One wonders if it is the sexual desire that the lover challenges or "Nikki's" initiative.

On a more somber note, Chicago poet Carolyn Rodgers is concerned with self-knowledge—as a black person and as a poet, but more ambivalent about her desire for artistic autonomy. Her 1969 poem "Breakthrough" hardly acknowledges gender except in the speaker's relationship to "littl [sic] bruthah" and "my man"[24] though the speaker's "partial pain" comes from her silence about being a woman writer. She best exposes her dilemma in the lines:

u see, the changes are so many
there are several of me and
   all of us fight to show up at the same time[25]

Are the "changes" producing "the several of me" or are the changes already produced by the losses of certain kinds of possibilities? Is there a resistance to the "dialectics of [black] women's lives," that is, the contradictory and complex affiliations that vie for black women's commitments?[26] Audre Lorde once longed for a place she could go where all of who she was would be accepted—that is, those female selves, namely mother, lesbian, feminist. Does Rodgers' anxiety about the "several of me" mask her anxiety about self-assertion, particularly if that self-assertion is as a woman? And as Lorde says "within the confines of Black society . . . the punishment for any female self assertion is still to be called a lesbian and therefore unworthy of the attention or support of the scarce black male."[27]

The speaker's pain is primarily related to the all-consuming requirements of blackness, which she quite poignantly laments:

I am very tired of trying
and want Blackness which is my life, want this to be
easier on me, want it not to suck me in and
out so much leavin me a balloon with no air, want it
not to puff me up so much sometimes
that I git puffed up and sucked in to the
raunchy kind of love Black orgy I go through.[28]

"Breakthrough" is the poet's longing to be understood for who she is by the people for whom she is writing.

    I really hope that
if u read this u
will dig where I'm at
and feel what i mean/that/where
    i am
and could very possibly
    be
    real
at this lopsided crystal sweet moment . . .[29]

Untypically, Rodgers uppercases her first person pronoun, "I," throughout the poem until the sixth and seventh lines from the end. This shift to a lowercase first person, "i," could possibly be a typographical error or the poet's subversion of her self-assertion.

The insistence on heterosexuality causes one of the great tensions between the poems of the Black Arts and lesbian feminist movements. Audre Lorde's 1971 "Love Poem"[30] a metaphoric tour de force about oral and digital penetration, counters the obligatory nods to heterosexuality. Though a bold post–Black Arts Movement move, the speaker's identity is still coded.

fingers whispering sound
honey flowed
from the split cups
impaled on a lance of tongues[31]

Using as a model Black Arts' poets' critiques of white people and white institutions, Pat Parker's 1978 poem "Exodus (To my husbands and lovers)" quietly refuses marriage, the cornerstone of heterosexual culture:

i will serve you no more
in the name of wifely love
i'll not masturbate your pride
    in the name of wifely loyalty[32]

Movement In Black, a collection of Pat Parker's poetry originally published by Diana Press in 1978, is constructed as a black woman's emotional and political journey. Sometimes the poems are autobiographical. "Exodus" appears in the first section, "Married," and marks the speaker's refusal to be bound within an institution she likens to slavery: "Hidden within folds of cloth / a desperate slave."[32]

Kay Lindsey, one of the contributors to Toni Cade Bambara's anthology, *The Black Woman,*[34] rejected the black nationalist assertion that women should be the custodians of the revolution:

I'm not one of those who believes
That an act of valor, for a woman
Need take place inside her.

My womb is packed with mothballs
And I hear that winter will be mild.[35]

The Black Arts Movement demanded that black men *and* the
"race" become men, as evidenced in Nikki Giovanni's popular
1968 poem "The True Import of the Present Dialogue, Black vs.
Negro."[36] Whether read by Giovanni or any other reader *schooled*
in the word, during its heyday "Present Dialogue" left audiences
breathless with its incantatory query, "Nigger / Can you kill / Can
you kill." Black arts poets, such as the black preacher, allowed
audiences to engage in what Lawrence Levine calls "ritualistic hyp-
nosis."[37] The shifts in address from "you" to "we" signify the dis-
sensions in the movement over the instrumentality of violence.
Obviously being "a nigger" is inconsistent with manhood and rev-
olutionary behavior. One wonders if the speaker is including
women in the invocations of "you" and "we." Perhaps women fall
into the "nigger" category, as "nigger" is only instrumental to the
understanding of what a man (or a revolutionary) is not? Thus, I
agree with Phillip Bryan Harper's argument in *Are We Not Men:
Masculine Anxiety and the Problem of African-American Identity*
that the "insistent use of the second person pronoun" in much of
black arts poetry by men and women, and particularly in "True
Import," represents "the implication of intraracial division within
the black Aesthetic poetic strategy."[38]

Giovanni chooses not to invoke gender until the poem's last

line, when the "we" is masculinized through the "killing" of the "white" and the "nigger."

> Can we learn to kill WHITE for BLACK
> Learn to kill niggers
> Learn to be Black men[39]

Perhaps Giovanni is projecting an urgency for unity, for everybody to be "one nation in a groove," not to focus on any identities that might rend one from pursuit of blackness *cum* manhood. The "race" must be masculinized, and women are erased in the race's race to manhood.

In her poem "Of Liberation" the irrepressible Giovanni, exploiting the stereotypes of lesbians and gays as weak and cowardly, tries to shame the indecisive subject, "black people," into organizing:

> Dykes of the world are united
> Faggots got their thing together
> (Everyone is organized)
> Black people these are facts
> Where's your power?[40]

The volume in which this poem appears, *Black Judge/Ment,* was published in 1968, a year before the Stonewall rebellion in New York City, which ushered in the gay liberation movement. Perhaps we can credit Giovanni with prefiguring the new demands for homosexual rights. This poem is striking for its appropriation of what would become the reclaimed terms of lesbian and gay liberation to advance timeworn stereotypes of black people as unorganized, trifling, "3/5 of a man/100% whore."[41] Giovanni, whose poetry is a running critique of the unreadiness of black people for liberation, became one of the chief female enunciators of the new black consciousness, the "princess of black poetry," according to the acerbic Michele Wallace in *Black Macho and the Myth of the Superwoman.*[42]

Audre Lorde's poem "Who Said It Was Simple"[43] theorizes on the complexity of privilege and oppression. It opens with the cautionary words about the dangers of repressed anger:

There are so many roots to the tree of anger
that sometimes the branches shatter
before they bear.

The narrative tells of an "almost white counterman" who passes a "waiting brother" to serve first a group of white "ladies [who] neither notice nor reject / the slighter pleasures of their slavery." Conflicts and contradictions will destroy revolutionary possibility as long as privilege is unexamined. Issues of color, class, sex, and gender collide as never before in this terse and packed eighteen-line lyric. "Simple" is one of the earliest black feminist testaments of the simultaneity of oppressions and one of Lorde's many critiques of a core Black Art tenet, to "be black first."[44]

By 1973, Lorde had allied with the lesbian feminist movement, though she always maintained contacts with other progressive and radical movements. Like many political poets of the era, Lorde, writer, teacher, librarian, lent her strong voice to many progressive causes. *From a Land Where Other People Live* was nominated for a National Book Award, along with Adrienne Rich for *Diving into the Wreck* and Alice Walker for *Revolutionary Petunias*. Rich won and insisted on sharing the award with her sister feminists, Walker and Lorde. All three books cross the restricted borders of race, sexuality, gender, and class. All three texts critique heterosexual, white, and/or male institutions, for example, motherhood, marriage, and nation.

From a Land Where Other People Live exemplifies these critiques. Most of the poems were written between 1969 and 1971 and signal black feminists' break with black nationalist politics and mainstream white feminism.

Lorde's 1973 poem "Now" signifies on black power by rejecting its primacy:

Woman power

is

Black power

is

Human power[45]

Refuting the black nationalist charge that feminism ("Woman power") and blackness are binary opposites, Lorde makes them equivalently human. The title of the poem implies there is no time like the present, that is, "Now," to accept the multiplicity of who one is.

Compulsory manhood and heterosexuality marred and limited the accomplishments of the Black Arts Movement. However, the assertive and militant literacy, assumed provocatively by the black women poets, enabled black lesbians to open a space within the circle of lesbian feminism for themselves and other women of color. Now, the essay will move forward to discuss black lesbian feminist applications of black arts literacies.

Nikki Giovanni's "True Import" finds its parallel in Lorraine Bethel's poem "What Chou Mean *We*, White Girl," with its fantasy of an autonomous black lesbian feminist community suggested in its expansive subtitle, ". . . Or, The Cullud Lesbian Feminist Declaration of Independence/(Dedicated to the Proposition That All Women Are Not Equal, i.e. Identical/ly Oppressed)." This poem critiques the tokenism within the lesbian feminist movement and utters very bitter commentary on the material privilege of white lesbian feminists and their institutions, "Volvos, country houses, town apartments, health centers, stores, magazines, universities' compared to the virtual lack of resources which often limited black women's participation in movement culture.

I am so tired of talking to . . .
the "I really want to know what your life is like without/
giving up
    any of my privileges
to live it" white women
. . . while we [black women] wonder where the next meal,
    job,
payment on/
    our college loans
    and other bills,
the *first* car, Black woman-identified bookstore, health/center,
magazine, archives, bar, record company, newspaper, press,
forty/acres and a mule,

    or national conference
    are going to come from.[46]

Though white lesbians are demonized for their acquisitiveness by the speaker, she longs for many of the same acquisitions for black lesbians. Black women "who won't deal with *real* sista love,"[47] that is, whose lovers are white women, come in for several rounds of vilification. Like the black nationalist claim on the sexual loyalty of black people to one another, Bethel's vision of a black lesbian nation won't include the ones

who've accepted and glorify in myth roles
Black bull dyke stud or Black
lesbianfeministgoddesstokenstar
of the white women's community
modern day political and apolitical minstrels in colored girl
    face . . .
We will leave them[48]

The poem's chanting enjambment, its black vernacular ease, its spillage of depredations of the enemies of "Black people Black women Black lesbian feminists"[49] pay homage to the Black Arts poets and are indicative of the speaker's desire to see a tradition of black culture.

They will come
from us loving/speaking *to* our Black/Third World/
sisters not *at* white women
They will come
from us taking Black woman energy presently being used
to legitimize your [white women's] movement[50]

The poem's yearnings for a black lesbian nation are every bit as serious as, say, Sonia Sanchez's call for a revolutionary black culture in many of her Black Arts era poems. Harper very astutely sees Sanchez's "blk/rhetoric"[51] as "writing beyond the end" of Baraka's poem "SOS," in which "all black people" are called presumably to join the "nation," but the poem never says. Harper continues with his intertextual interpretation of Sanchez's poem as a "calling into question what will ensue among the black collectivity after it has heeded the general call."[52] Sanchez asks: "who's gonna give our young/blk/people new heroes. . . ."[53] As in "True Import" and the Bethel poem, we see the concern for correct behavior, as the speaker catalogues activities in which young black people should not be engaging: "wite whores," "drugs," "new dances," eating "chitterlings," drinking "a 35 cents bottle of wine," "quick/fucks in the hall/way/of wite/america's mind." These latter references, especially "white whores" and "quick fucks in the hall/way," offer a critique of male behavior cleverly concealed in the category "young blk people." The elision allows for the critique to be heard by those who need to hear it without endangering the poet's status within the circle of blackness. This is rather different from Harper's theory of the speaker inside the circle of blackness defining intraracial distinctions, so that "Black Arts poetry . . . achieves its maximum impact in a context in which it is understood as being *heard* directly by whites, and overheard by blacks."[54] Both the white people who hear the signifying directly and the blacks who overhear it are "without the circle." However, Bethel's speaker defies both theories, for she situates her speaker outside the space of privileged white lesbian feminists and "'Black/lesbianfeministgoddesstokenstar[s]," and whoever white or black hears or overhears her signifying will not endanger her status.

Nationalist Nostalgia and Revisionist Motherhood

The important "A Black Feminist Statement," written in 1977 by the Combahee River Collective, is a manifesto that posited black feminism as radical praxis and ideology.[55] It opposed the "bourgeois feminist stance" of the National Black Feminist Organization (NBFO), founded in 1973; the Combahee River Collective had been the NBFO's Boston chapter in 1974–1975. The Combahee statement helped stimulate the development of black lesbian feminist organizing, but although it emphasizes racism, sexism, and classism as the political "province" of black feminist struggle, homophobia and heterosexism are not referenced at all, even though the writers refer to themselves as "feminists and lesbians." The submersion of the lesbian into the feminist identity functions in a way similar to Sanchez's elision of any direct critique of black male behavior discussed above in the poem "blk/rhetoric." Because the Combahee statement accuses black men and black people of being "notoriously negative" toward and "threatened" by feminism,[56] the manifesto writers might have worried that a strong statement about the antigay and antilesbian attitudes of the black community would risk driving another wedge between black (lesbian) feminists and the rest of the black community. The manifesto also erases all but negative history of work with white feminists. While it says black feminists "must struggle together with black men against racism" and "struggle with black men about sexism,"[57] "[e]liminating racism in the white women's movement is by definition work for white women to do."[58] In the Combahee statement, as in "What Chou Mean *We*, White Girl," a nostalgia for a black nationalism is expressed, even though both lesbian separatism and black nationalism are rejected by the Collective.

Black feminists were not the only black people who posited a nationalist longing. In *how i got ovah*, Carolyn Rodgers' fourth book of poetry since 1968, she critically reexamines her contributions to the black cultural revolution, her relationship to blackness, and, in many of the poems expresses concerns about her heterosexuality. Five of the poems, were published previously in her 1969 volume, *Songs of a Black Bird*. A singularly stunning poem in this collection is "I Have Been Hungry," which the author tells us in a preface

> was written because I was asked to contribute to an anthology of black and white women, and the title of the anthology was *I Had Been Hungry All My Years*[59]

Published three years before Lorraine Bethel's "What Chou Mean *We*, White Girl," it expresses some of the same tensions, though from a decidedly antifeminist and antilesbian perspective. The poem is a good example of how feminism had permeated the poetry of nonfeminist black women. "I Have Been Hungry" expresses the same anger at black women's instrumentality to white women. While Bethel's poem expresses anger at being a token, Rodgers's poem is suspicious of sisterhood with white women because

there is still the belief that
i am
a road
you would travel
to my man.[60]

Despite the loneliness, always a recurring theme in her poetry, Rodgers rejects sisterhood because of her fantasy of women's liberation as sterile lesbianism:

do not tell me
liberated tales of woman/woeman
who seek only to *satisfy them selves*
with them selves, all, by them selves
I will not believe you
I will call you a dry canyon
them, a wilderness
of wearying failures . . .[61]

"Hungry" talks about relationships with men as a "puffing out," without which a woman is deflated, hungry, insubstantial. Of course by 1975 artistic cross-fertilization had taken hold, despite sacred and secular nationalisms and strident separatisms. Feminist ideas, though not often identified as such, began to influence contemporary black women's writing, if only in terms of hostile responses. "Hungry" seems to chide feminists for stating the obvious, the always already fact that women are women:

> ah, here i am
> and
> here have i been
> i say.[62]

Conventional motherhood came under heavy examination during the '70s both by white and black feminists and lesbian feminists. Yet, at the same time, leading poets such as Adrienne Rich, a mother of three sons and a lesbian, and Audre Lorde, a self-defined black lesbian feminist mother of two, were busy reinventing and renegotiating motherhood. Rich, during this time, had published a major feminist statement, *Of Woman Born*.[63] Lorde's references to children in her poems are myriad; children are future, regeneration, and liberation from the old paradigms. And her treatment of motherhood sometimes borders on essentialism. At the base of lesbian-feminist critiques of motherhood is the struggle to separate sex from procreation. Rich and Lorde, however, gave voice to the sensual and sexual feelings involved in mothering. Lorde, particularly, believed that women, feminists, lesbians should not give up mothering and constantly challenged women not to limit mothering to the biological and to "Speak proudly to your children / wherever you may find them."[64]

Regeneration had been a key theme in the poetry of women and men of the Black Arts Movement. Regeneration for women not only meant childbearing capacities, but also strength, indestructibility, infinite powers. Mari Evans's poem "I Am a Black Woman" epitomized, in unimpressive, spare enunciations, the provincial black arts perception of black womanhood: "I / am a black woman . . . strong beyond all definition."[65] Nikki Giovanni's humorous and hyperbolic "ego tripping" continues this trend: "My strength flows ever onward."[66] The relentless reified "I" of "ego-tripping" finds itself lowercased in Sonia Sanchez's "for blk/wooomen: the only queens of this universe," an encomium of black women's "blk" omnipotence; and like Evans's black woman, she can cause the world to be "shaken" and "reborn."[67] Perhaps influenced by the Black Arts Movement, white poets also celebrated birth—a birth of new consciousness—despite the lesbian feminist rejection of conventional motherhood. Using imagery of the birth process, Jan Clausen's poem "A Christmas Letter"[68] manifests this interest, as the speaker warns her mother of her own impending breach with the old ways: "we can't sit around talking / in the womb anymore / for i already have / begun to be born."[69]

Black Women Poets and the Public

The African American freedom struggle of the 1960s sought to redefine Africans in North America and in so doing to transform the

African American psyche. Black writers and other artists were integral to the transmission of this new black consciousness. The sixties revolution in black arts, that is, the writing, theatre, music, and rhetoric of African American people, cleared a large space—almost two hundred years' worth—for poetry's complex tutelage; and poetry became a deep resource for the 1960s' black revolution in letters.

The dialogic relationships of black nationalist poetries and black lesbian feminist and lesbian feminist poetries continued throughout the '70s. Black Arts women reified heterosexuality and nation, black and white lesbian feminist poets reified lesbian sexuality and lesbian "ways of knowing." But as we have seen, feminism was not lost on black arts women poets nor was black autonomy lost on black lesbian feminists. Even those non-feminist women who remained for a time within the circle of the Black Arts Movement offered coded critiques of the sexism of black men as in Sanchez's "blk/rhetoric" and Giovanni's "Seduction" and "True Import."

The literacy gained from black movement poetry became a large house of resistance to patriarchal culture—black and white. Audre Lorde's 1978 collection of poetry, *The Black Unicorn,* is an amazing statement of a black lesbian "cosmology and mythology,"[70] rooted in Dahomey, West Africa, which is the place where Lorde traces her own lineage of woman-centered consciousness. Black lesbian feminism continued its expressivity throughout the 1980s, into the era of Reaganism and bourgeois narcissism. Black dyke pasts were recovered and invented by writers and critics like Jewelle Gomez, Gloria Hull, Ann Allen Shockley, and this writer—from within and without the accepted traditions of poetry and history. In "for muh dear," Carolyn Rodgers celebrates the black self's permeability to blackness, that is, "black lay backin and rootin."[71] Black Arts poetics "lay backin and rootin" in the vernacular and written culture of black lesbian feminists. Black lesbian feminist literacy of sexuality exposes the sexist and heterosexist (homophobic) commitments of Black Arts practitioners, and simultaneously pays homage to its revolutionary literacy.

Notes

1. Amiri Baraka, *Transbluesency: Selected Poems, 1961–1995* (New York: Marsilio Publishers, 1995), 142.

2. *Ibid.*

3. Audre Lorde, *Sister Outsider* (Freedom, Calif.: Crossing Press, 1984), 37.

4. LeRoi Jones, "Black Dada Nihilismus," in *The Dead Lecturer* (New York: Grove Press, 1964), 62.

5. Larry Neal and Michael Schwartz, *Visions of a Liberated Future: Black Arts Movement Writings* (New York: Thunder's Mouth Press, 1989), 184, 186.

6. COINTELPRO was the FBI's secret and well-known war against "black nationalist, hate-type groups . . . to expose, disrupt, misdirect, discredit, or otherwise neutralize" them. J. Edgar Hoover, "1967 Memorandum to Special Agent in Charge, Albany, New York," in *Modern Black Nationalism: From Marcus Garvey to Louis Farrakham,* edited by Van Deburg (New York: NYU Press, 1997), 134.

7. Ntozake Shange, *for colored girls who have considered suicide when the rainbow is enuff* (New York: Collier-MacMillan, 1977).

8. David Lionel Smith, "The Black Arts Movement and Its Critics," *American Literary History,* vol. 3, no. 1 (Spring 1991), 93–110.

9. The Montgomery (Alabama) bus boycott was spearheaded by several black constituents in Montgomery: NAACP president E. D. Nixon, Joanne Robinson, head of the Women's Political Council, and later the young minister Martin Luther King, Jr., who was asked by Nixon to head the Montgomery Improvement Association. The bus company observed a segregated seating policy, of course. Giddings reports in *When and Where I Enter: The Impact of Black Women on Race and Sex in America* (New York: William Morrow & Co., Inc., 1984) that a fifteen-year-old girl was jailed for refusing to move to the back of the bus just weeks before the famous incident with Rosa Parks. However, "[t]he girl's mother forbade her to appear in court, for her daughter was visibly pregnant—and unmarried" (263). Nixon believed that Parks's " case would be the better case to test the law. The time that she was arrested was not Parks's first transgression of the city's transportation segregation codes. "Parks . . . was previously evicted from a bus and sometimes drivers refused to pick her up," (262). According to Branch, in *Parting the Waters,* "All thirty-six seats of the bus she (Parks) boarded were soon filled, with twenty-two Negroes seated from the rear and fourteen whites from the front. Driver . . . seeing a white man standing in the front of the bus . . . called out for the four passengers on the row just behind the whites to stand up and move to the back" ([New York: Touchstone, 1988], 129). Rosa Parks, the only one of the four black riders, was arrested for refusing to give up her seat to the white man. Parks, secretary of the Montgomery NAACP, seamstress, and community activist, chose and was chosen to be "the symbol of the challenge to southern segregation" (Giddings, 265). After a year of organized boycotting of the bus system, black citizens won their right to sit where they wanted. Montgomery was a major victory in the struggle against segregation in the South and ushered in a whole new phase of the African American freedom

struggle. The Free the Soledad Brothers Movement in California had been organized to defend the rights of three black prisoners, George Jackson, John Cluchette, and Fleeta Drumgo, who had been accused of killing a prison guard. This prison guard, O. G. Miller, had just been acquitted on grounds of justifiable homicide, of killing three black prisoners in a prison-instigated melee. Angela Davis became one of the chief activists involved in their political defense activities. In 1970, also, Jackson's younger brother, Jonathan, along with three others, was killed in a shoot-out in the parking lot of the Marin County courthouse after trying to free two San Quentin prisoners in court on assault charges. In 1971, George Jackson was murdered in the prison yard of San Quentin Prison, where he and his codefendants had been transferred. Angela Davis, at the time of George Jackson's death, was in jail in Marin County preparing for her trial on charges of murder and kidnapping in connection with the Marin County shoot-out. Davis emerged victorious in 1972. Angela Davis, *Angela Davis: An Autobiography* (New York: Random House, 1974).

10. In *When and Where I Enter,* Giddings provides a rich feminist narrative of black women's historical leadership in the freedom struggles of Afro-Americans, particularly in her telling of the race and gender collisions at the height of the civil rights/black power movements, 1955–1965. See Mary King, *Freedom Song: A Personal Story of the 1960's Civil Rights Movement* (New York: William Morrow, 1987), and Sara Evans, *Personal Politics,* for white women's accounts of their experiences as members of SNCC. Anne Moody's *Coming of Age in Mississippi* (New York: Dell, 1968) remains a vivid story of a black woman's account of her SNCC experiences during the voting rights struggle in Mississippi. *A Circle of Trust: Remembering SNCC* (Cheryl Greenberg, ed. [New Brunswick, N.J.: Rutgers University Press, 1998]) is published from the taped sessions of the 1987 SNCC conference and reunion. Black and white women, such as Diane Nash, Mary King, Joann Grant, Bernice Johnson Reagon, Casey Hayden, and others share memories of their experiences as SNCC staffers and volunteers. The notorious 1964 position paper on women in the organization is contentiously discussed

in the chapter "SNCC Women and the Stirrings of Feminism." Joan Nestle, lesbian feminist writer whose lesbianism predates Stonewall, writes compellingly about her experience of the 1965 Selma to Montgomery march in "This Huge Light of Mine" from her book of essays, *A Restricted Country* (Ithaca, N.Y.: Firebrand Books, 1988): "I did not put the word *Lesbian* on my [white index] card. I put Jewish and feminist. . . . I did not talk about the bars I went to and the knowledge about bigotry I had gained from being a queer" (61).

11. Angela Davis, *Angela Davis: An Autobiography* (New York: Random House, 1974), 161.

12. *The Black Scholar* (May/June, 1975), 24–26.

13. June Jordan, "From the Talking Back of Miss Valentine Jones, No. 2," *Things I Hate to Do in the Dark* (New York: Random House, 1977), 152.

14. In his 1845 *Narrative of a Slave,* Frederick Douglass meditates on how he, as a slave, "did not understand the deep meanings of those rude, and apparently incoherent songs" which enveloped his childhood. Being "within the circle" of slavery necessitated a kind of self-protection from understanding the depth of the songs' expressions that once he was "without" the circle, that is, escaped from slavery, he could take in. Thus, being within the circle of blackness necessitates a self-protectiveness of the feeling/knowledge that, if known, would cause ostracism.

15. Barbara Smith, "Towards a Black Feminist Criticism," *Conditions: Two* (October 1977).

16. Black feminist critics and theorists have contributed mightily to the study of black women writers in the last twenty years. The late 1970s and 1980s was a watershed period of black feminist critical production. Truly, sometimes the criticism is as daring as the literary works themselves. Articles, anthologies, and books that have pushed me are: Akasha (Gloria) Hull, " 'Under the Days': The Buried Life and Poetry of Angelina Weld Grimke," *Conditions: Five, the Block Women's Issue* (1979), 17–47; Jewelle L. Gomez, "A Cultural Legacy Denied and Discovered: Black Lesbians in Fiction by Women"; Hull, "What It Is I Think She's Doing Anyhow: A Reading of Toni Cade Bambara's *The Salt Eaters*"; Linda C. Powell, "Black Macho and Black Feminism," all in *Home Girls* (1983) Smith, ed.; Hortense Spillers, "Interstices: A

Small Drama of Words," in *Pleasure and Danger, Exploring Female Sexuality,* edited by Carol Vance (San Francisco: Thorsons Publishing, 1991; June Jordan, *On Call: Political Essays.* (Boston: South End Press, 1985); Marjorie Pryse and H. Spillers, *Conjuring: Black Women, Fiction, and Literary Tradition* (Bloomington, Ind.: Indiana University Press, 1985); Hazel Carby, *Reconstructing Womanhood: The Emergence of the Afro-American Woman Novelist* (New York: Oxford University Press, 1987); Mary Helen Washington, "The Darkened Eye Restored: Notes Toward a Literary History of Black Women in." *Invented Lives: Narratives of Black Women, 1860–1960* (New York: Doubleday, 1987); Cheryl A. Wall, ed., *Changing Our Own Words: Essays on Criticism, Theory, and Writing by Black Women* (New Brunswick, N.J.: Rutgers University Press, 1989), esp. Hull's and Henderson's articles.

17. Smith, "Towards a Black Feminist Criticism," 33.

18. Elly Bulkin, Irena Klepfisz, Rima Shore, Jan Clausen founded *Conditions* as "a magazine of writing by women with an emphasis on writing by lesbians" in 1976 and published the first issue in 1977. *Conditions* closed its pages in 1990 because of flagging resources and editorial energy. During its years of publication, it became a repository of the multicultural lesbian literary culture. Its contributors included Paula Gunn Allen, Dorothy Allison, Gloria Anzalda, Jewelle Gomez, Judy Grahn, Joy Harjo, Audre Lorde, Cherrie Moraga, Minnie Bruce Pratt, Adrienne Rich, Sapphire, Shay Youngblood as well as Barbara Smith and this writer. *Conditions: Five,* however, caused the editors to rethink their commitments to lesbian communities. Not only must black women and other women of color see themselves on the pages of so-called lesbian publications, but they must also be involved in the decisions that produce those publications. In 1981, the editors recruited an eight-person collective, which included three African American women, one white working-class woman, one Latina, two Jewish women, and one white Anglo-Saxon Protestant lesbian. Successive collectives remained committed to this model as well as to each member's requisite lesbianism. This writer was a member of the collective from 1981 to 1990.

19. *Conditions: Five, The Black Women's Issue,* 12.

20. Jan Clausen, *A Movement of Poets* (Brooklyn: Long Haul Press, 1982), 17.

21. Leroi Jones and L. Neal, eds. *Black Fire: An Anthology of Afro-American Writing* (New York: William Morrow & Co, 1968), 255

22. Nikki Giovanni, *Black Feeling, Black Talk, Judgment* (Detroit: Broadside, 1970).

23. Ibid,. 38.

24. Carolyn Rodgers, "Breakthrough," in *how i got ovah* (Garden City, N.Y.: Anchor Press, 1976), 36.

25. Ibid., 35.

26. Deborah K. King, "Multiple Jeopardy" (1995), 300.

27. Audre Lorde, "Age, Race, Class, and Sex," *Sister Outsider: Essays and Speeches* (Freedom, Calif.: Crossing Press, 1984), 121.

28. Rodgers, *how i got ovah,* 36.

29. Ibid.

30. Audre Lorde, "Love Poem," in *Undersong: Chosen Poems, Old and New, Revised* (New York: W.W. Norton, 1992).

31. Ibid., 141.

32. Pat Parker, *Movement in Black* (Ithaca, N.Y.: Firebrand Books, 1985).

33. Ibid., 37.

34. Toni Cade Bambara, *The Black Woman* (New York: New American Library, 1970).

35. Ibid., 17. Emphasis added.

36. Giovanni, *Black Feeling, Black Talk, Black Judgment* (New York: William Morrow & Co., 1970), 20.

37. Lawrence Levine, *Black Culture and Black Consciousness: Afro-American Folk Thought from Slavery to Freedom* (New York: Oxford University Press, 1977). Levine pays close attention to the impact of black music on the physical and psychic survival of African Americans: "Secular

work songs resembled spirituals in that their endless rhythmic and verbal repetitions could transport the singers beyond time, make them oblivious of their immediate surroundings, and create a state of what Wilfrid Mellers has referred to as 'ritualistic hypnosis.' " (213).

38. Phillip Brian Harper, *Are We Not Men: Masculine Anxiety and the Problem of African-American Identity* (New York: Oxford University Press, 1996), 47.

39. Giovanni, *Black Feeling, Black Talk, Judgment,* 20.

40. Giovanni, *Black Judge/Ment* (Detroit: Broadside Press, 1968), 2.

41. Ibid.

42. Michelle Wallace, *Black Macho and the Myth of the Superwoman* (New York: Dial Press, 1978), 166.

43. Audre Lorde, "Who Said it Was Simple?" in *From a Land Where Other People Live* (Detroit: Broadside Press, 1974).

44. Don L. Lee, "Introduction: Louder but Sofdter," in *We Walk the Way of the New World Black Fire* (Detroit: Broadside Press, 1970), 180.

45. Audre Lorde, *Chosen Poems: Old and New* (New York: W.W. Norton, 1982), 88.

46. Lorraine Bethel, "What Chou Mean *We,* White Girl," in *Conditions: Five, the Black Women's Issue* (1979), 87–88.

47. Ibid., 89. Emphasis added.

48. Ibid., 90.

49. Ibid., 91.

50. Ibid., brackets mine.

51. Sonia Sanchez, "blk/rhetoric," *We a BaddddDDD People* (Detroit: Broadside Press, 1967).

52. Harper, *Are We Not Men?,* 43.

53. Sanchez, "blk/rhetoric," 15.

54. Harper, *Are We Not Men?,* 46.

55. Combahee River Collective, "A Black Feminist Statement," first published in *Capitalist Patriarchy and the Case for Socialist Feminism,* edited by Zillah R. Eisenstein (New York: Monthly Review Press, 1979).

56. Combahee River Collective, "Beyond the Margins: Black Women Claiming Feminism," in *Words of Fire,* edited by Beverly Guy-Sheftall (New York: The New Press, 1995), 237.

57. Ibid., 235.

58. Ibid., 239.

59. Rodgers, *how i got ovah,* 49.

60. Carolyn Rodgers, "I Have Been Hungry," in *how i got ovah.*

61. Ibid., 51. Emphases added.

62. Ibid., 52.

63. Adrienne Rich, *Of Woman Born* (New York: W.W. Norton, 1973).

64. Audre Lorde, "For Each of You," in *Chosen Poems* (New York: Norton, 1982), 43.

65. Marin Evans, *I Am a Black Woman* (New York: William Morrow Publishers, 1970), 12.

66. Nikki Giovanni, *The Women and the Men* (New York: William Morrow, 1975), 20.

67. Sonia Sanchez, "bit/rhetoric," *We A BaddDDD People,* 6.

68. Jan Clausen, "A Christmas Letter," in *Amazon Poetry2,* ed. Elly Bulkin and Joan Larkin (New York: Out & Out Books, 1975,) 52.

69. Ibid.

70. Fahmaisha Shariat, "The Black Unicorn" in *Conditions: Five, the Black Women's Issue* (1979), 173–176.

71. Rodgers, *how i got ovah,* 1.

Part Five
The Days of Good Looks:
2000–2005

Living as a lesbian underground, fin de siecle

here under this pile of 20th century,
my ass is sore from
taking in air on the underside of this mask.
so close i have worn it since the defoliation
of 14th street.
a high blown and wasted blues.
the same vamp after sorry vamp.
and burning indochine flesh.

Bald Woman

I am growing bald in a place hidden from ordinary sight
—except mine—and
held in memory most of the time.

I ask my lover if she is losing hers?
She laughs. And sleepily I grab at her sweats.
She kisses me 'nightie night' and climbs the two flights to
   bed.

I always knew I'd be here resenting the changes,
comparing them to others like my lovers the same age
and wondering do I look like I'm bald in a place
I could run my fingers
through
once.

Billie Holiday

mostly was thinking
about singing the song
once she got to carnegie,
columbia,
or cafe society
not
some fbi john back at
the attucks or the grampion
taping opium to the back of the commode
and stealing her money.
it's an intellectual process and
'in-dee-pendent-lee bloo-oo-oo.'
Calculating future
to tell the story this time
never the same way twice.
sung or heard
so many times the same story
but bent or slant
so constant and so uncertain.
the perfect tongue-in-cheek of
'to whomever you love.'
the empress pops prez.
a lost-wax process

PLEASE READ.

Pulaski, Tenn., July 15, 1883

DEAR FRIENDS:

I am trying to find out where my children are. Please help me. Their names are Diana, Henry, Drucilla and George Washington. Before the war we belonged to Mr. W. M. Thompson, in Rutherford County, North Carolina. About thirty years ago, after the death of our old Mistress, Diana and Drucilla were taken from me and carried into Georgia. George Washington was taken away from Jackson County, Alabama, by the soldiers during the war.

I, their mother, was Hannah Thompson, but have since married a man named Powers.

Please read this notice in the churches, and any one knowing of my children will confer a favor by writing to me.

Address,
HANNAH POWERS,
 Pulaski, Tennesee.

james dean longing

during a hard nod one night in 1972:
jerome johnson, red-eyed and aspiring
to film sibilant from his hot director's chair,
declaims:
    'jimmy was the first feminist!'
(confusing 'feminist' with 'faggot,' i think baldwin.)

later that year:
jerome johnson
gunned down in columbus circle
is framed for the evening news
butt facing the camera
the body of a famous mafioso on him
his brooch with cameo portrait of jimmy
snatched purposefully from his chest
by one of the assassins.

Inside the brooch:
james dean longing
his scowl and protean lips
tucked and disheveled
white trash and preppie
bloody

drunk

queer

(sal mineo

natalie wood

and rock hudson

pose for sex

just beyond the take)

Urban Epitaphs After 9/11/01

i. Kyra Mills
6 years old
last seen hold-
ing her mother's hand on the 92nd floor of Tower One.

ii. Chopra Dias
works on the 107th floor.
Last seen: 9/11
is diabetic
and wearing college ring on left hand.

Dreams of South Africa

i. Geography 1958
Photograph representing South African Apartheid to
    Catholic grade school children
in a second hand geography textbook
of a line of black black men
shirtless, frowning,
sitting down from the drudgery
of whatever menial work they'd been allowed to do
for the day with
racist middle school captions scribbled by previous users
        under each man: 'your boyfriend,' 'liver lips,' 'blackie.'

ii. South Africans
are white.
Does that mean whites are Africans
not Afrikaans? Whites are Africans.
That blows my mind given my current state of ignorance.

iii.
I was an aspiring petite bourgeoise in my second year of
college when the Unilateral Declaration of Independence
occurred in Rhodesia, now Zimbabwe. Ian Smith,
Rhodesia's president/dictator has the same name as a Holly-
wood Brit who played King Arthur among other character

roles in the 1930's. The progeny of Cecil Rhodes has a lot
to answer for.

iv.
I had a really serious auto accident the day I was to meet
Desmond Tutu's daughter in 1988. Sideswiped on the left
front by a tractor-trailer. The damage was such an eyesore
that my close friend, an agnostic, grabbed me and thanked
God I was alive. Bishop Tutu's daughter rode graciously to
and from the airport in that car. I asked after her father: 'He's
behaving himself,' she said grimly smiling. She damned
Apartheid eloquently and liked to smoke cigarettes after. She
defined family under apartheid as dedicated to its overthrow.

v. The two
Were actors.
One played a father, whose daughter dies in the revolution.
The other played his neighbor, an informer who redeems
himself. I drove them to the City that night after their inti-
mate two man performance. They would return to Johan-
nesburg before the week was out.

They were brown happy-talking men like the jaunty
	porcupine before she gives up her quills.
One 40-ish, the playwright;
the other 60-ish and handsome.

Both bore deep facial scars and keloid lesions.
Marks of apartheid. The drawer slammed shut on your
 sister's naked nipple.

To have a theater. To speak another truth.
They'd made many journeys alone and together, any one
could have meant certain death. Despite this they were
happy-talking men and brown.
'Is Fugard the only South African playwright you people
produce here?' the 40-ish brother called cheerily back to
me after our warm goodbyes.

vi.

A thirty day strike lends itself easily to poetry. 'Divest,' the
students told us. I was on their side though passing. I
unloaded gallons of spring water from my station wagon
every night at the site of the take-over. I read poetry,
rousing to cheers a sleepy crowd of 'township' members
after 15 days and nights camped on the commons, which
they renamed 'Biko Township.' The aim of poetry: to
silence obligatory clapping. Some chick before me plodded
self-righteously through a lecture on the plight of South
African women—black and white. Not so hard an act to
follow. She commended me for my poetry: 'You even
stirred this crowd.' She was an empirical chick and clearly
 skeptical until our encounter.

vii.

I was to do a reading somewhere in Manhattan. On the
program as well a member of the ANC talking on the
economics of Apartheid, how blacks fared, and what we,
in the 'West' could do.

He was a stocky, tight, brown spring, grossly preoccupied,
breathing audibly—what Fanon would call 'combat
breath'—and young not so young as Tutu's daughter,
but still younger than 40. And kind.

viii.

Having spent 17 long, wide, and tight days in the province
of Kwa Zulu Natal very close to the ground, the fevered
pitch of resistance can be heard and the lost bones of
children touched, back in Jersey City, an industrial berg
across from Manhattan on the Hudson, I accept the loss
of the Twin Towers on this frighteningly beautiful day. I
watch askance from the car on the Newark Bay Exten-
sion the Second Tower implode behind me and disinte-
grate in the space between my right shoulder and
earlobe.

A Sister's Lament as She Poses for an AP Photograph Holding Her Dead Sister's Portrait

Black women are accustomed to being firsts, and here you
　　go again being first:
Sgt. J. L. Winters,
'first [African] American [u.s.]/[black] servicewoman [of
　　mixed ancestry] to die since the war [against/with
　　Afghanistan] began.'

Says family friend, Ron:
'The price we have to pay for what happened on 9-11.'

Why?
Is your body to be bartered, levied, or charged? Does he
　　know it was priceless and peerless and that you knew
　　what you were stepping to?

and here I stand
for the public
holding this picture of you in your uniform
looking so pretty in it
and your eyes aren't convinced
or resigned
to being 'the price.'

Nor are mine.

We look eerily identical

but opposite.

I don't half-smile or look into the camera with old glory

    displayed behind me.

I fairly suck my teeth and stare piss-faced

askance with a suburban chimney as backdrop.

I look like a ventriloquist

holding this portrait instead of you in my arms.

I'm lonely as a convict out here outside of Gary,

while you are crashed into a mountainside in Pakistan.

A mysterious mistake.

Not 'hostile fire,' say the secretaries

and generals.

Were you thinking it'd end this soon?

We look eerily identical.

The days of good looks

i.

Slipping only back into Newark
on the rails I slip further back.
To my grandmother, Pearl.
Down.
Across that funky line.
And deeper in
where the 'Southern cross the Yellow Dog.'
And on back North, way North with
her never to look back
at that Carolina dirt again.
1918 and too good looking
to be moored to
its red hills.
My grandmother was a black black woman
in the days of good looks.

ii.

In the days of good looks I liked what I saw
and so did anybody else who looked at me.
    'You almost as pretty as your mother . . .
    Only almost. You're darker.'
I thought I was prettier than my mother and too
good lookin' to be a butch.

Not all mannish

like the studs on Seventh Street,

who I didn't like told me I wasn't good lookin' enough.

'You might as well git rid of that binding, and go git you a
     man.'

In the days of good looks staying on top was

work.

iii.

All got up in my butch

my Raleigh racer

and some silly brother

yelling running chasing me (on my racer)

     'Hey, good looking . . .

     Let me be your bicycle seat,

     baby. . . . yo' seat.'

Hollering down the whole block

not to be spurned somewhere in central Jersey

     'Hey, hey, big butt,

     yo' bicycle seat.

     I'll be yo' bicycle seat,

     Yo! Let me be yo' bicycle seat.'

July in a boisterous end of town in 1979

on a bicycle would make you commit mayhem in a car:

     'Hey, hey, bulldyke on a bike!

    Yo, little man.

    Let me be

    yo' little she

    dagger.'

In the days of good looks, a bicycle seat made for a tight
    fast butt.

iv.

The days of good looks are going

and it ain't just the lack of blood.

'Step out of your car

    and empty your pockets, ma'am.

    I smell Mary Warner.

    She's an illegal substance, you know.'

In the days of good looks I am always suspect.

v.

waiting to exhale

definitely on the make

a hooded hip-clad biracial-bisexual-moreno-filipino-
    nuyorican maroon 17

and destined for Christopher Street

gives me a V-sign

gesturing for a smoke—

not peace or victory—

at the train station
on a post-modern day in a pre-colonial berg.

Showing my flush pack
like a flush hand, I invite him to 'help yo'self, daddyo.'
He draws fire from my lit faggot, swivels his hips, and
    adjusts his head phones.
Reticently slips himself another blunt for the long night
    abroad.

'Good lookin,' he exhorts as if I too am on the make,
    exhaling that perilous silver stream.

vi.
In this hostile corridor
a quickening nostalgia suffuses
me, this late evening at the fin de siecle
between two endangered sites.
The marvelous
have been
blighted by
a blood borne scourge.
Flamboyantly frail, still marvelous,
you nourish these failing geographies.
As I face you over the counter
of this nasty KFC

and am dazzled by your articulated brows,
the delicately applied mascara,
the discrete texture of your facial skin.
Cultivated nails.
You recognize me too
by my precise haircut.

Lesbianism, 2000

THIS BRIDGE CALLED *My Back: Writings By Radical Women of Color* is a powerful presentation/representation of multicultural expressivity—one of the earliest and one of the best. *This Bridge* offered direction to so many women of color writers, predominantly lesbians in the successive years of lesbian-feminist publishing, and still remains a life-changing text. My deepest and long-overdue thanks to its original editors, Cherrie Moraga and Gloria Anzaldua. You gave me the opportunity to write and to publish the endlessly popular "Lesbianism: An Act of Resistance" back in 1979. From its very beginning, the essay took on a life of its own and caused contention within, among, and across diverse communities of women—queer, of color, white, straight, and otherwise, particularly college students. Every year since its publication, I have been invited to either a women's studies, black studies, or queer studies, cultural studies class to answer up to the assertions studding that essay. A writer could have no greater accomplishment than that her work gets read and talked about by many of the people for whom it is intended. And that's what happened with "Lesbianism: An Act of Resistance," and I am having a ball.

"Have you complexitized your ideas since you wrote this essay? I was turned off by them, because I'm excluded. I'm biracial and bisexual. What's in it for me?"

Five or six years ago (at this writing) a young woman student confronted me with this question. She objected to my characterizations of bisexuals and mixed-"race" people as impostors, poseurs, and passing as dominant. The passage to which the student refers follows and is one in a series of several complicated and problematic analogies of "lesbianism" and "blackness" assayed in "Lesbianism: An Act of Resistance":

> There is the woman who engages in sexual-emotional relationships with women and labels herself bisexual. (This is comparable to the Afro-American whose skin-color indicates her mixed ancestry, yet who calls herself 'mulatto' rather than black.)

The irreverence is absolutely intentional. Besides, who would want to call herself "mulatta/o" rather than "black" anyway? The student did not care for being the brunt of my Malcolm-X-Leroi Jones/Imamu-Baraka-type signifyin(g). She believed that I was advancing a purism about identity, sexuality, and race that contradicted the mestizo-ism of *This Bridge*, enunciated by the late Toni Cade Bambara in her 1979 "Foreword" to the first edition:

Blackfoot amiga Nisei hermana Down Home Up Souf Sis-
tuhsister El Barrio suburbia Korean The Bronx Lakota
Menominee Cubana Chinese Puertoriqueña reservation
Chicana campañera . . . Sisters of the yam Sisters of the rice
Sisters of the corn Sisters of the plantain putting in telecalls
to each other. And we're all on the line. (vi)

And I suppose the student was also wondering what makes me a
"radical" woman of color if I cannot get beyond the racialist and
monocultural norms of everyday life in U.S./North America. But
that was 1979 and I was "coming out"—not as "black" or as "lesbian"
—but as a "black lesbian writer," and brash spoken and written decla-
mations of identity were the primary tools I used to "break the
silence(s)"—as they had been used to break so many other silences.
"You hadda be there," I cajoled. "It was a stage," I continued to retort.
The student was still not convinced of lesbianism as an act of resist-
ance. I encouraged her and the rest of the class members to read the
essay in the context of the full *This Bridge* text. *Bridge*'s letters, journal
entries, poems, essays—"telecalls"—were flowers of declamation and
contamination, shouts of multiplicity, fire-words challenging all our
notions of identity, oppression, struggle as fixed modes of action. But
in "Lesbianism: An Act of Resistance" I chose the poetics of reification
—a strategy used so successfully by black arts movement practi-
tioners (roughly 1963 to 1975) to advance black nationalist practices.
This paradox-of-sorts critiques its practices of exclusion, sexism and

homophobia in black communities, and racialist judgementalism among black lesbians, and falls short of "theorizing" a multicultural lesbian-feminist future. Make no mistake, I am not going to "theorize" that here now.

Twenty years later I can say I don't give up black for African-American, don't give up gay for queer, and want to reaffirm my lesbian practice: "I am a mannish dyke, muffdiver, bulldagger, butch, feminist, femme, and PROUD." I don't give up feminist, which is a doppelganger for lesbian and always gives me a way to move. I do not wish to be a lesbian without feminism. Feminism still means roughly: the revolution that will liberate all women (and men) from patriarchal oppression. Lesbians need to be feminists, as do any really serious progressive people, and struggle to take on hybridity, to take on queer, to take on diasporas, to "work across" sexualities." And struggle to admit the always-already unready.

As much as I deplore the insertion of the self into the self's essay, I do feel the need to qualify. I have gone back and forth on the angle of this piece for *This Bridge We Call Home* (Routledge, 2000). Do I talk about the life of the essay "Lesbianism" over the last twenty years? Do I call this current essay "Lesbianism: An Act of Resistance 20 Years later"? Or do I pick up where I left off twenty years ago?— talking about loving ourselves as "the final resistance." (No, no, I won't pick up from there.) Or do I "complexitize" the ideas presented in the original, as the young bisexual, biracial woman recommended. (Others have already done that, e.g., Cathy Cohen, Evelynn Hammonds.) Do I cop to my "put downs": of light-skinned people of color, bi people as the "niggers in the woodpile" of heterosexuality, black lesbians who "castigate" other black lesbians for sleeping with white lesbians, black men who are "rabid heterosexual[s]," and heterosexuals who are enthrall to an institution that is the foundation of the "master-slave relationship between white and black people in the United States." No, I don't even want to take myself on. What I wrote stands on me as I stand on it.

Lesbianism has emerged at this time in my life as more of a strategy and less of a hard-and-fixed-identity-politics-that-I-am-going-to-be-no-matter-how-it-gets-deconstructed. One never knows how one may have to "live as a lesbian" trafficking in conservative-family-maniacal U.S. capitalist hegemony, do one? Lesbianism and feminism are mutually instrumental practices. In fact, I said earlier —they are "doppelgangers." Each stands in for the other. I prefer what dykes are putting down. (Dykes are feminists too.) But not every feminist has to prefer it, do it, or be it. Dig it? Dig it. Everybody ain't able. But everybody needs to be a feminist for her own good. I believe this more than ever, particularly since battering, rape, and other forms of violence against women (and children) are no less frequent—only less unheard of—than they were twenty years ago. Be feminists—it may just save your lives. Be feminists— and you may just save some other women's lives.

When *This Bridge* was being put together by its editors—more than twenty years ago—I was living a double life in the suburbs of New Jersey with a very suburban white feminist lover, her two daughters, writing sometimes, doing graduate work, and trying to be a black lesbian feminist. Read my biographical statement in another classic text of the period, i.e., Bulkin and Larkin's *Lesbian Poetry* (1981). I'd attended several black feminist retreats and meetings in Massachusetts, Connecticut, New York, and New Jersey, organized initially by black feminists in Boston. The twenty or so of us who joined each other at those retreats had histories in black civil rights, women's liberation, new left, black nationalist, black women's studies, black church. I'd been involved in one of the New Jersey defense committees for Assata Shakur. All of us had learned from the black power movement that we had to speak directly and publicly to our communities. We'd learned that we had to hold accountable all our people for our collective justice. We knew that a larger body of writing had to be created. We'd learned the power of words, angry words. We believed in the power of "mothers" and "sisters," i.e., the power of recovering the words of black women writers—past and present, live and dead. Audre Lorde was one of those sisters, amazons, warrior women we extolled; and she was very much a poet— "out there," in the street, hanging tough, palpable, reading her liberatory work, standing up and in for freedom, being a lesbian, being a feminist. Reread her 1978 collection of poems, *The Black Unicorn. Unicorn* is certainly a critical context and crucible for *Bridge,* as it throws down Lorde's challenge in "Solstice" to "never forget the warning of my woman's flesh."

Some of us are not brave.

However, we recovered, discovered, and paid long-overdue homage to others: Angelina Weld Grimke, Mae V. Cowdery, Alice

Dunbar Nelson, Zora Neale Hurston, Nella Larsen, Toni Morrison; and appropriated their characters: "Irene Redfield"/"Clare Kendry," "Big Sweet," "Sula" and "Nel," "Meridian," the "Ladies in Red, Yellow, Green, Brown, and Purple." Alice Walker gave us "Celie" and "Shug Avery." (Defying the behavior codes of straight black womanhood in U.S./North America, Ntozake Shange and Walker took a lot of heat for their gifts). We felt they belonged to us, and we had the right to read "lesbian" into the motive of every black woman writer and imagined black woman, including Morrison and "Sula." Morrison didn't like it one little bit. Also, some of us felt we should require allegiance to lesbian expressivity of all black women writers who claimed black women as their subjects. And we created quite a stir when we thought anyone was hedging or getting it wrong. As evidence, see the following excerpt from a 1982 taped conversation of fledgling black feminist critics about *This Bridge,* on the dilemmas of only writing homage:

> **L:**The search for perfection is something which also affected my view of *This Bridge Called My Back: Writings by Radical Women of Color.* With all the 'hooplah' which attended its publication, one would have expected it to be the definitive work on the issues of women of color in the United States. I suppose I also resented being defined as a woman of color, because I feel my blackness is subsumed. I guess I took that resentment out on the book. . . .
>
> **J:** . . . I don't feel blackness is subsumed in the 'women of

color' designation. . . . I would have liked more space devoted to women as artists and political beings. . . .

E: I feel *This Bridge* would have been much stronger had class and economics been addressed. . . . [but] I'll go on record about *This Bridge.* It is a valuable beginning.

B: Then I'll go on record about *All the Blacks are Men, All the Women are White, But Some of Us are Brave,* since it was the first composite of black women's studies. . . . [When I reviewed it] I wanted people to look at it themselves. I wanted . . . to say: "You have to look at it. Don't think it's wonderful in the world, but you need to look at it.". . . .

C: . . . . Sometimes I can't see my own value judgments getting in the way. Audre Lorde confronted me. . . . She said, "How come you criticize what isn't there? It's like you put the burden of the whole world on me." And my response to Audre was, "Well, now, Audre, you know we expect you to be perfect. "

In 1973, after four years of reckless heterosexuality, I collided high speed with lesbians and lesbianism. I spoke of this as an epiphanic moment in "Lesbianism: An Act of Resistance."

For me personally, the conditioning to be self-sufficient and the predominance of female role models in my life are the roots of my lesbianism. Before I became a lesbian, I often wondered why I was expected to give up, avoid, and trivialize the recognition and encouragement I felt from women in

order to pursue the tenuous business of heterosexuality. And I
am not unique. (134)

But now I am inclined to embellish this narrative with the fact of
my relationship with a jazz-loving, freaky, myopic white boy that
helped me cross over the burning sands of group disapproval/dis-
sension. I always wanted to be wild, after my sheltered bourgeois
black upbringing, and the "interracial" and the "lesbian" put me
right out there. Then that same year, 1973, Assata Shakur burst
on the scene after the notorious "shoot-out" on the New Jersey
Turnpike, just up the road from where I lived in New Brunswick,
N.J. Assata, a revolutionary black woman, became the symbol of
resistance against racist, capitalist, imperialist patriarchy for which
all progressive women longed. When Assata became pregnant by
one of her New York co-defendants while awaiting arraignment on
one of the many bogus charges the Government rigged up against
her, I, for one, was disappointed. I wanted her to "come out," like
Susan Saxe, as a revolutionary black amazon. Of course that wasn't
going to happen, because black nationalist organizations policed
her loyalties, marginalized her female lover, and ferociously
guarded her image as a black heterosexual revolutionary. None of
that would matter by 1977, when Assata escaped from Clinton
Prison, a minimum security facility for women in New Jersey, and
finally to Cuba.

You go, girl!

So, I came to appreciate how far out there lesbianism could send one—erotically and politically. I opted for above-ground agitation, lesbian visibility, and theoretical decentering of whiteness, maleness, heterosexuality. I was not crazy (or courageous) enough to be a warrior, and I was too nonconformist to be a soldier. By the time I was writing "Lesbianism: An Act of Resistance," I had become convinced that there existed multicultural bevies of lesbian communities just waiting for the words of lesbians. As a dyke prison activist once said to me, "So little has been said to us, everything is appreciated"; or as a well-known dyke organizer said quite recently at a public event, "To get applause from a lesbian audience, all you have to do is walk onto the stage." So, here was my moment to take that stage, to be the writer I'd always wanted to be, since my days of apprenticeship to blackness, to do it for lesbians about lesbians with lesbians. I could signify on the black intelligentsia (a favorite and frequent target of black writers), expose some funky little truths, and air some dirty laundry. These were the strategies that came together in "Lesbianism: An Act of Resistance" as well as its nearly-as-well-known companion piece, "The Failure to Transform: Homophobia in the Black Community" (*Home Girls,* 1983).

The time was then to illuminate the failures of one's groups. The time is now as well. I learned from the black arts to be direct, relentless, and mocking. Plus, if I could cop as pompous a tone as, say, Baraka, Larry Neal, or Nikki Giovanni—a form of what my sister calls "beration therapy"—I would have struck a black blow for lesbianism and feminism, as Audre Lorde and June Jordan had been striking for years. Oh, to be in that company! This performance of

Black Arts style catapulted my message all over black queer communities. And I have been thanked over and over by black queer people for the performance of this style. What was this "style" a performance of? Anger. Anger—the righteous "eye to eye"—projected at the sources of one's people's woes—racist, heterosexist, capitalist patriarchy (i.e., homophobic, misogynist, woman-destroying patriarchy); at one's own communities when they submit to co-optation, assimilation, or self and self's groups' destruction; at self for self's collusion in all of the aforesaid. Anger as instrumental as lesbianism, as feminism, as blackness; fluid as sex; as essential as fire. "How to train that anger with accuracy rather than deny it has been one of the major tasks of my life," poses Audre Lorde.

Anger is the challenge I should have ended "Lesbianism" with, instead of that corny "love" thing. Anger and rage are heavy challenges in *This Bridge,* directed at white feminists who won't check their racist ways, social and cultural institutions which exclude and damage, mothers who won't accept daughters' differences, and legacies of powerlessness. And anger, a still relatively unexplained and unexplored phenomena, has to become a tool of action, correction, and reflection. We need to re-read Lorde's "Uses of Anger: Women Responding to Racism" (written in the same vein as her blockbuster essay "Uses of the Erotic"):

Every woman has a well-stocked arsenal of anger potentially useful against those oppressions, personal and institutional, which brought that anger into being. Focused with precision it can become a powerful source of energy serving progress and change.

Go from there, project it out again to shock women into checking themselves out even as they still deny what they see: e.g., capitalist hegemony, perilous enmeshment of church and state powers, global colonization, global genocide, global violence against women, murderous homophobia. White people—including white feminists—still do not want to be held accountable for their history and their privilege. With the exception of black gay men, black men have still not affirmed their solidarity with black women—and even black gay men must continue to check their masculinist tendencies and male privilege. The homophobia of the black middle class community is still prevalent and most telling in the lingering silence surrounding AIDS/HIV, except by some of the most conservative black policy brokers and faith healers in the country and by diverse underfunded grassroots organizations in urban areas hardest hit by the disease. Straight black women are still afraid to reject the trappings of conventional heterosexuality and be feminists. Bisexuals as a political constituency still do not hold themselves accountable for their heterosexual privilege. While some lesbians and gays are redefining and revolutionizing same-sex unions and childrearing, too many liberal lesbians and gay men seem content to reproduce bankrupt heterosexual institutions—weddings, commitment ceremonies, and showers.

Anger, yeah. Use it. Be used by it. Or lose it.

Pomo Afro Homo Vexing of Black Macho in the Age of AIDS

Once we reclaim the camp and crazy 'carnivalesque' excesses of Little Richard—the original Queen of Rock 'n' Roll—we can appreciate the way black men in popular music have parodied the stereotypes of black masculinity to 'theatricalize' and send up the charade of gender roles.

(Mercer and Julien, 173)

SO SAID ISAAC Julien and Kobena Mercer eleven years ago. But even Richard Penniman would not have been possible without Louis Armstrong. Did Little Richard—(Elvis and James Brown, too)—not learn his excesses from Pops? What excesses were there like Pops'excesses? Remember his Zulu King at the Mardi Gras parade in New Orleans in 1949? He claims to have been awakened from a nap by "'something crawling around my chops.'" A member of the Zulu Social Aid and Pleasure Club, Pops' longtime fraternal association, was steadily making him up in preparation for the parade. After the member applied the whiteface, Pops "donned . . . a wig, red velvet tunic, yellow grass skirt, black tights, and a crown adorned with red feathers. . . . A grotesque sight," according to Laurence Bergreen, one of Armstrong's more recent biographers. To preserve the luster of Pops' heterosexuality, Bergreen is quick to mention the "retinue of female assistants" who attended him as he "mounted" the Zulu Float (444). Was this "carnivalesque enough?"

In 1986, Audre Lorde's warrior poem, "Sisters in Arms," theorizes suggestively that "the men will follow" the women into battle. Black feminism's impact on the work of black gay men cannot be overstated. Four years earlier, in the first volume of *Yemonja,* a New York City black gay journal, writer Isaac Jackson calls for "an autonomous black gay movement," stating that "the white gay male movement is not equipped to help me integrate my gayness and my blackness" (1982:4).

Because silences regarding sexuality are still so deadly within black communities, this piece wants to be a conversation that begins to sort out what it means to remember the black gay writers who sent up "the charade of gender roles" in this age of AIDS.

Essex Hemphill (1957–1995) stakes his claim on the body of Afro-American writing, taunting the black heteronormative canon with his homo-lyric blues. Hemphill faces off black macho prescriptiveness by asserting his phallocentric masculine "place." He awakens to "recognize the authenticity of my Negritude" (read as "my homosexuality," *Ceremonies,* 1992:5) by declaiming his membership in the black gay nation and laughing off the dangers of a homophobic white supremacist culture: "in america, / I place my ring / on your cock / where it belongs" (*Conditions,* "XXIV," 1986:24). Let not our brother's canonization in the *Norton*

Anthology of African-American Literature mark our forgetting of his crucial and beautiful writing[1]?

"Lover Man, Oh Where Can You Be?

Gone? Dead? Killing me? Sylvester (1947–1988) "rose on a ramp from beneath the stage" of the San Francisco War Memorial Opera House, "in a blue sequined number" (Gamson, 2005:171) dead in the spotlight and singing "Lover Man, Oh, Where Can You Be" (Davis, Ramirez, and Sherman), a song first recorded in 1944 by Billie Holiday and her only hit, and historically sung by the likes of Sarah Vaughn, Ella Fitzgerald, Dinah Washington, Blossom Dearie, Barbara Streisand, and even Linda Ronstadt, among others, but, of course, not *sung* by a man and rarely performed instrumentally by men—except for Duke, Monk, or Dizzy—unless the "girl singer" was up front for cover. Sylvester helps us negotiate that third or "in-between" space of ambiguous difference (King, 2000) disrupting our longing for a grounded racial and sharply gendered sexuality. Sylvester was the first black gay singer—after Little Richard—to cross over and be "out" or, as Gamson says, "himself," a queen (188). That night in 1979 at the Opera House, his rich falsetto version of "Lover Man" made history as it insinuated itself into the annals of pop music, up against a do-wrong black patriarchal/matriarchal community that would come to marginalize its own—the homosexuals, whores, crack and heroin addicts, single mothers, and others with AIDS.

Is it possible to raise any questions about black men—including straight ones—and not talk about AIDS?

BGM Looking for Same

Isaac Julien's *Looking for Langston: A Meditation on Langston Hughes* and Marlon Riggs's *Tongues Untied* remain two critical and crucial independent films released in 1989 on the state and status of gay men of the African diaspora. Both Riggs (1958–1994) and Julien explore the terra incognita of black homosexual masculinity. As Julien terms his film a "meditation," full of surreal footage and overdubbing, I'd term Riggs's film an "ejaculation" of his own subjectivity as a black gay man, and a more autobiographical script than that of his British peer. Riggs occupies much of the footage. Julien appears in one scene in the opening sequence of a funeral, ostensibly James Baldwin's, but it is Julien's face we see, playing the death mask, as the camera revolves around the top of the casket. Essex Hemphill (1957-1995) is the linchpin of both films for the lines from "Part VIII" of his multipart poem "Conditions:"

Now we think
as we fuck
this nut
might kill us.
There might be

> a pin-sized hole
> in the condom.
> A lethal leak

Both films acknowledge the scourge of AIDS and the scourge of violence, including murder, against black gay men.

Joseph Beam (1954–1989) entitles his introduction to the anthology *In the Life,* "Leaving the Shadows Behind," playing upon the twentieth-century metaphor of the "veil," established by DuBois in 1903. Beam claims that his feminism, radical masculinity, and eroticism were fed by the courageous works of diverse lesbian and feminist writers. The anthology contains work by newer writers like Craig Harris, Donald Woods, Essex Hemphill, Assotto Saint—all of whom would die of AIDS by the mid nineties—and more established writers like Melvin Dixon, who died of AIDS in 1993. When Beam died of AIDS in 1988, he passed on his sheaf of submissions to Essex Hemphill for the second anthology of writing by black gay men, *Brother to Brother,* to be published in 1991.

In 1987 the black queer world mourned the deaths of James Baldwin, Bayard Rustin, and Bruce Nugent. (Black freedom-fighter Ella Baker also died that year.) Nineteen-eighty-seven also marked the debut demonstration on Wall Street of ACT-UP (AIDS Coalition to Unleash Power) New York, whose "camaraderie was central to its activism, and it fostered strong bonds between gay men and lesbians that gave substance to newly emerging notions of queer identities and politics," according to Ann Cvetovich, and whose "in-your-face activism" caused black lesbian video-maker Jocelyn Maria Taylor to join its ranks, "even though it was a predominantly white gay male organization" (McKinley and Delaney, eds., 1995). A year later, the journal *Other Countries: Black Gay Voices, A First Volume,* published by the Other Countries Collective in New York, was intended to be a periodic resource for emerging black gay writers in New York City. The brothers still felt maintaining separate space to express their black gay selves was crucial to their development. This first issue is dedicated to Baldwin, Rustin, and Nugent and contains one of the last interviews Rustin gave, and, among many other topics, including the Civil Rights Movement, he talks about AIDS and his vision of stimulating "a conference . . . which would create in our own localities ways to relieve suffering" (Jeanmarie, 13).

The Age of AIDS

In 1988, the only members of the black community who were organizing around the AIDS epidemic in black communities were black gay men and some black lesbians. (Fresh in my memory is becoming a founding member of New Jersey Women and AIDS Network, because over 50 percent of the people with HIV/AIDS in New Jersey were women and seventy percent of that were women of color. But this was a straight organization, though lesbians were in the leadership and became the organization's directors). Colin Robinson, poet and activist, was one of those who early on committed himself to working in the New York City community as a gay activist and an AIDS activist, caring for sick and dying friends, many of whom were in the publications of the time and in the professional field of AIDS research and education. He was also the production coordinator for this issue of *Other Countries,* in which his poem "For CJ" appears. Robinson's speaker follows the tutelage of his lesbian sisters not only in the writing but also in the acting. The opening lines "to love you like / a lesbian like a / man make love to you like / worship" (20), in which the genders are merged, posit an "in between space of kinship" for lesbians and gay men. Mindful of AIDS, the speaker catalogues body fluids, secretions, and emissions. Robinson takes seriously the lessons of lesbian writing and lovemaking, as in Lorde's "Recreation" (1979), and my own "Kittatinny" (1986), which he places in conversation with "For CJ's" overrunning lines, sans punctuation, and funky language. All enhance the surging desire, sans penis, reclaimed in the age of AIDS.

In 1993, the Other Countries Collective returned with Volume II, *Sojourner: Black Gay Voices in the Age of AIDS.* Its cover presents the book's title in various configurations of red, black, and green; and to the right displays an image of young black men's faces and with closed eyes; and the names of the many who have died of AIDS appear in white reversal lettering. "Red, black, and green—they stand for liberation," sang Gil Scot Heron at the height of black nationalist expressivity. The editors have "stolen" this masculinist sign as a gesture of their own struggle and contribution to black survival—"common sense black nationalism" (Lubiano). After the front matter, in a section entitled "Standing on the Shoulders of Our Ancestors," are the names of nearly four hundred men known to the editors, who have died of AIDS, from earliest to most recent deaths. White letters are foregrounded on black, evoking the Vietnam War Memorial. Sylvester's name is at the end of the third line of the first page.

Through their deployments of literacies drawn from the teachings of black feminists and black nationalists, "black gay renaissance" writers (1982–1996) negotiated the rough terrain of black, queer, and man, disillusioned or not by the politics. Will we reckon with the tremendous toll AIDS has taken on black communities in the United States? The vexing of black macho has had to do with the absence caused by AIDS, shifting gender expression, and strategic silences—"I won't tell you who I am"— e.g., when Sylvester appeared on the *Tonight Show* on New Year's Eve 1986, tacky hostess Joan Rivers asks him, "'So, what did your family say when they found out you were going to be a drag queen?'" Sylvester exclaims dramatically, "'I'm not a drag queen! I'm Sylvester'" (Gamson, 12). In its vexing of black macho, black queer masculinity often means, as Marlon Riggs (1958–1994) asserts in "Reflections of a SNAP! Queen," living on a continuum of multiple identities which, as philosopher Élias Farajaje Jones says (1992), are strategies that enable one to do one's work, to know the danger and go there anyway. The vexing of black macho has further involved taking the same risks of being black and "as much man" as one's straight black brothers but being willing to pass to avert discovery of one's sex or gender preferences or HIV status—we wear the mask, too. The vexing is a refusal to be any other identity than that of black gay man, despite the instability of both racial and sexual signs: i.e., "BGM looking for same," as implied in a scene from *Tongues Untied.*

The vexing is a manipulation of the two signs, silence and invisibility (Bambara, 1988), which penetrate Afro-American life and culture. Silence does not always equal death. The vexing eschews the protection of nationalism, evangelism, and the mainstream. Often the vexing has meant an indeterminacy of gender and a fixing of gender identity, as in the separate male spaces invoked in the two films, *Looking* and *Tongues* and all of the anthologies and journals. Or for a time to give up risk, as the wary and ironic speaker in Craig Harris's (1958–1991) unpublished poem, "Sacrificial Cock:"

I no longer invite

strangers in

I am afraid

I am confused

I am cautious

. . . .

I no longer sing:

'Va, Loco, Loco Valadi'

sacrifice my cock.

offer rum libations

I offer this unquenching libation.

This is an abbreviated version of a longer article written for the Masculinities, Femininities Seminar in 2003–2004 conducted by the Institute for Research on Women at Rutgers University. A version of it also appeared in the Institute's Working Papers, published in the spring of 2004. Many thanks to Wesley Brown, who commented on the paper, as well as all the members of the seminar for their insights and comments. I'll close by thanking Mr. Steven G. Fullwood, Manuscripts Librarian, for his pioneering work in developing the Lesbian, Gay, Bisexual, In the Life Archive at the Schomburg Center for Research in Black Culture. I was able to gain a strong sense of context for this piece in the brief time I spent with the archive. I look forward to returning to spend more time poring over the contributions of queer black writers to black culture.

Works Cited

Bambara, Toni Cade. From a lecture at Sweet Briar College, Sweet Briar, Va., 1988.

Beam, Joseph, Ed. From "Introduction: Leaving the Shadows." *In the Life: A Black Gay Anthology.* Boston: Alyson Publications, Inc., 1986.

Cohen, Cathy J. *The Boundaries of Blackness: AIDS and The Breakdown of Black Politics.* Chicago: University of Chicago Press, 1999.

Cvetkovich, Ann. "Legacies of Trauma, Legacies of Activism: Act-UP's Lesbians." In David Eng and D. Kazanjian, eds., *Loss* (Berkeley, University of California Press, 2002).

Gamsun, Joshua. *The Fabulous Sylvester: The Legend, the Music, the Seventies in San Francisco.* New York. Henry Holt & Co., 2005.

Harris, Craig G. "Sacrificial Cock" (undated, unpublished poem).

Hemphill, Essex. "VIII" and "XXIV." *Conditions.* Washington, D.C.: BeBop Books, 1986.

Jones, Elias Farajaje. From a talk at Rutgers University, 1992.

King, Jason. "Any Love: silence, Theft, and Rumor in the Work of Luther Vandross." *Callaloo: Gay, Lesbian, Transgender Literature and Culture.* Vol. 23, No. 1, Winter, 2000.

Looking for Langston: A Meditation on Langston Hughes. Dir. Isaac Julien. Waterbearer Films, 1989.

Lubiano, Wahneema. "Black Nationalism and Black Common Sense: Policing Ourselves and Others." Ed. W. Lubiano, *The House That Race Built: Black Americans, U.S. Terrain.* New York: Pantheon Books, 1997.

Mercer, Kobena. "Black Masculinity: A Discourse On Images of Black Male Sexuality" (with Isaac Julien). *Welcome to the Jungle: New Positions in Black Cultural Studies.* N.Y.:Routledge, 1994.

Lorde, Audre. "Recreation." *The Black Unicorn.* New York:W.W. Norton, 1978.

—. "Sisters in Arms." *Our Dead Behind Us.* New York:W.W. Norton, 1986.

Other Countries: Black Gay Voices, A First Volume, 1988.

Other Countries: Sojourner, Black Gay Voices in the Age of AIDS, Vol. II, 1993.

Riggs, Marlon. "Black macho revisited: Reflections of a SNAP! queen." *Brother to Brother New Writings by Black Gay Men.* Ed. Essex Hemphill (and conceived by Joseph Beam). Boston: Alyson Publications, Inc., 1991.

Robinson, Colin. "For CJ." In *Other Countries: Black Gay Voices, A First Volume,* 1988.

Sylvester. "Lover Man (Oh, Where Can You Be). Written by Jimmy Davis, Ram Ramirez, Jimmy Sherman, published in 1942. *Living Proof.* Fantasy, 1979.

Taylor, Jocelyn, Maria. "Testimony of a Naked Woman." In Catherine E. McKinley and L. J. Delaney, eds. *Afrekete: An Anthology of Black Lesbian Writing* (New York: Random House, 1995).

Tongues Untied. Dir. Marlon Riggs. Frameline's Lesbian and Gay Cinema Collection, 1989.

The Prong of Permanency,
a Rant

THIS PIECE IS written from my perspective as a dyke (a perspective I've been writing from for 25 years). I do not name each of the communities who have broadened and contributed to the gay and lesbian movement for liberation, i.e., bisexual, trans, questioning, ambiguously/ambivalently sexed and gendered people; for gays and lesbians are in the vanguard of this movement for marriage equality. Regardless of how our partnerships have enriched, restored, and rehabilitated communities all across this country, gays and lesbians are the focus of this critique. And so, I won't hold back.

Their Eyes Were Watching God, a foundational black women's literary text written by Zora Neale Hurston in 1937, comes to my mind these days, especially the character Nannie. "Love is the very prong colored women gets hung on," Nannie tells her 16-year-old granddaughter, Janie, the novel's protagonist, whom she quickly marries off to a bachelor three times her age. Like "love" for black women, permanency for gays lesbians, and other same-sex variants is the very prong we "gets hung on" when the arguments for marriage equality come up. We want that forever thing or the thing forever. We use the law, land, and furniture to make it so, don't we? Long demonized by/in the West, lesbians and gays long for longevity. "Longevity has its place," said Martin Luther King prophetically and critically, shortly before his untimely murder at the age of 39.

Admittedly, permanency has its place—replacing "promiscuity," the other, sexier p-word still applied to our communities. But let's not turn our whole movement over to the locking-in of the same-sex dyad. Need we dedicate our pride marches to marriage, as was the case in this year's New York Pride March [2004]? "We decided we had to attend the *parade* this year. We had to let people know we're here," said one 20-30-something New Paltz–married lesbian and her partner. First of all, young sister-dyke, it's a "march" not a "parade." Secondly, we've had a movement for 35 years, letting people know we're here. Can't help it if your pride was just born yesterday. This dangerous and ahistorical speaking and thinking burns me in our march toward marriage—or bust. This desire for permanency is driving us into state-sanctioned marriages. Same-sex folk want to be able to deploy marriage in as equivalent a way as opposite-sex folk do to bind each other to their relationships. Our pride marches could have been dedicated to ending the war in Iraq or the homophobic torture of Iraqi prisoners of war at Abu Ghraib, or to getting homeless youth off the streets, fifty percent of whom are queer, or lobbying against the cutting of funds to fight HIV/AIDS.

I am calling upon bulldaggers, dykes, faggots, feminist femmes, fierce sissies, and other outrageous progressive queers to have a major multicultural sexual liberation confabulation to take our movement back from liberals. Because marriage equality with its rhetoric of sameness is not why we came out of the closet in 1969 or before. We came out to dismantle marriage as an institution. (Yeah, like gays in the military; we shouldn't be prevented from joining because we're gay—but our whole movement shouldn't be contravened nor the lives of those queer service people endangered because liberal queers want to make political hay.)

Yes, I want permanency as much as the next queer. Who wants to risk being left when we're old and ugly? But must we sabotage our liberation just so that six-figure-salaried gay or lesbian elopes across the border to Massachusetts to lasso his/her six-figure-salaried lover into nuptial oblivion and tax shelters? And, yes, as I said above, lesbian and gay partnerships have changed the cultural, political, and material landscape of this country. But must we be married? And even if we are together 12, 17, 28, 32, 40 years as the lesbian and gay couples suing for marriage equality in New Jersey are—and I am full of admiration for them—we still want to lasso our partners into that vain institution, where the church and state converge and congeal. Marriage trivializes our partnerships.

Even though more than half of straight marriages in this country end in divorce, we still want leaving and taking up with the next same-sex lover with a SUV (or U-Haul) and a good dental plan to be just that much more difficult for our lovers. But according to the May–June issue [2004]of *The Advocate,* divorce attorneys are gearing up to handle gay and lesbian divorces. I am almost ready to agree with Double-Ya: get a constitutional amendment to preserve marriage for heterosexuals. Let heterosexuals have it. Marriage is a bankrupt remnant of the bondage of women and children. Remember also, marriage was denied enslaved black people, and was even denied interracial couples in many Southern states until the 1970s. Even heterosexuals, except those in Hollywood, think we're bonkers to invest in it.

Let us, the queers—and anyone else who wants to constitute a domestic partner relationship or civil union with whomever you choose, if it be your next-door neighbor—have those benefits that automatically accrue to married heterosexuals (and now married homosexuals in Massachusetts for the time being where institutions and corporations have rolled back domestic partner benefits for same-sex couples because we can get married now). And better yet, if we had universal health care, perhaps fewer of us would be so caught up in the marriage syndrome.

I tried out my premise of permanency on a dyke couple, I'll call Y. and B., who have been together for 19 years, are raising an 11-year-old daughter, own property together, and are both professionals with good insurance plans and politically against marriage. They laughed in all the right places when I read this piece to them, but Y. disagreed with my premise:

"I'll tell you why we want marriage," Y. proffered.

"Yeah, why?" I asked.

"Self-hatred."

Ecstatic Fallacies: The Politics of the Black Storefront

"you think i accept this Pentecostal church
in exchange for the lands you stole"
—(Jayne Cortez, "Do You Think," 1978)

CRUCIFIED JESUS. STOLEN, enslaved, and forced Black bodies: a stunning "imitation" of the suffering Son of God. I resisted the ecstasy of the black church; its unconditional love of my slave body. Though the stripes on my breasts, back, and buttocks attest to my worthiness, I took no consolation from that old rugged cross nor found any balm (only boredom) in the somber Latin-said masses of my faked childhood meditation on that distant Lord, his bloody sweat, crown of thorns, studded palms pulped into that stolen gold crucifix up there on its silk covered marble slab.

But I do so love a good gospel choir.

Ecstatic. Charismatic. Vatic. Don't want to go that far back. The demand on the soul (which I do believe in, like the Big O singing "I been loving you too long to stop now") is too perilous. One gets tired of a prophet. All my life, from the time of my post-Reconstruction

North Carolinian maternal grandmother's fixation on the white proto-"televangelist" Oral Roberts of Tulsa, Oklahoma, I've laughed at Bible-beating proselytizers, or, in my young, bourgeois Roman Catholic days, thought them ignorant of the Canon, trashy, and country with all that sweating and shouting and spitting. Now, they are running the country. And I'm back on the dock of the bay.

Still and all, why does Bishop Harry R. Jackson Jr. (Note: they're often "Jr.'s," so we'll assume their mothers were *married* to their fathers?)—author of the "Black Contract With America on Moral Values" and pastor of Hope Christian Church, a so-called "megachurch" of 2,000, in College Park, Md.,—think that by offering up gays and lesbians on the altar of "marriage protection" (or in the lesbian feminist terms of Adrienne Rich, "compulsory heterosexuality"), he's got a place at the table (*Sunday Times,* March 6, 2005, p. 23; *Free Republic,* 4/25/2005, www.freerepublic.com/focus/f-news/1391049/posts; "Black Contract with America on Moral Values," HIMPACT/ High Impact Leadership Coalition," www.thehopeconnection.org/contract.htm; Blumenthal, "Justice Sunday Preachers," *The Nation,* www.thenation.com/doc.mhtml/blumenthal).

All this, because 7 percent more black people voted for Bush in 2004 than in 2000? Bishop Jackson's a little taken with his ecstatic fallacy. He is said to be collecting a million signatures endorsing his "Contract" to present to President Bush on February 1 of 2006. He was among the Judas black preachers Bush invited to the

White House in January and the only black preacher at Justice Sunday—a campaign holiday for Bill Frist.

Meanwhile, the United States has kept not a one of its own contracts (e.g., viz., the Constitution and its assorted amendments) with its Black citizens. Why would it honor one drawn up by a coalition of black preachers, conservative though they be? Blacks in the funky U.S. can't use a contract of "moral values." Given our history here, we have a surfeit of moral values and no dearth of contracts with America. I hope Bishop Jackson is not mistaken for an intruder as he proceeds toward the White House in February of 2006, briefcase brimming with those million signatures: rather like Ellison's Invisible Man, carrying the *New York Times* and a briefcase with the message, "Keep this nigger running," hidden inside.

There's dissension in the King family. Rev. Bernice King—a preacher too and youngest daughter of Martin Luther King, Jr.— led a cynical march with the Bishop Eddie Long, homophobic pastor of the New Birth Missionary Baptist Church, a *mega* megachurch of 25,000 (!), through Atlanta in December of 2004 to support a constitutional ban on same-sex marriage: "I know deep down in my sanctified soul that he [Dr. King] did not take a bullet for same-sex unions," said the young Rev. King. Well, in a way Dr. King did die so that gay people could be free. Liberations stand in for one another—(just like oppressions). (Black liberation is Queer liberation.) Joseph Lowery and John Lewis, two of King's close associates, both said Dr. King would never have marched for a constitutional ban on gay marriage. I believe King—whatever his sexual performances and proclivities— would have preferred a world in which he could receive all the counsel he needed from Bayard Rustin, a black gay man and mentor to the Civil Rights Movement, without censure and blackmail. And I believe both the Rev. Bernice King and Bishop Eddie Long doth protest too much.

Nine months before her daughter's ecstatic fallacy last December, Coretta Scott King stood up for the right of gays and lesbians to marriage equality: "Gay and lesbian people have families and their families should have legal protection, whether by marriage or civil union. A constitutional amendment banning same-sex marriages is a form of gay bashing and it would do nothing at all to protect traditional marriage" (GayPASG.org., "Split in Martin Luther King's family reflects gay marriage debate," Jan. 16, 2005).

> I learned to love the gospel music
> swelling up past garbage cans in the summer
> backyards of my childhood Armageddon.
>
> ("About Religion," Audre Lorde, 1978)

But who could have predicted this black turn to what Martin Kilson identifies as "Christian fundamentalist atavism," reaching back to Old Testament values to justify hatred of queers and women and to wedge their way onto the Republican agenda. Easier to do that than for "the black storefront" to face other realities Black people are living with: in almost forty years the seven year disparity in life expectancy between whites and blacks in this country only decreased six-tenths of a percent; the foundering under-funded urban public school systems (yeah, who does love the children Jesus suffered to come unto him, especially the poor ones) are wasting the minds of another generation of students of color; the crisis of AIDS, which along with heart disease, cancer, cirrhosis, diabetes, murder, and car accidents account for more than 80 per cent of all "excess deaths" in African-American communities. The gross disparity of incomes—even between the rich and the richer. And so many people making so little money. Tens of millions without health insurance. And a real dire need for all of us to do something for our queer children of color. Wherever we find them, as Audre Lorde says, the children are our children too. Yet, the "black storefront" keeps throwing up "the family" in our faces as the answer. The family, especially the nuclear family, is not sufficient, efficient, or safe for children.

Keith Boykin, gay activist and former Clinton aide, speaks on homophobic black preachers, in a pithy piece of writing, "Gay Rights, Civil Rights":

> [A] black minister in Chicago told the *New York Times,* 'If the KKK opposes gay marriage, I would ride with them.' Dozens of other black ministers have gone on national television and radio programs to condemn homosexuality. . . . If that's not enough to spark black LGBT activism, I'm not sure what is (Wharton and Philips, eds., *I Do/I Don't: Queers on Marriage,* 2005).

I remember reading that amnesiac preacher's ecstatic fallacy and thinking, *This is a crazy enemy. His blackness notwithstanding.* And yes, I ask myself the same question Mr. Boykin begs: *Where is black LGBT activism?* But that isn't enough either. National Black Justice Coalition notwithstanding.

A number of prominent black Christians, like Mrs. King, Rep. Lewis, Rev. Lowery, have refused the "Black Contract with America on Moral Values" and the buffoonery of other black preachers promoting homophobia in the black community? They know, for example, that the new white right is the old Invisible Empire? Suits and Gucci pumps instead of capes and hoods. (Alabama native and lesbian writer Minnie Bruce Pratt whispers to me, "You could always tell a klansman by his shoes."). They've been summoned inside the Beltway from the dark ghosts wailing in the Delta to press the flesh of the "white corporate oligarchs" (Kilson 2005). Homophobia stands in for and "structures" racism, xenophobia, and anti-Arab and anti-Muslim profiling and surveillance. Traditional Values Coalition is the White Citizens Council. Homeland Security is COINTELPRO.

But can Black Christians (many of whom are queer) take back the church, that has been your shelter when you had none, your sanctuary from the snare of enemies, your nation within a hostile nation, your courage in the face of attack dogs, fire hoses, tear gas, beating, jail, and horrific death? Or, like *Beloved*'s Baby Suggs (Morrison 1983), start a new one.

Acknowledgments

Poems in "Part One" have appeared in: Lewis, ed. *Bluestones and Salt Hay: An Anthology of Contemporary New Jersey Poets,* 1990; Morse and Larkin, eds. *Gay and Lesbian Poetry in Our Time*, St. Martin's Press, 1988; Linthwaite, ed. *Ain't I A Woman*, Virago Press, 1987.

The essays in "Part One" appeared in the following publications: "Lesbianism: An Act of Resistance" in Moraga and Anzaldua, eds. *This Bridge Called My Back: Writings by Radical Women of Color*, Persephone Press, 1981. "The Failure to Transform: Homophobia in the Black Community" in Smith, ed. *Home Girls: A Black Feminist Anthology*, Kitchen Table: Women of Color Press, 1983; "New Notes on Lesbianism" in *Sojourner*, Jan. (1983) and reprinted in Kahn, ed. *Frontline Feminism, 1975–1995*, Aunt Lute Books, 1995; "Black, Brave, and Woman, Too" (review essay), *Sinister Wisdom: 20*, 1982.

Poems from "Part Two" have appeared in the following publications: Donoghue, ed. *Poems Between Women: Four Centuries of Love, Romantic Friendship, and Desire*, Columbia University Press, 1997; Coss, ed. *The Arc of Love: An Anthology of Lesbian Love Poems*, Scribner, 1996; Howe, ed. *No More Masks*, Harper Collins, 1993; Lewis, ed. *Bluestones and Salt Hay: An Anthology of Contemporary New Jersey Poets*, Rutgers University Press, 1990; Sheba Collective, eds. *Serious Pleasure: Lesbian Erotic Stories and Poetry*, Sheba Feminist Publishers, 1989; *Ikon: Art Against Apartheid Issue*, 1986; Bulkin and Larkin, eds. *Lesbian Poetry*, Persephone Press, 1981.

Essays in "Part Two" have appeared in the following publications: ". . . She Still Wrote Out the Word Kotex on a Torn Piece of Paper Wrapped Up in a Dollar Bill . . ." in McCorkle, ed. *Conversant Essays: Contemporary Poets on Poetry*, Wayne State University Press, 1990. "Knowing the Danger and Going There Anyway," *Sojourner: The Women's Forum*, v. 16, n. 1, 1990; "Saying the Least Said, Telling the Least Told: The Voices of Black Lesbian Writers," *Lesbian and Gay Studies Newsletter*, Toronto, February, 1990; "Silence and Invisibility: Costly Metaphors," *Gay Community News Black History Month Issue*, February 19-25, 1989; "Two Rich and Rounding Experiences" (review essay), *Callaloo*, Vol. 11, No. 2, 1988; "Coming Out" (speech), *Black/Out*, Fall 1986.

Essays in "Part Three" have appeared in the following publications: "Living The Texts Out: Lesbians and the Uses of Black Women's Traditions" in Stanlie James, eds. *Theorizing Black Feminisms: The Visionary Pragmatism of Black Women*, Routledge, 1993; "The Homoerotic Other," *The Advocate,* February, 1991; "The Everyday Life of Black Lesbian Sexuality in Warland, ed. *Inversions: Writing by Dykes, Queers, and Lesbians*, Press Gang Publishers, 1991.

Poems in "Part Four" also appeared in the following publications: *Callaloo: A Journal of African American and African Arts and Letters, Special Issue: Queer Studies*, April 2000; *The Lesbian Review of Books*, 1999; Lassell and Georgiou, eds. *The World in Us: Lesbian and Gay Poetry of the Next Wave*, St. Martin's Press, 2000; Finch, ed. *A Formal Feeling Comes*, 1994; *The World: Publication of St. Mark's Poetry Project*, 1992; *Feminist Studies,* 1992; *Hellas: A Journal of Poetry and the Humanities*, Vol. 3, No. 2, Fall 1992.

Essays in "Part Four" have appeared in the following publications: "Transferences and Confluences: The Impact of the Black Arts Movement on the

Literacies of Black Lesbian Feminism" in Brandt, ed. *Dangerous Liaisons: Blacks and Queers Fighting for Equality*, New Directions, 1999; "A House of Difference: Audre Lorde's Legacy to Lesbian and Gay Writers" in Douglas et al, eds. *Maka: Contemporary Writing by Queers of African Descent*, SisterVision Press, 1996.

The poems in "Part Five" have appeared in the following publications: *Bloom*, 2004; *Long Shot: The Beat Bush Issue*, 2004.

The essays from "Part Five" have appeared in the following publications: "Ecstatic Fallacies: The Politics of the Black Storefront" in *Sodom and Me: Queers on Fundamentalism*, Suspect Thoughts Press, 2005; "The Prong of Permamency, a Rant" in *I Do/I Don't: Queers on Marriage*, Suspect Thoughts Press, 2004; "Lesbianism, 2000" in Anzaldua and Keating, eds. *This Bridge We Call Home*, Routledge, 2000.

About the Author

Poet and activist Cheryl Clarke was educated at Howard University and Rutgers University. Her books of poetry include *Narratives: Poems in the Tradition of Black Women* (1983), *Living as a Lesbian* (1986), *Humid Pitch* (1989), and *Experimental Love* (1993). Her poems and essays have appeared in numerous journals and anthologies, including *The Black Scholar, The Kenyon Review, Belles Lettres, The World in Us: An Anthology of Lesbian and Gay Poetry,* and *Persistent Desire: A Femme-Butch Reader.* Her most recent book is a history of the Black Arts Movement of the 1960s titled *After Mecca: Women Poets and the Black Arts Movement* (Rutgers, 2005). Clarke is the Director of the Office of Diverse Community Affairs and Lesbian-Gay Concerns at Rutgers University. She lives in Jersey City, New Jersey.